TATTOO DESIGN

BY LIFE DAILY STYLE

Table of Contents

INTRODUCTION

Tattooing has always been more than a craft. It is a conversation between inner vision and outer expression — a collaboration between the artist who interprets and the person who chooses to carry the image for life. Behind every line and every shade lies intention. Behind every symbol, a story. And behind every finished tattoo stands a long chain of inspirations, sketches, references, and influences that prepare the ground for that final moment when needle meets skin.

Artists know this well: creativity doesn't appear on command. It grows through exposure — to images, to shapes, to moods, to the visual language of different eras and styles. Inspiration is collected, not summoned. It builds slowly through repetition, experimentation, and the willingness to explore outside what feels familiar. That is the purpose of this book: to give you a space filled with imagery that can spark ideas, unlock new directions, and become a foundation for your own artistic interpretation.

The pages you're about to explore are intentionally diverse. They do not follow one path or restrict themselves to one mood. Instead, they travel across different visual worlds — from the intensity of dark fantasy and gothic themes, to the atmospheric shadows of cinema-inspired imagery, to the rhythm and texture of music-based elements, and finally into the timeless honesty of traditional tattoo motifs. Each chapter is designed to stand on its own, yet all of them share a common thread: clear storytelling potential. Every design hints at a narrative, offering possibilities rather than fixed solutions.

This book is created as a working tool. Something that can live beside you at the studio table, in your travel bag, on your workstation, or next to your digital setup. It's meant to be opened, marked, referenced, traced, adapted, reimagined. Many artists find that a single visual spark can unfold into an entire custom piece or provide the missing idea that completes a client's concept. The goal here is not perfection — the goal is usefulness. Inspiration that moves your hand forward.

While browsing these pages, allow yourself time. Sit with the imagery without pressure. Notice the shapes that immediately resonate with you. Notice the themes that make you pause. Notice the ideas that slowly start forming as you move from chapter to chapter. Tattoo art thrives on these subtle moments — the quiet flash of an idea that wasn't there before, or the feeling that a certain style is calling you to explore it deeper.

Whether you are an established artist with years of experience or someone new to the world of tattooing, this book meets you where you are. You can use it to test visual directions with clients, to challenge your own style boundaries, or to simply refuel your creativity on days when inspiration feels far away. Every artist needs reference points. Every artist needs visual input. And every artist, no matter how skilled, benefits from having a wide reservoir of ideas close at hand.

Let this be a space where your imagination can breathe.

Let it be a tool that pushes you toward new designs and stronger artistic identity.

Let it support your workflow, your style development, and your storytelling.

And above all — let it remind you why tattooing remains such a powerful, enduring form of art.

DEMONIC PORTRAITS

The world of demonic imagery has always held a powerful place in tattoo culture. These forms — twisted, seductive, unsettling, or strangely beautiful — reflect the deeper layers of human emotion. They represent fear, strength, rebellion, duality, temptation, transformation and the unknown. In many ways, demonic portraits are mirrors: they show the parts of ourselves that are often hidden, exaggerated, or amplified into myth.

In tattoo art, demons are not simply monsters. They are characters. They carry expression, attitude, personality and storytelling potential. A single face can shape an entire tattoo composition — through the tilt of a jaw, the intensity of the gaze, the curve of a horn, or the fractured detail of a mask. This chapter explores those faces in many forms: elegant and cruel, sorrowful and fierce, grotesque and ethereal. Each portrait pushes the boundaries of imagination, blending human features with the supernatural to create visual tension and emotional depth.

These designs are meant to be used as foundations and springboards. A good demonic portrait can evolve into a full sleeve, serve as a focal point in a back piece, or anchor a smaller composition with strong visual impact. Whether you refine the details, combine motifs, or reinterpret the character entirely, the goal is the same: to create art that feels alive on the skin.

Use this chapter to explore shape, emotion, exaggeration and energy. Study the silhouettes, the expressions, the shadows, the cracks and the interplay between beauty and distortion. Let these portraits guide you into designing your own creatures — ones that speak with your style, your atmosphere, your artistic voice.

This is the realm where imagination becomes myth.

This is where the face of a demon becomes a canvas for storytelling.

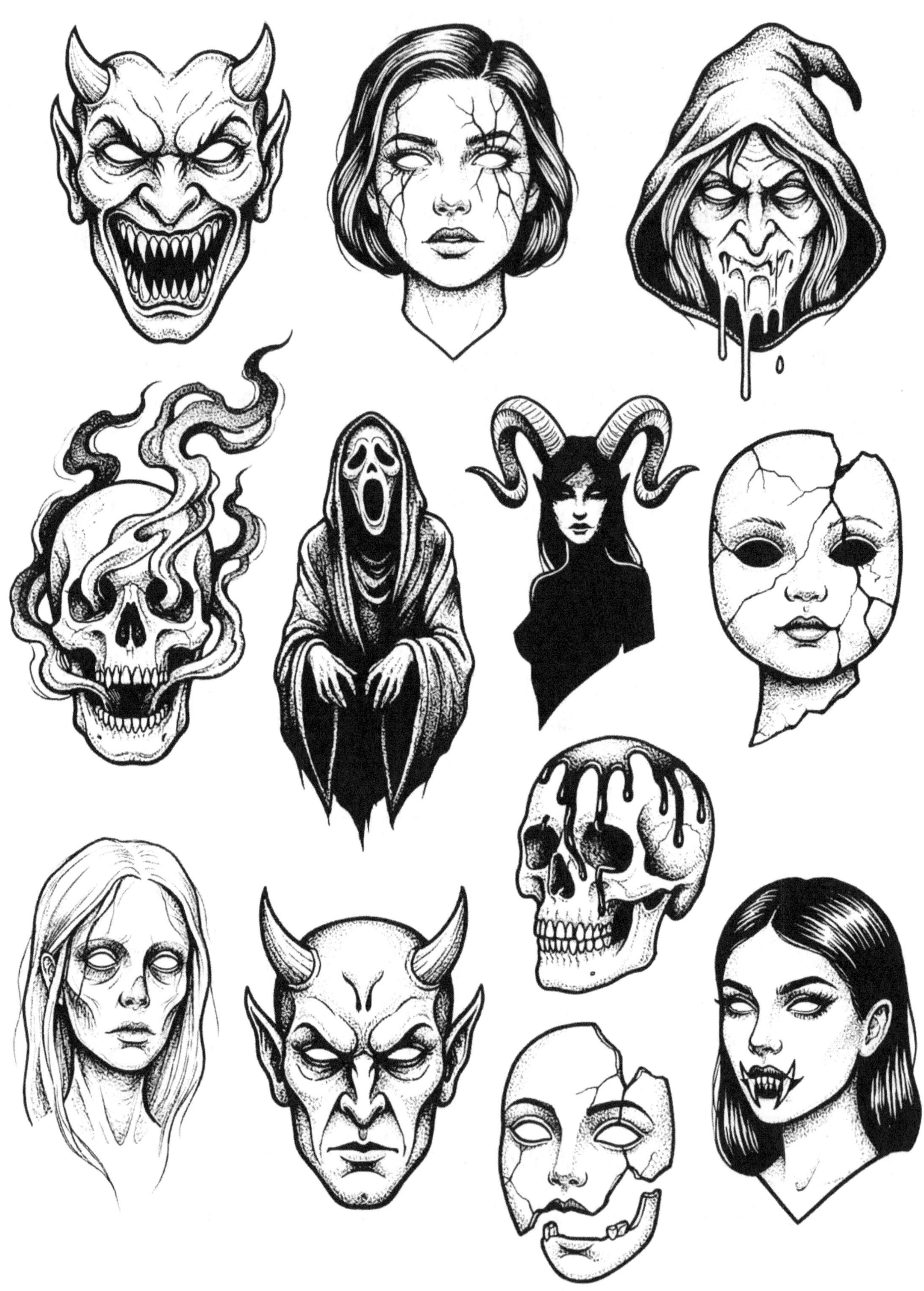

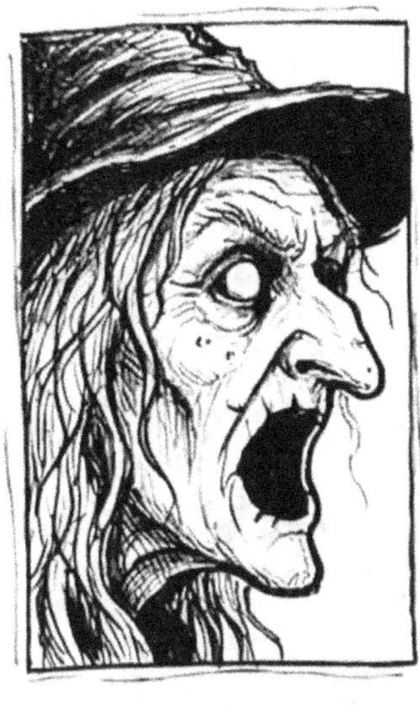
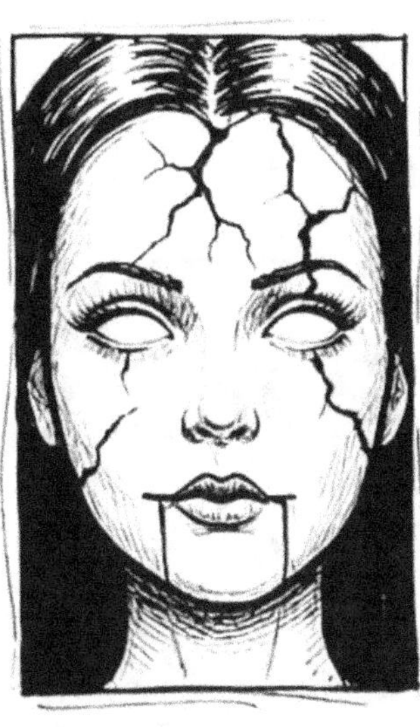
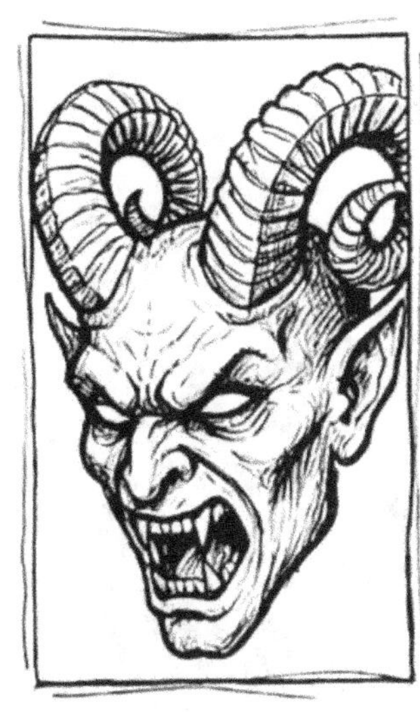
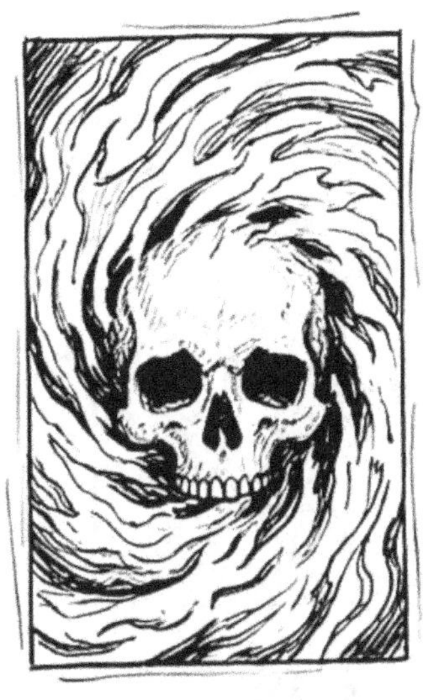
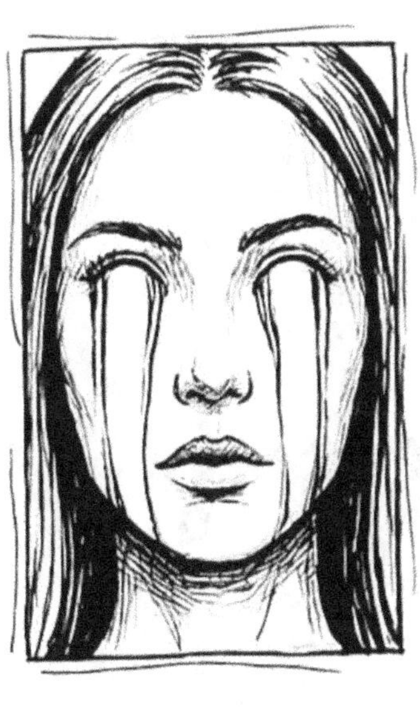
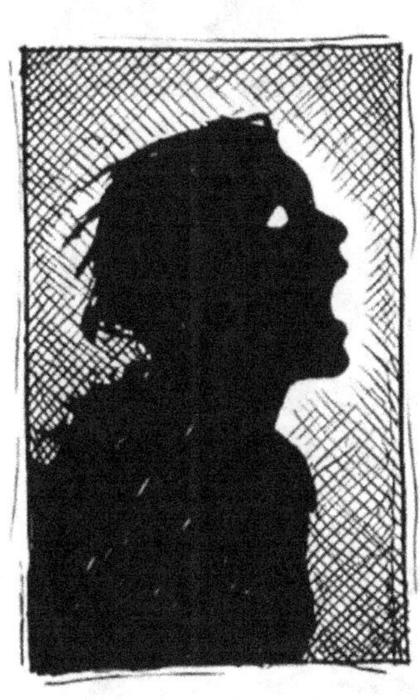
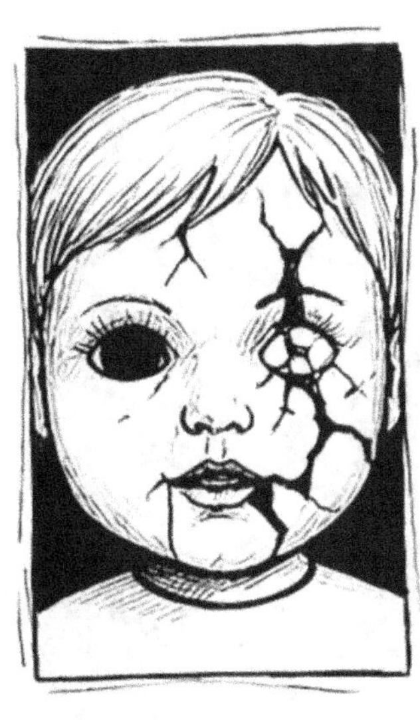
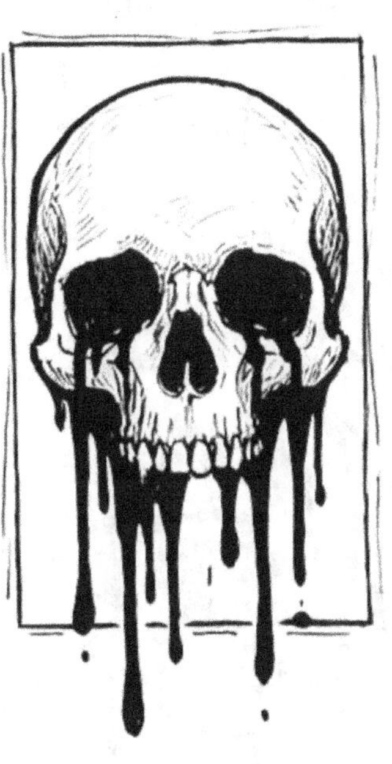
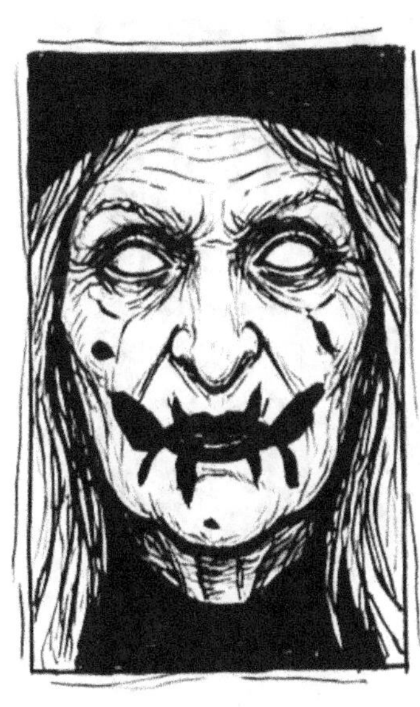
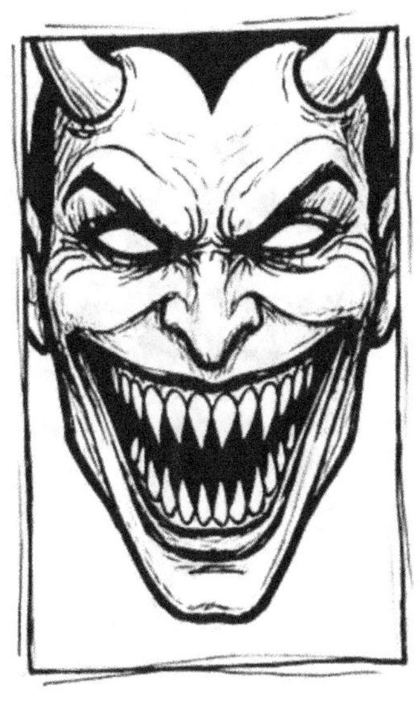
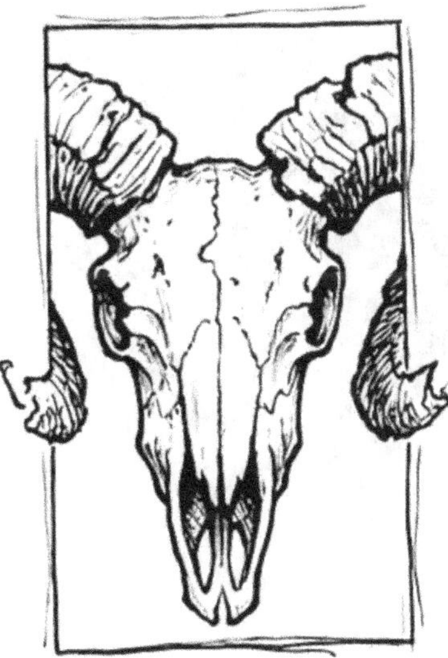
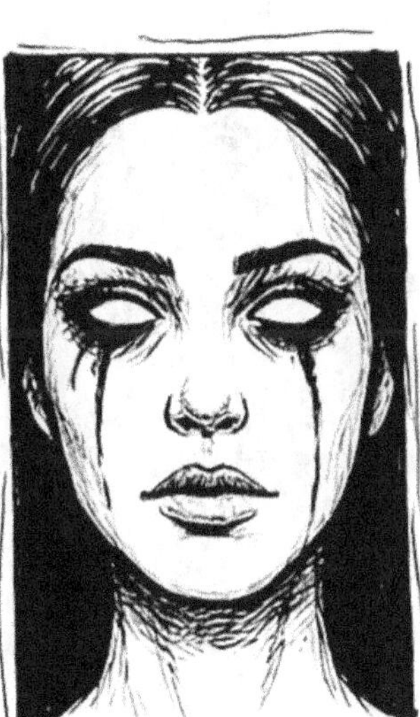

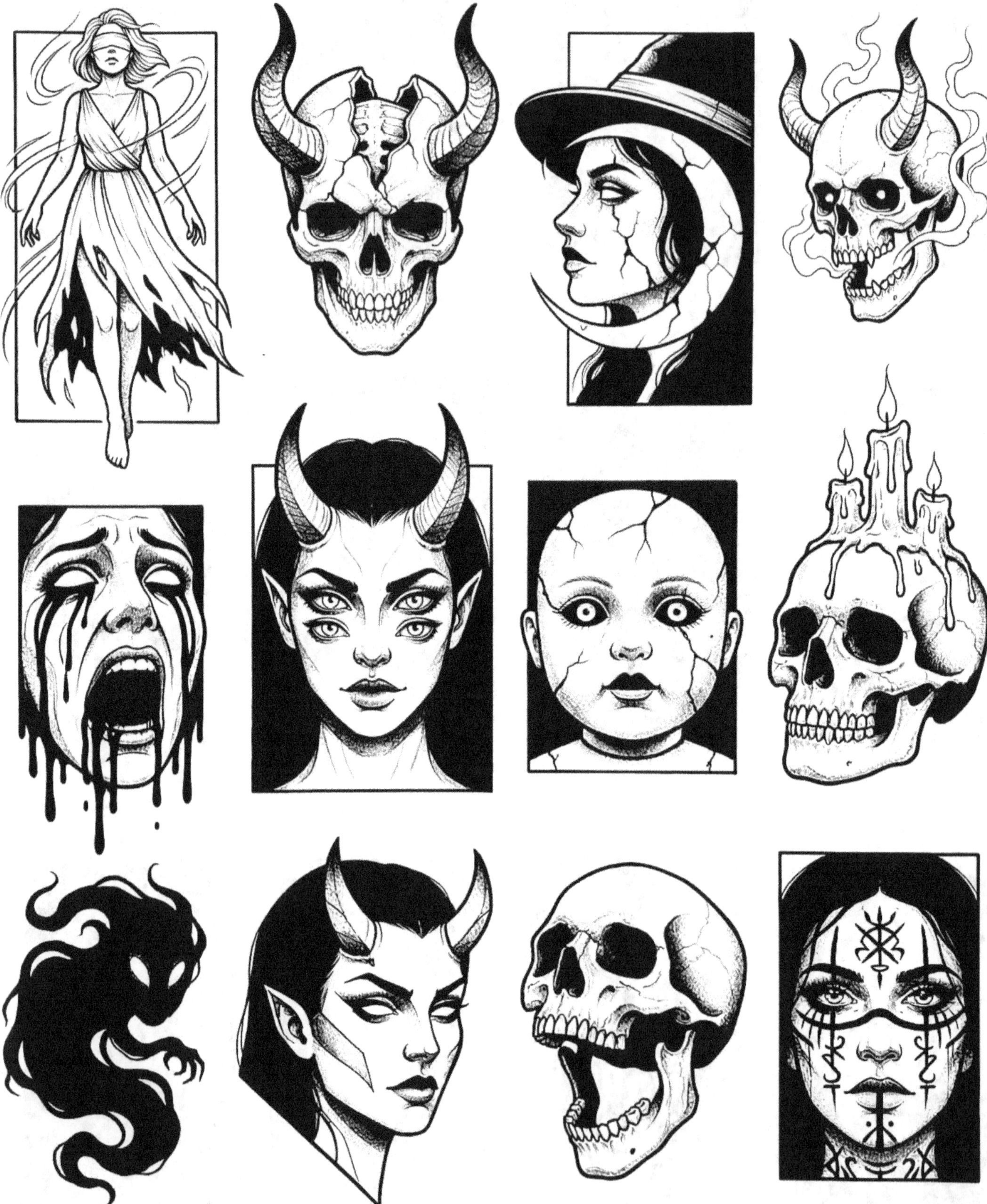

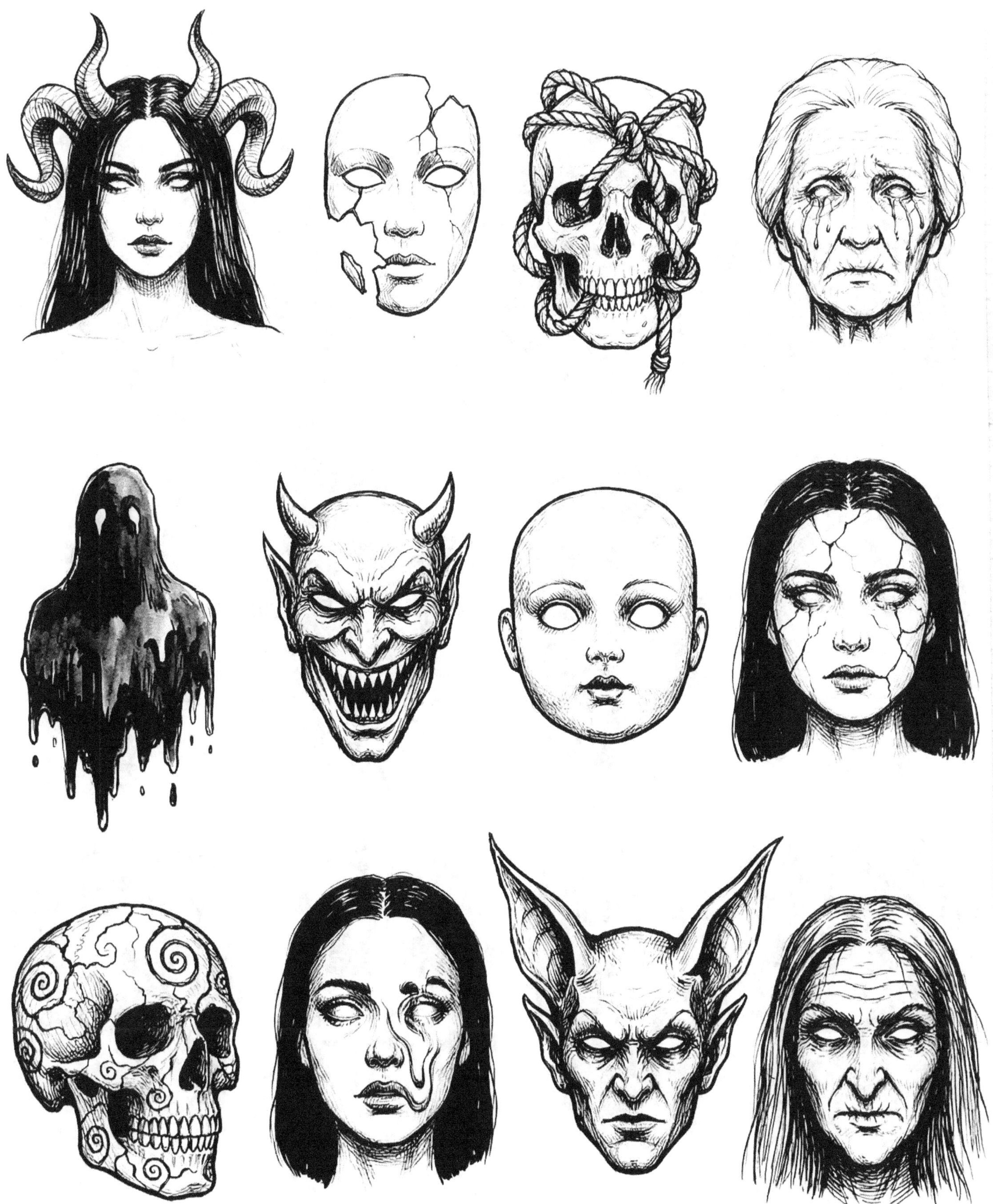

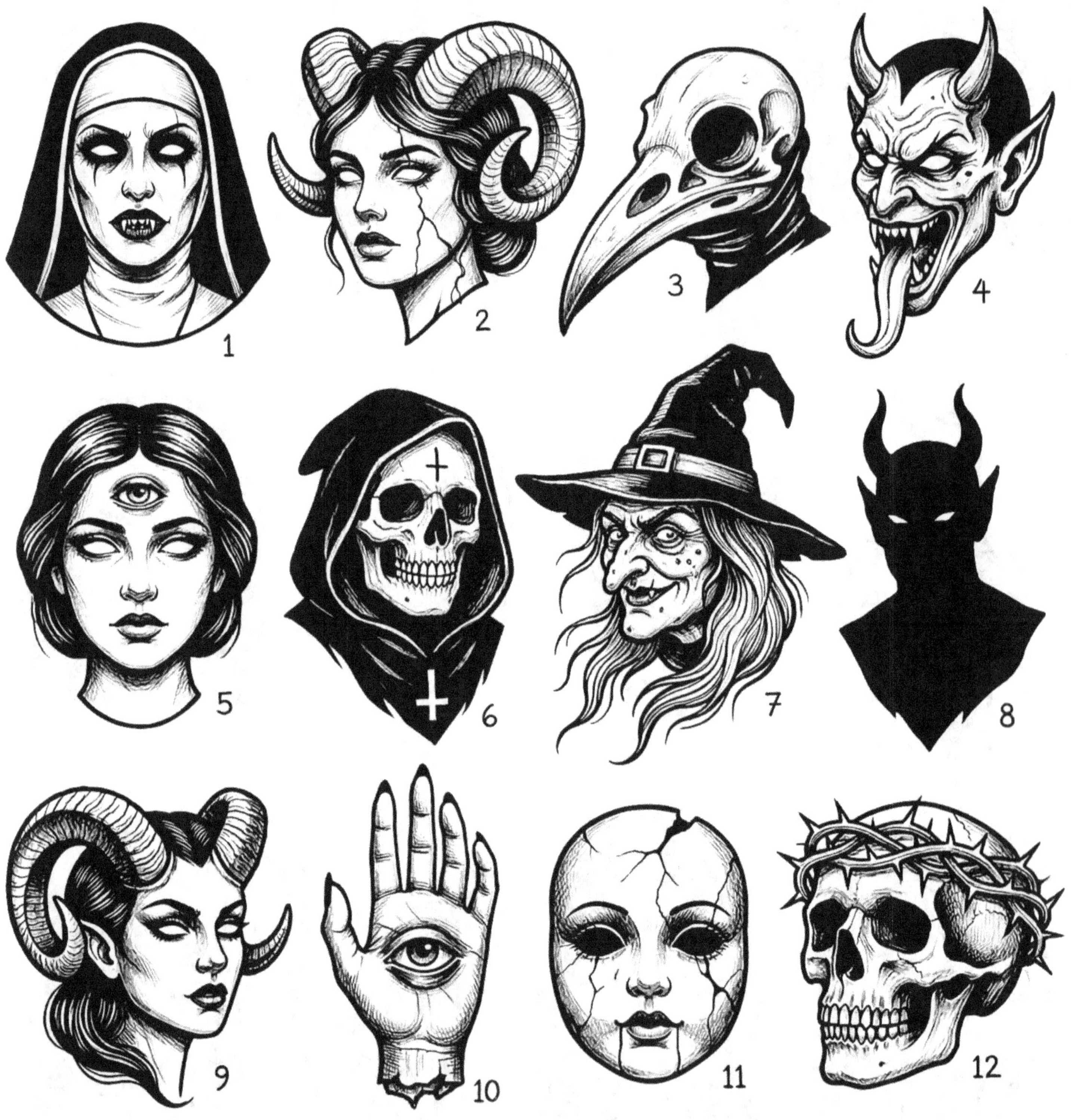

1
2
3
4
5
6
7
8
9
10
11
12

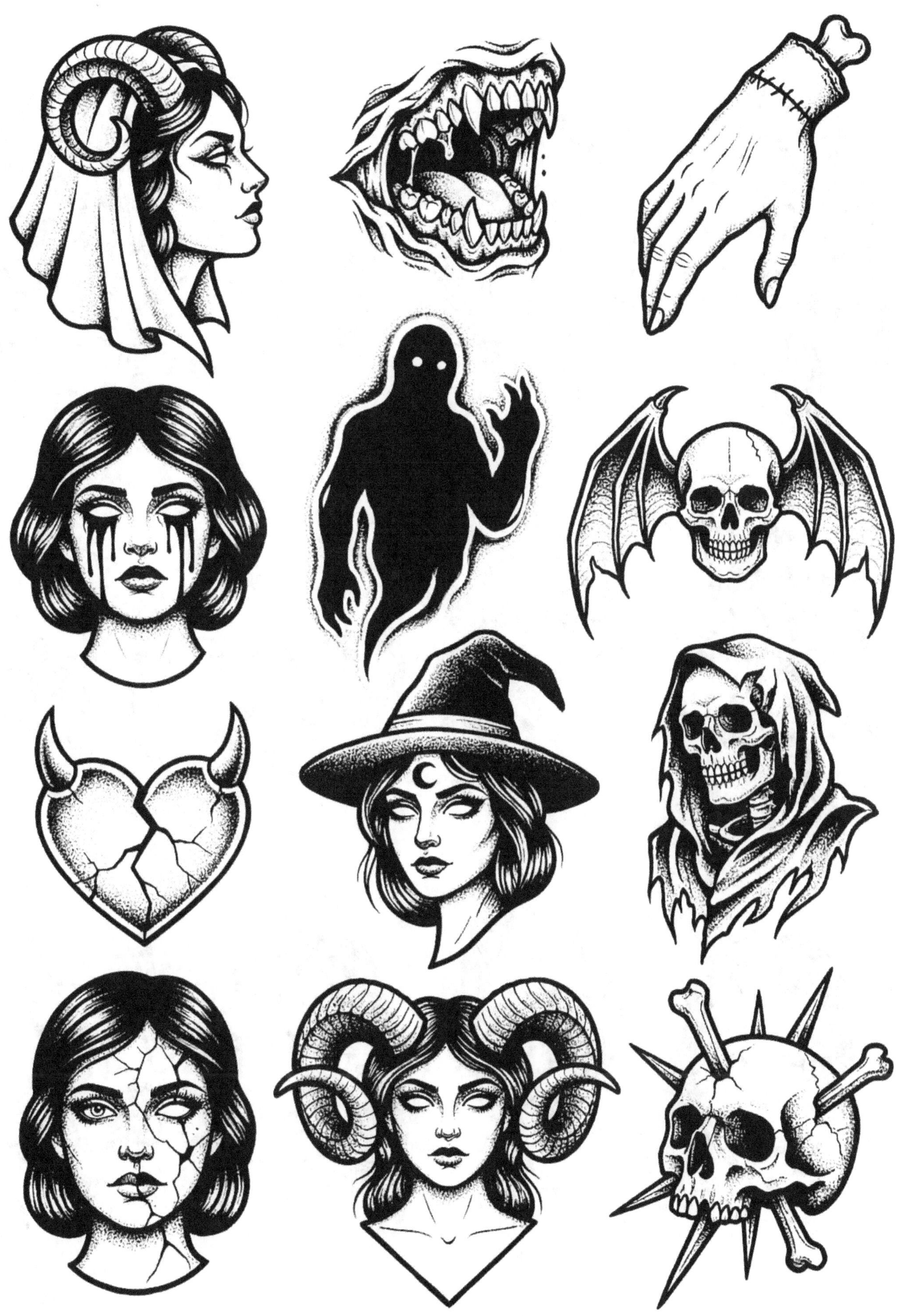

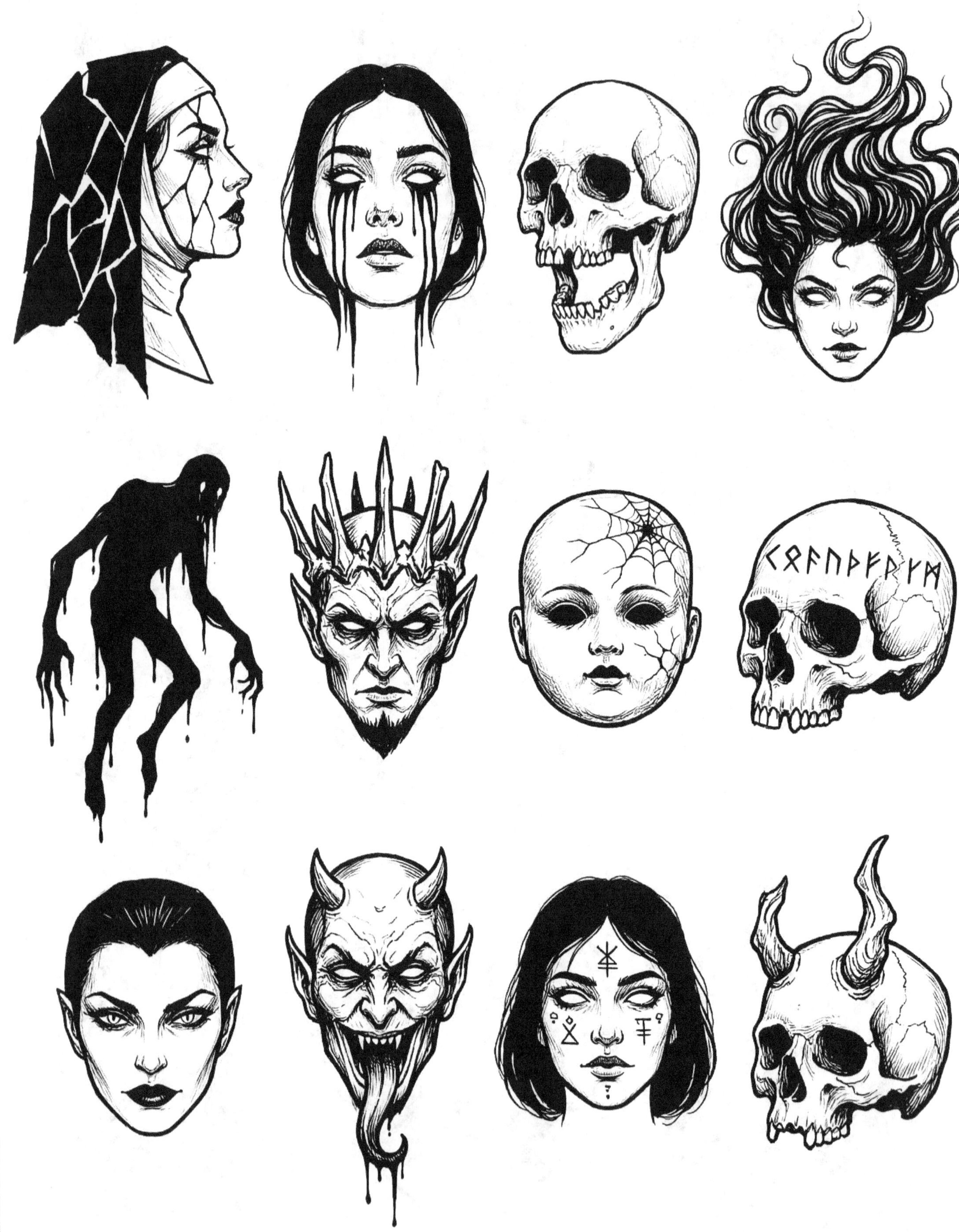

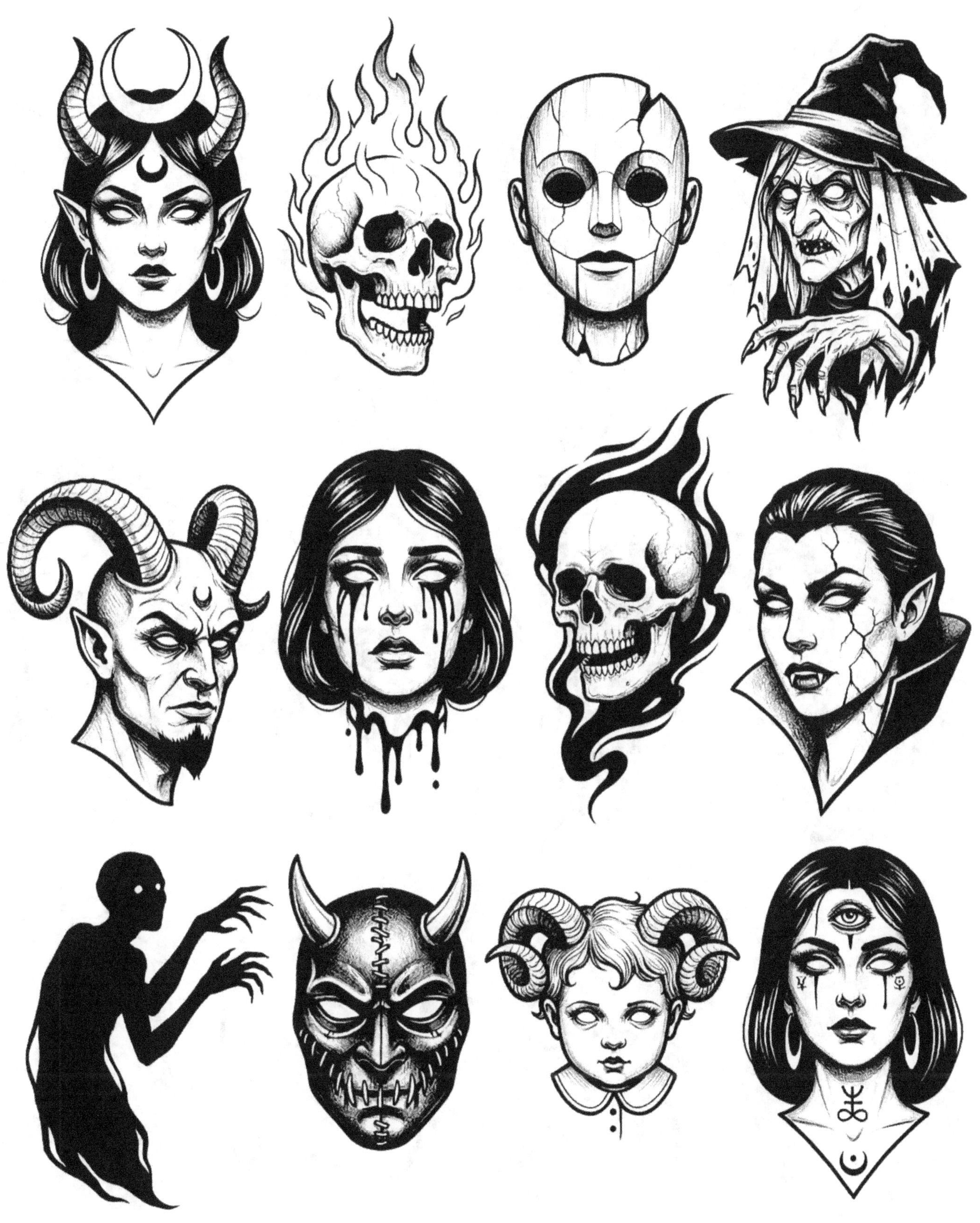

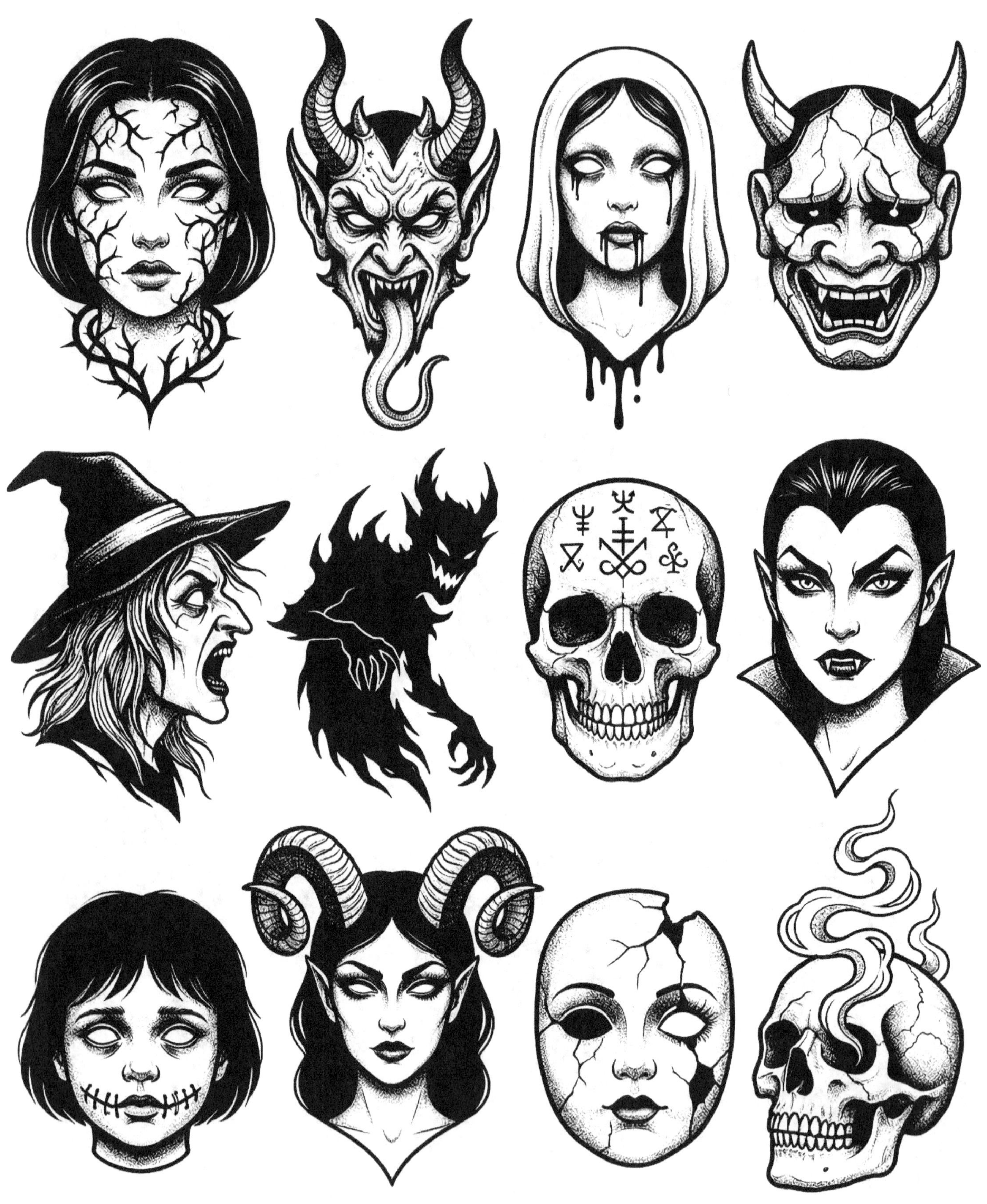

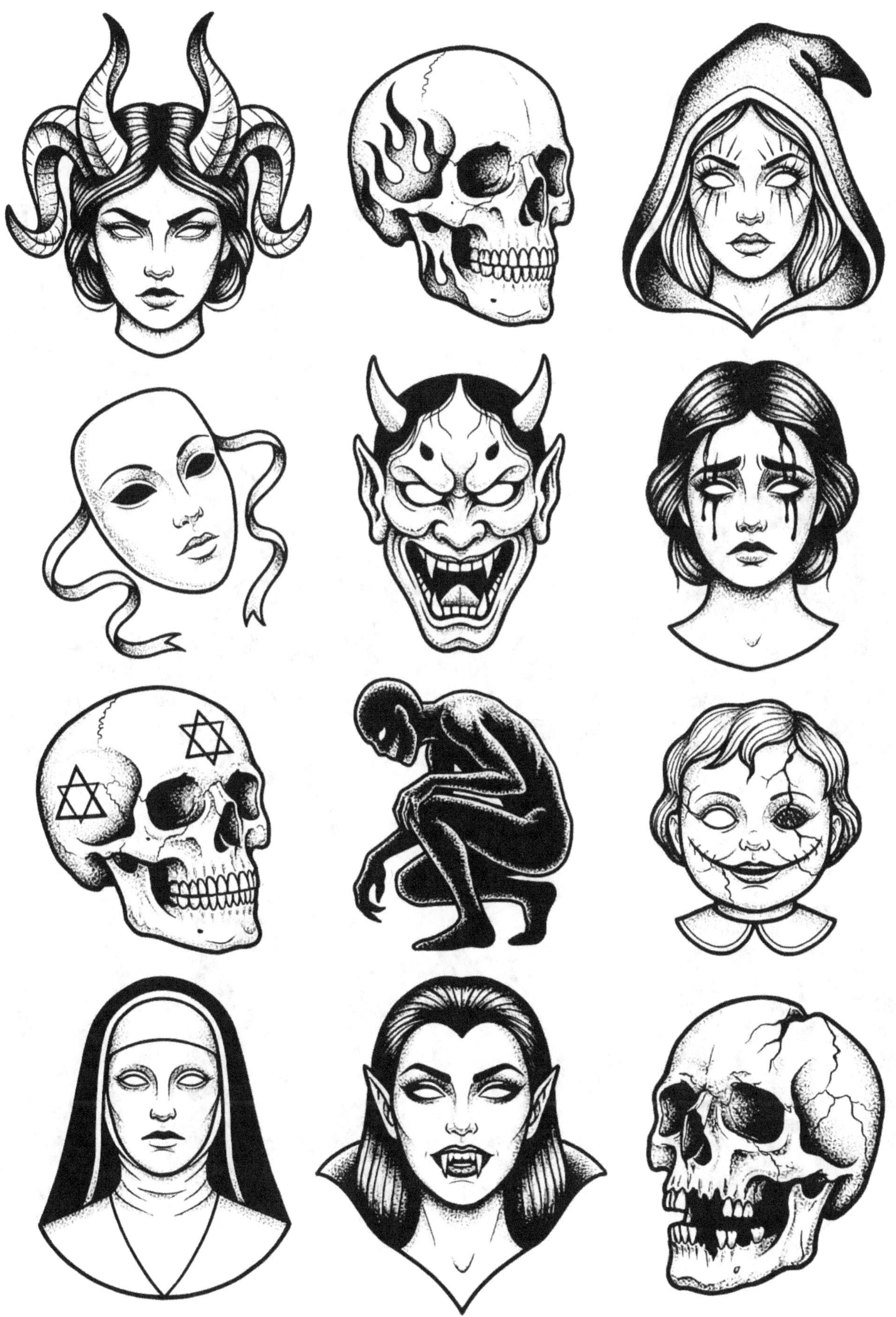

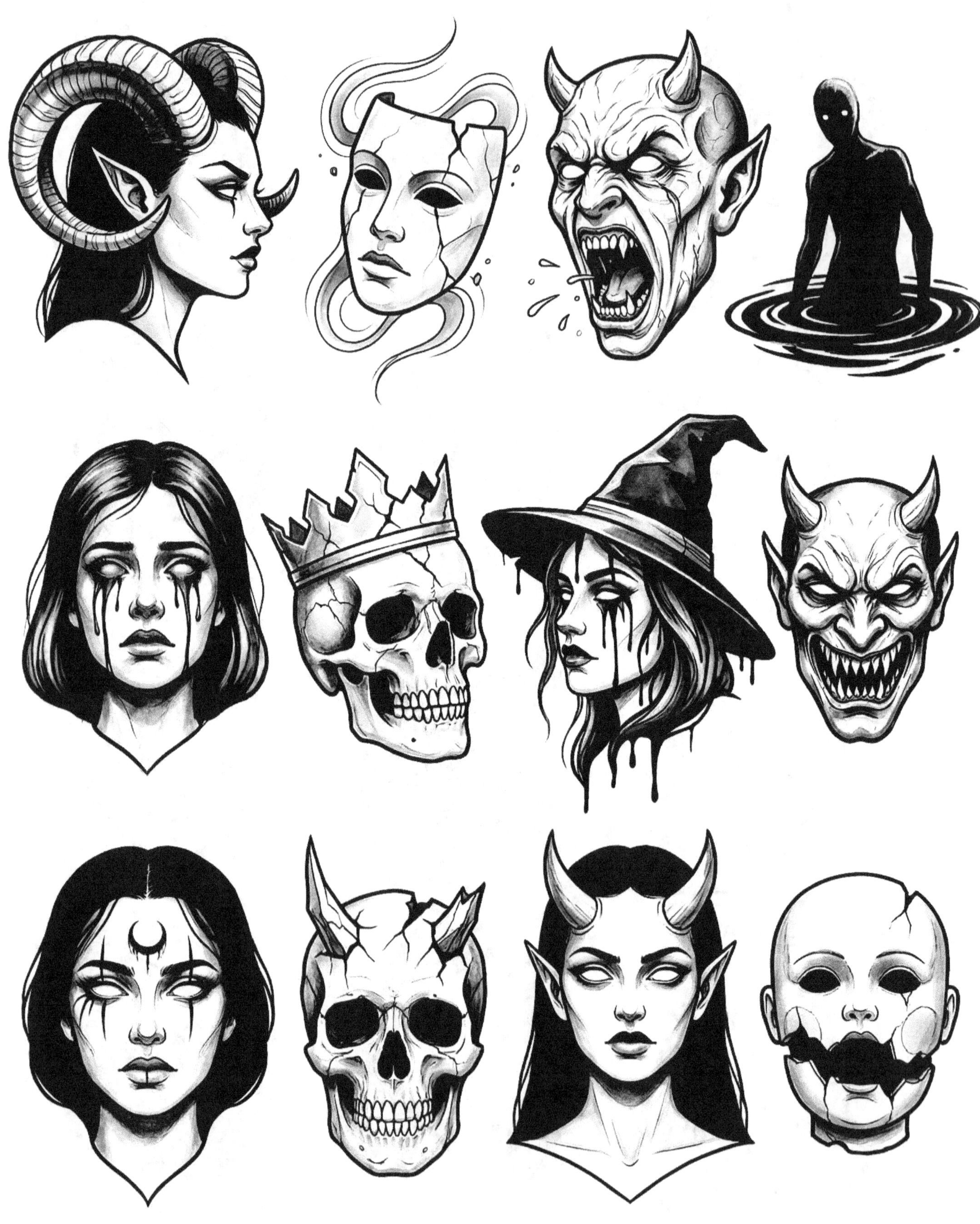

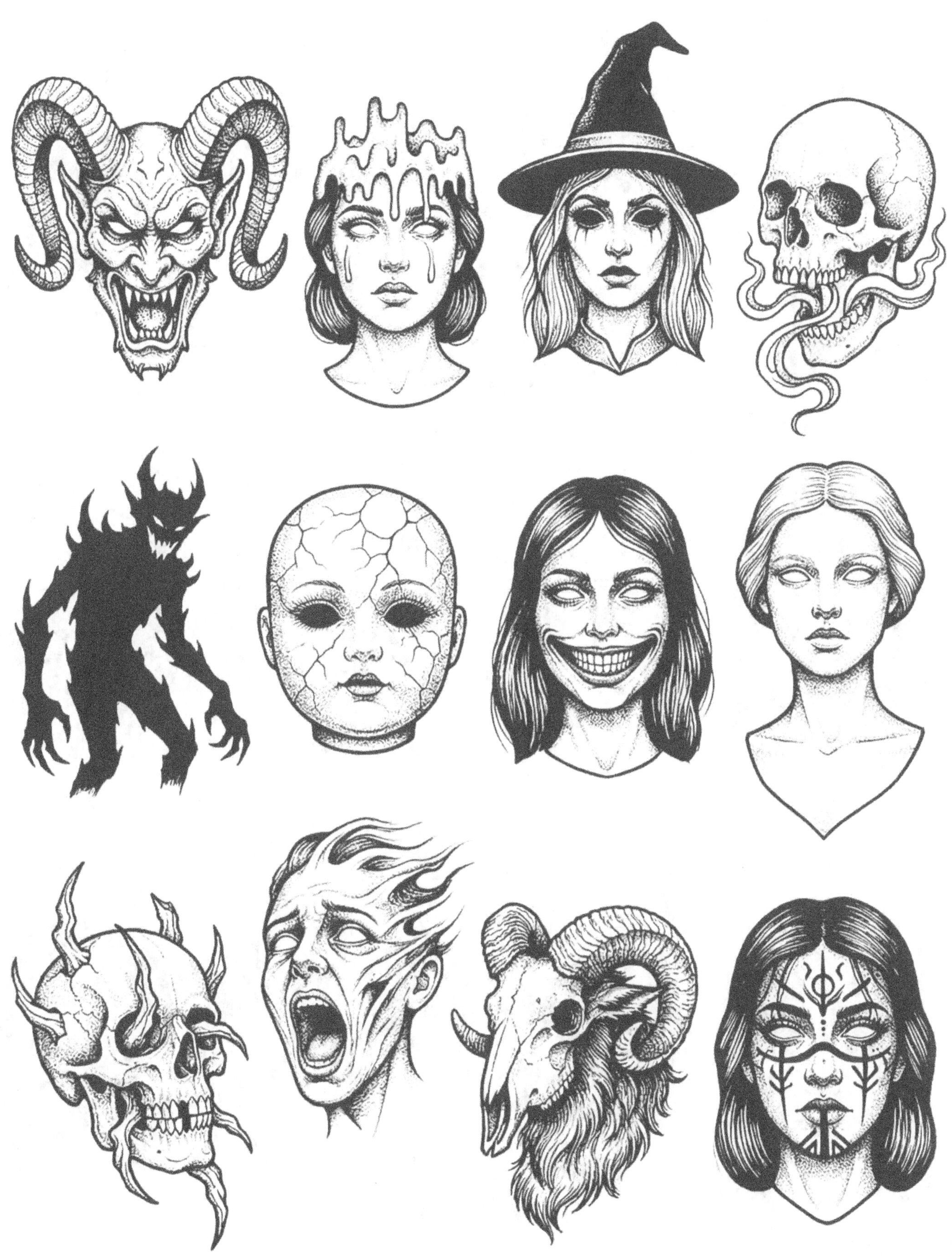

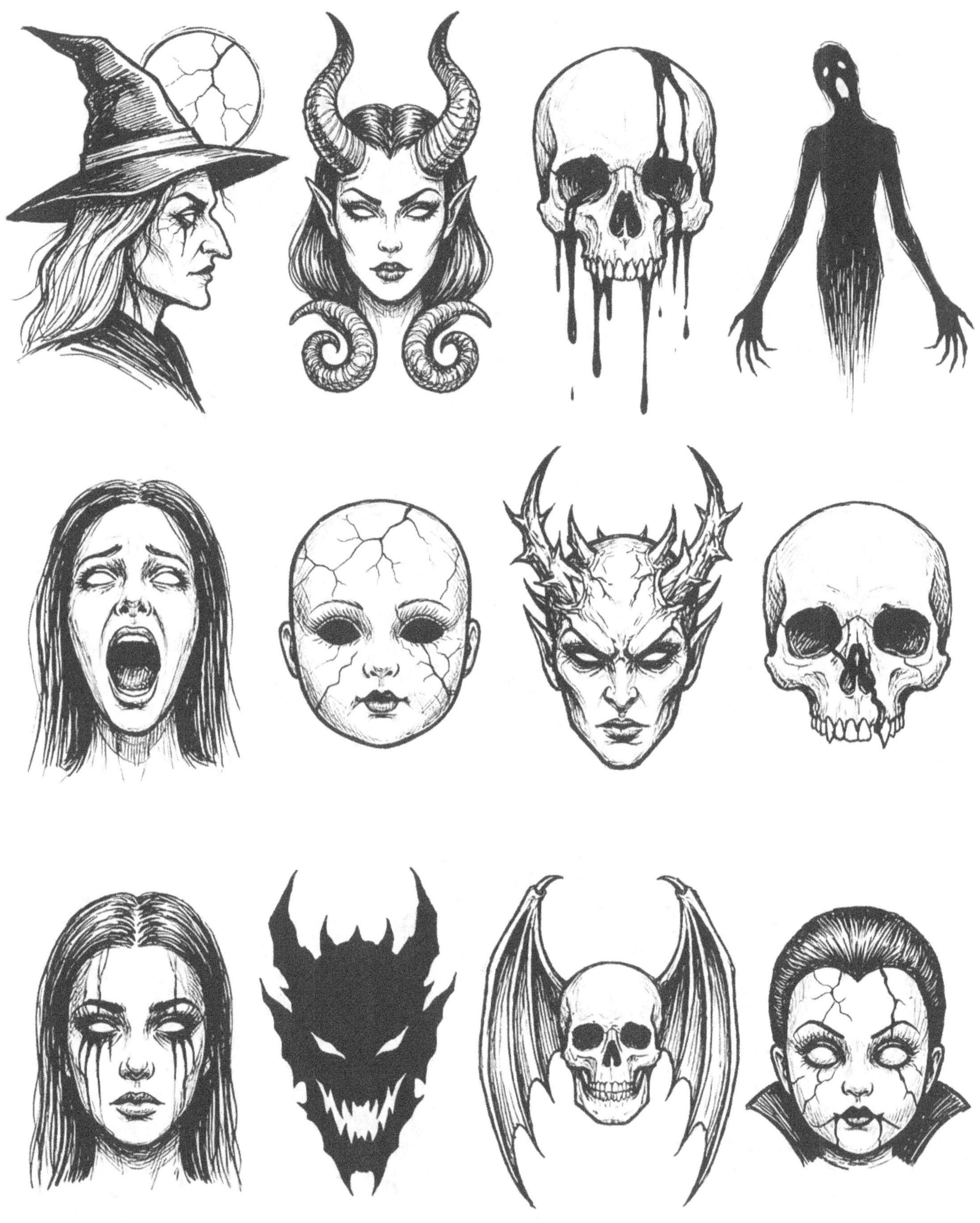

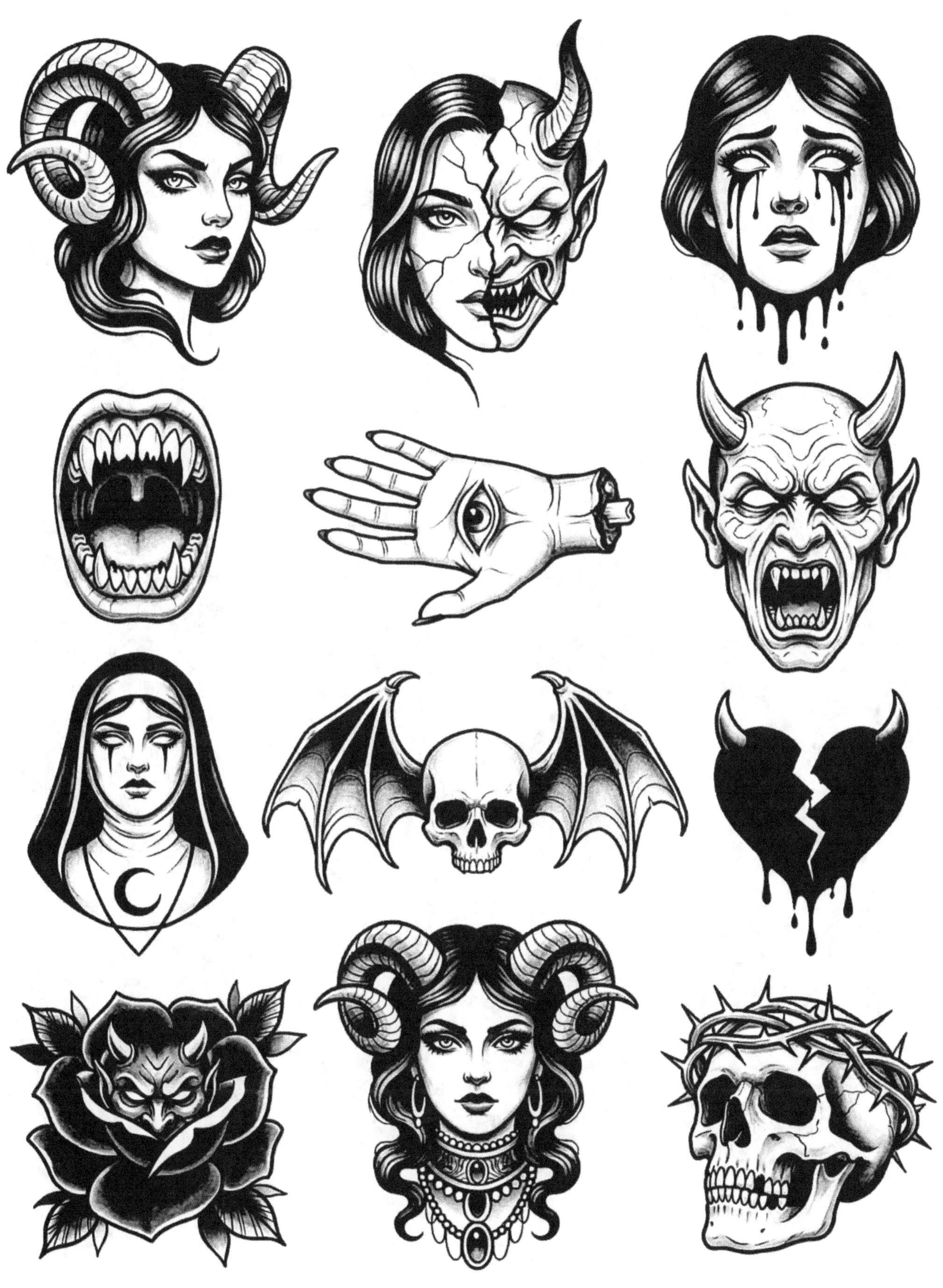

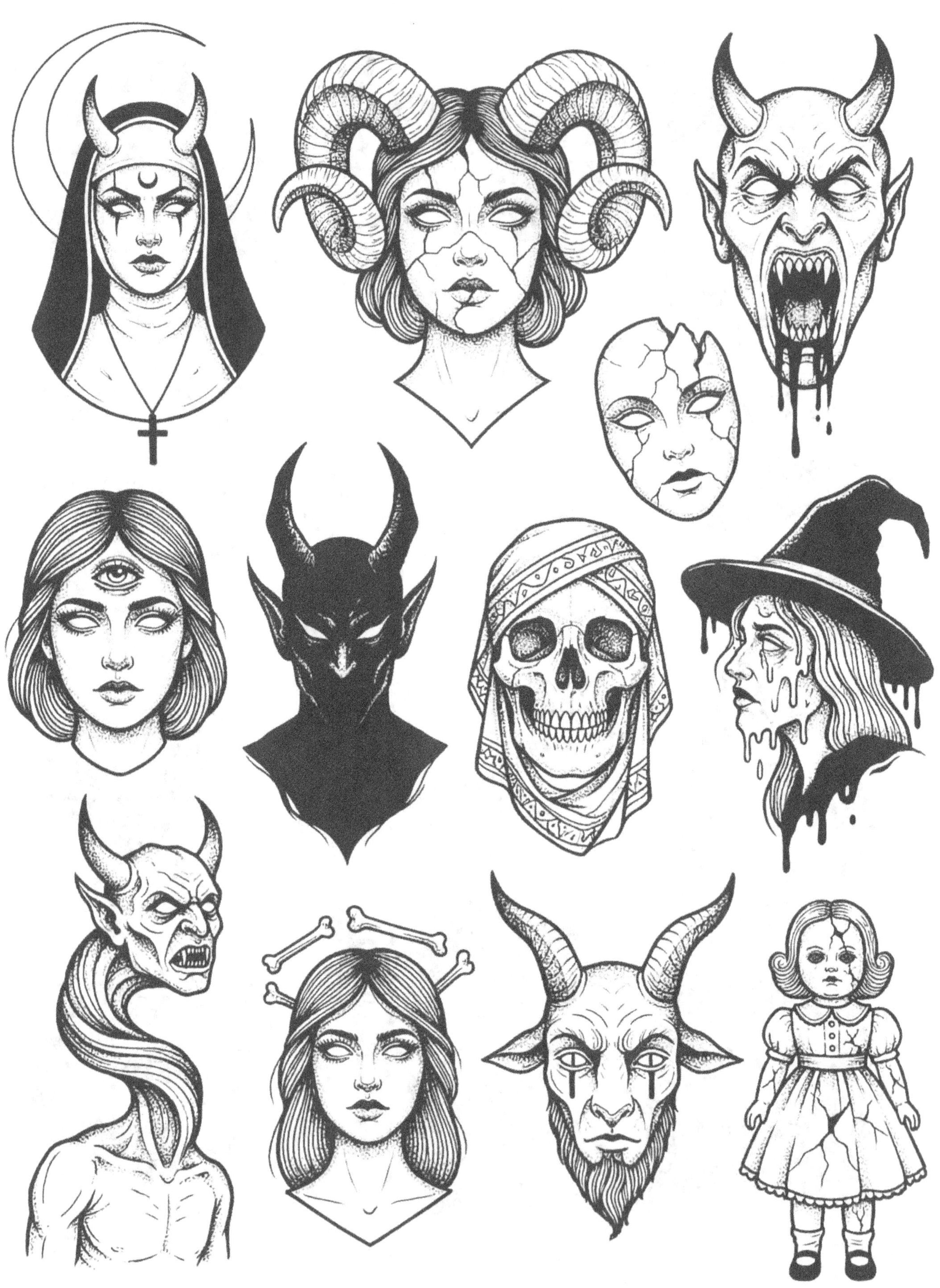

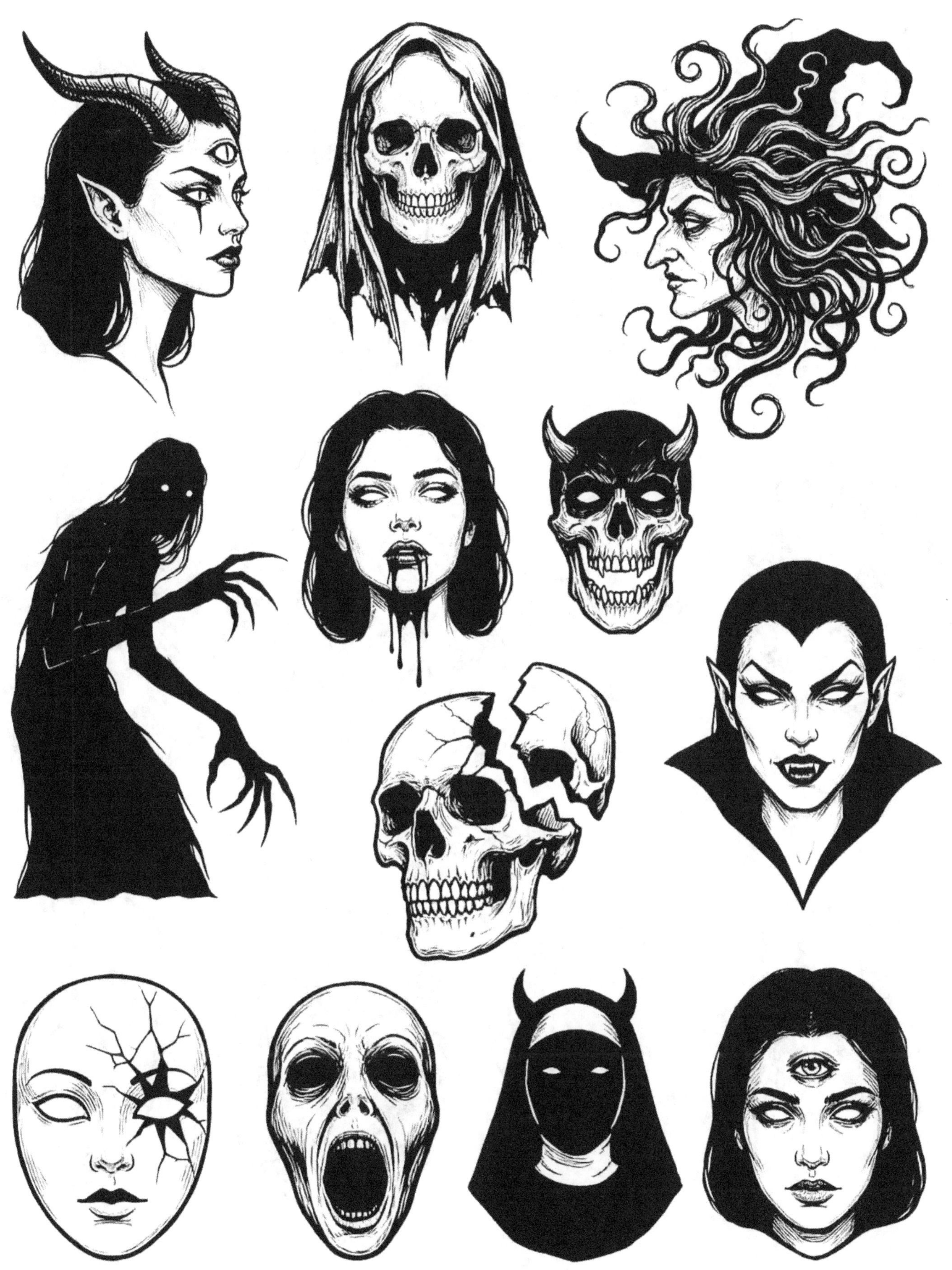

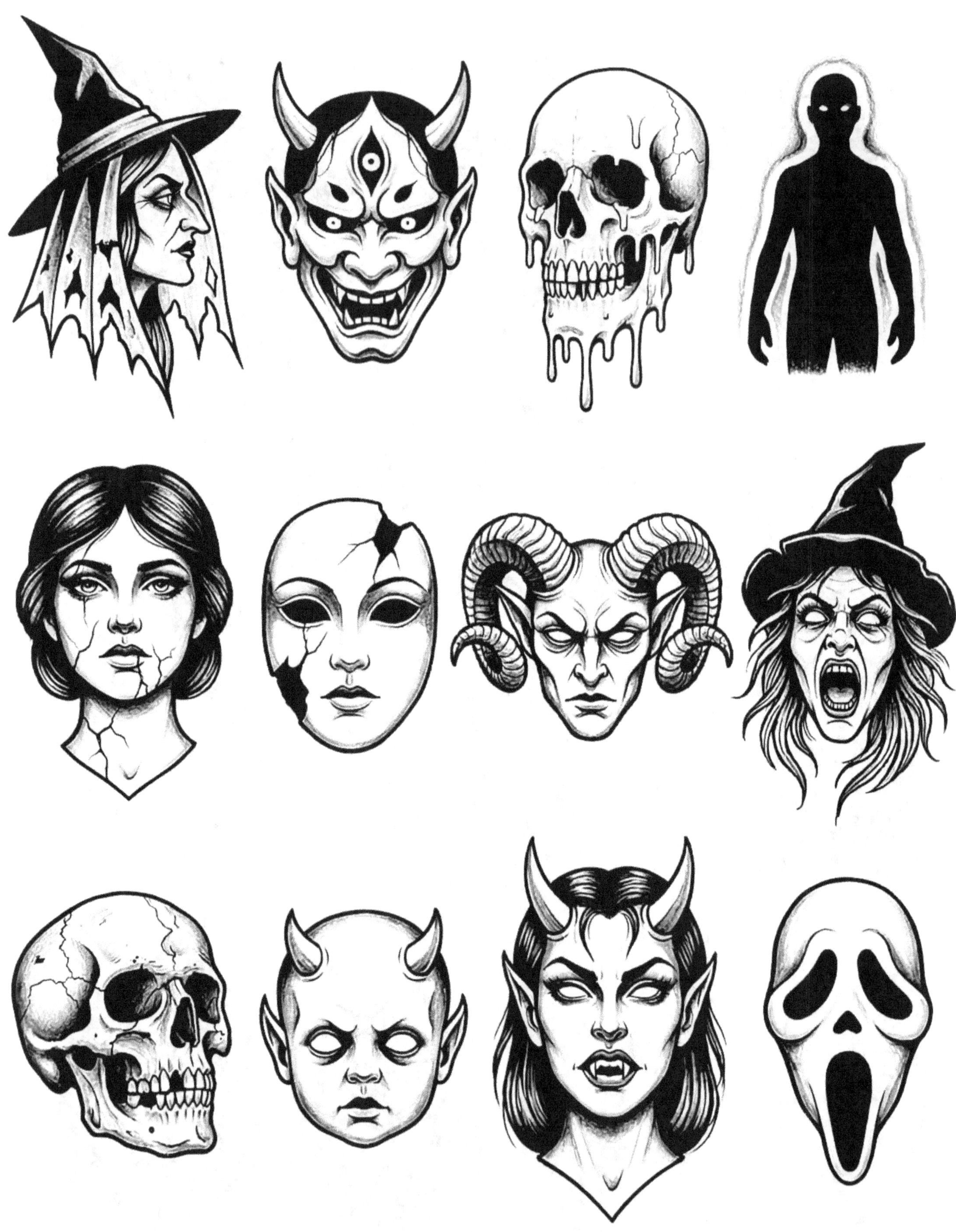

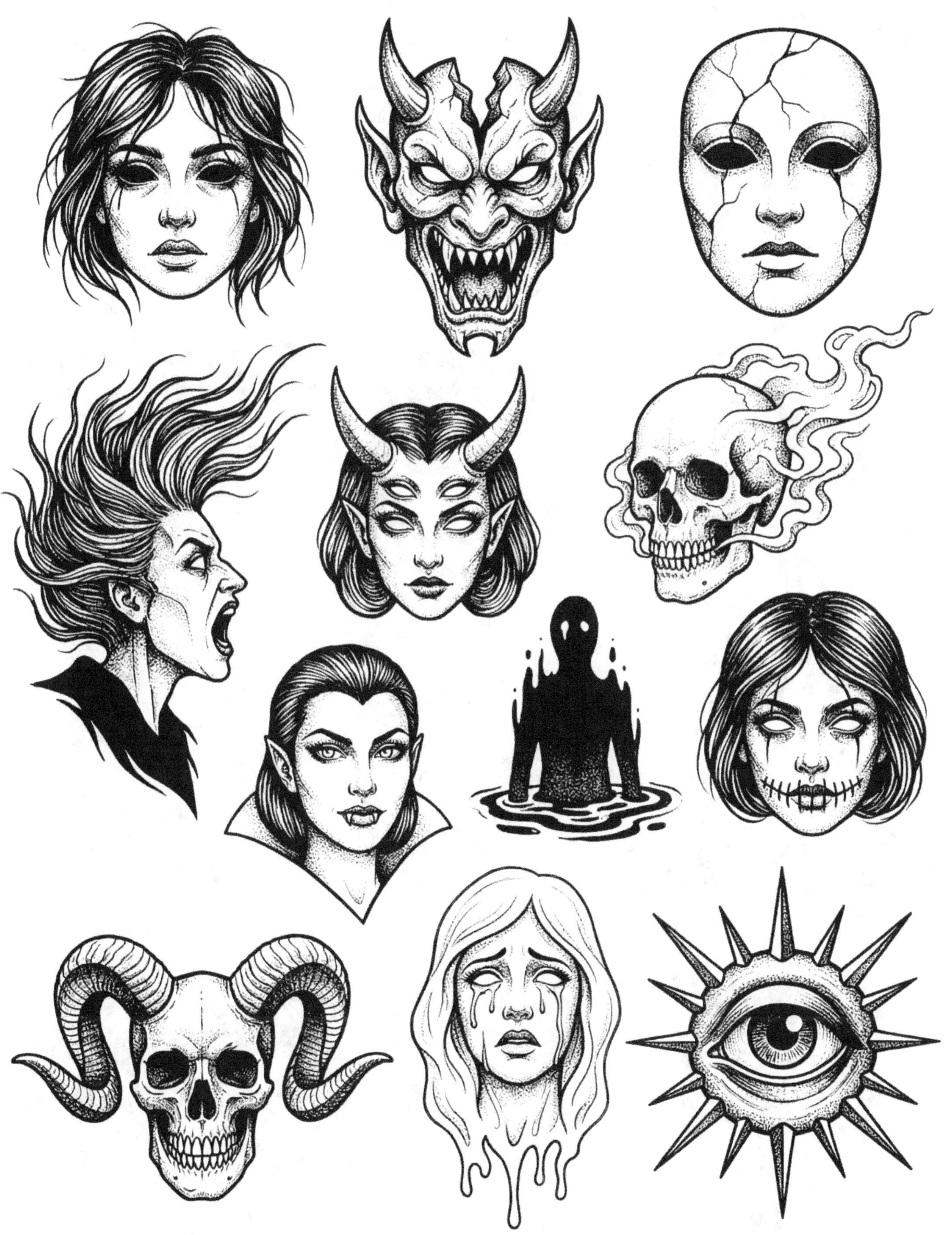

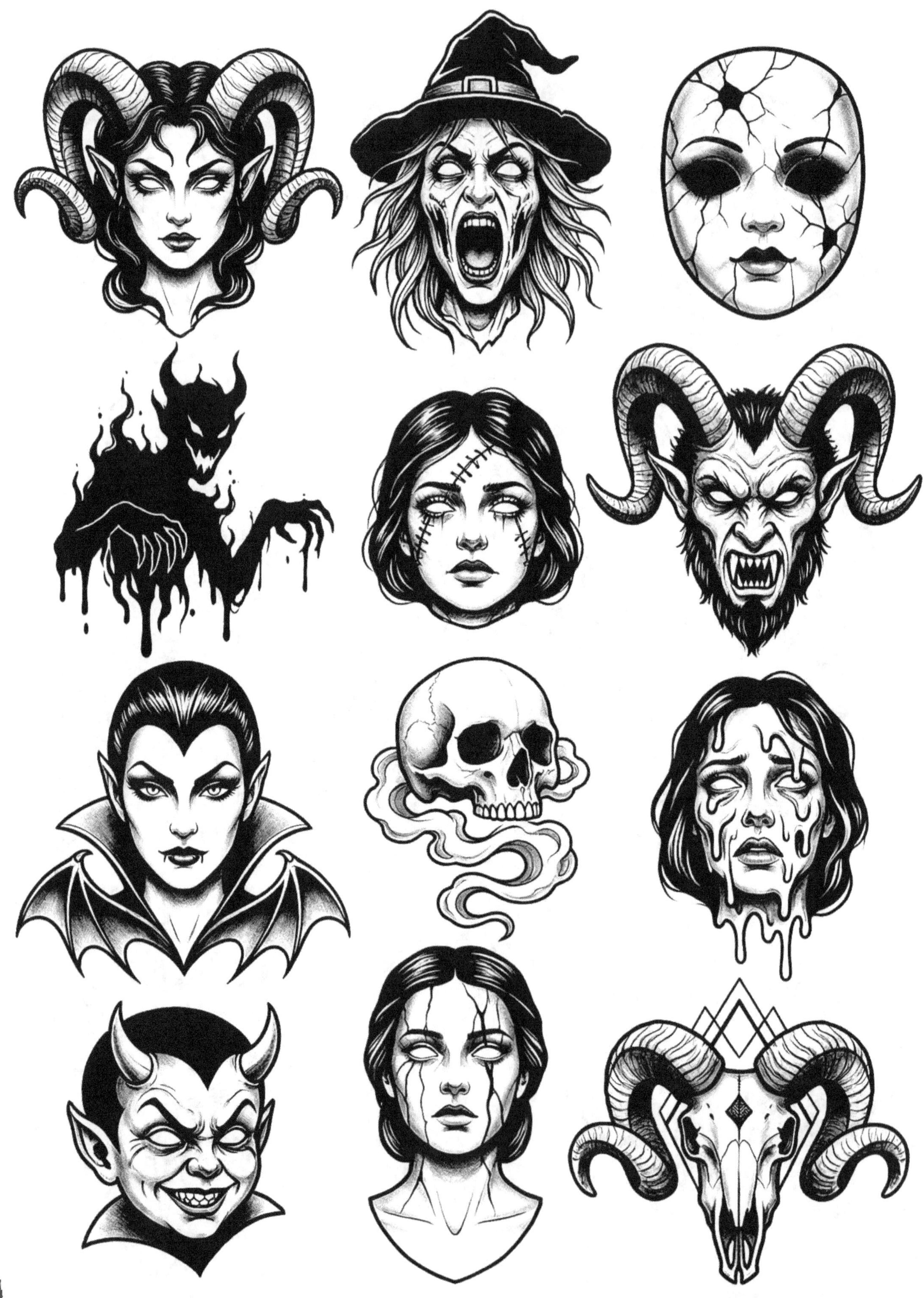

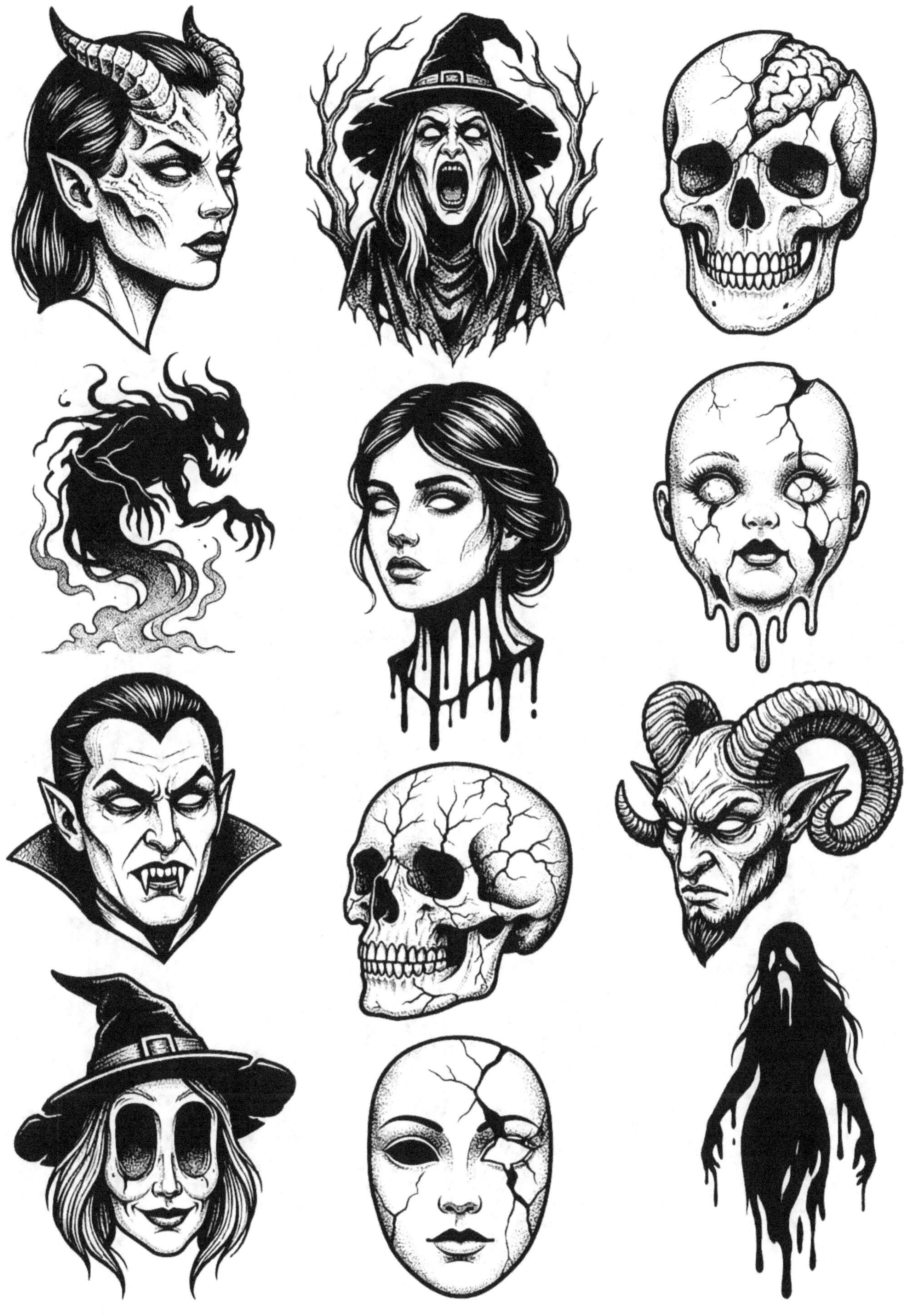

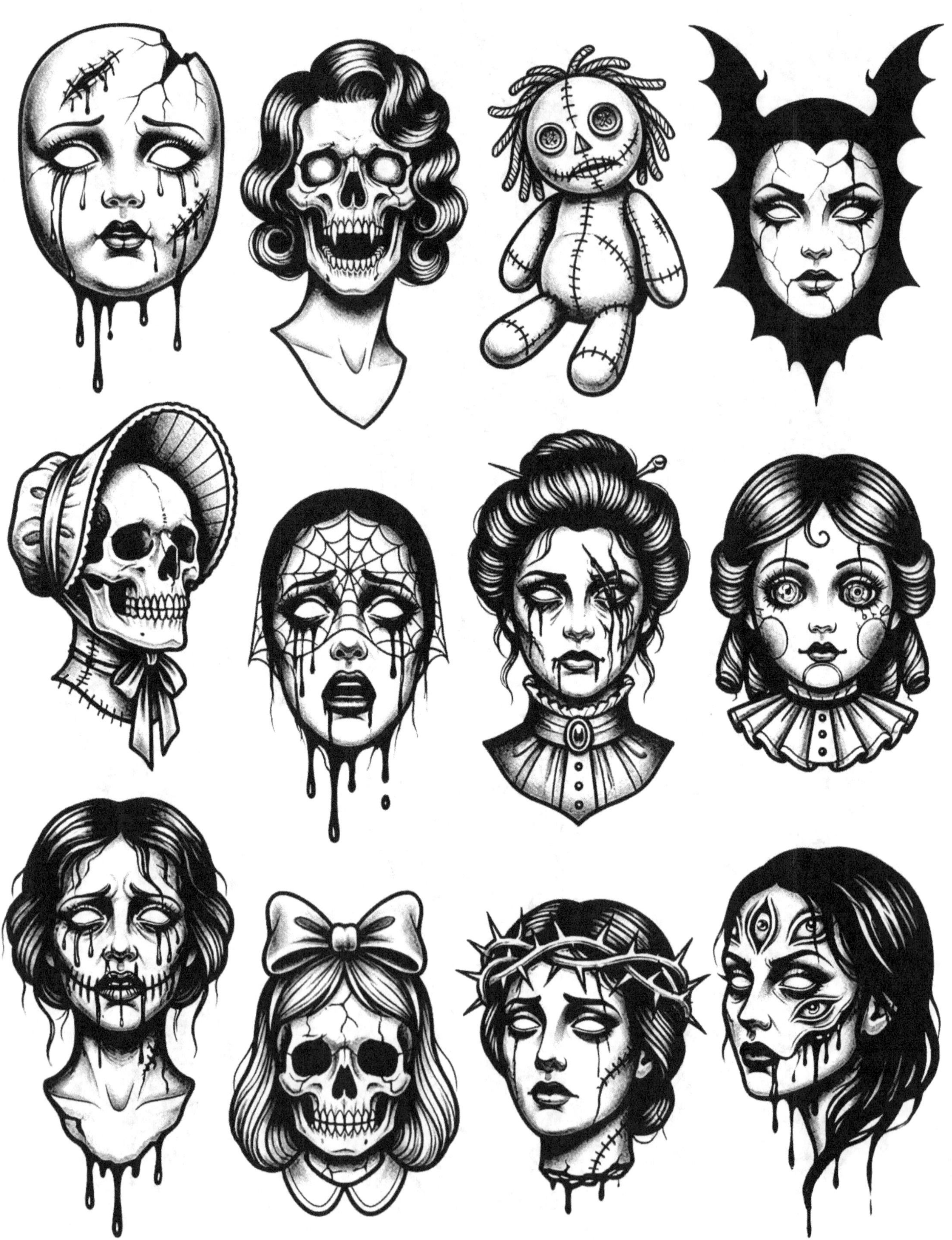

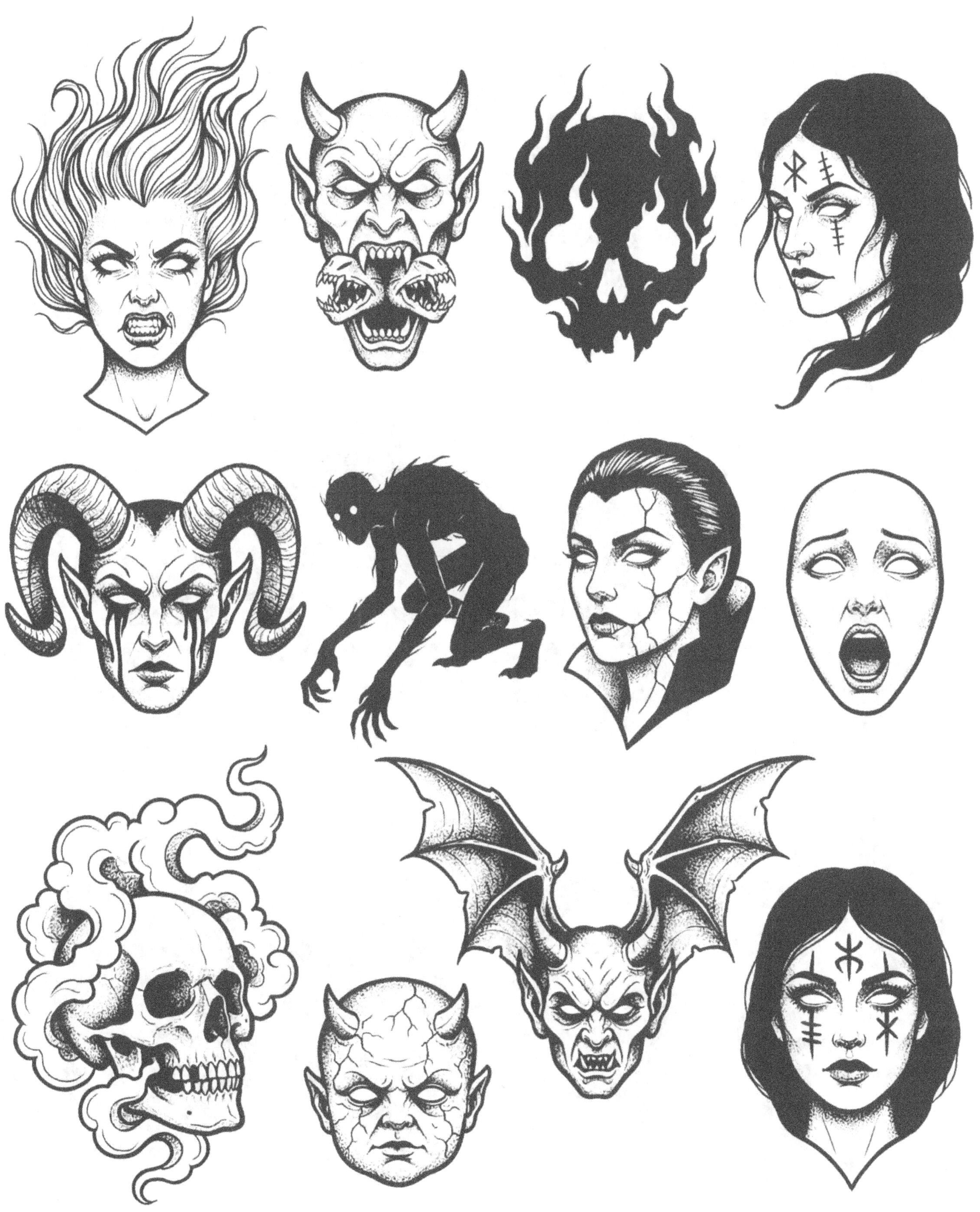

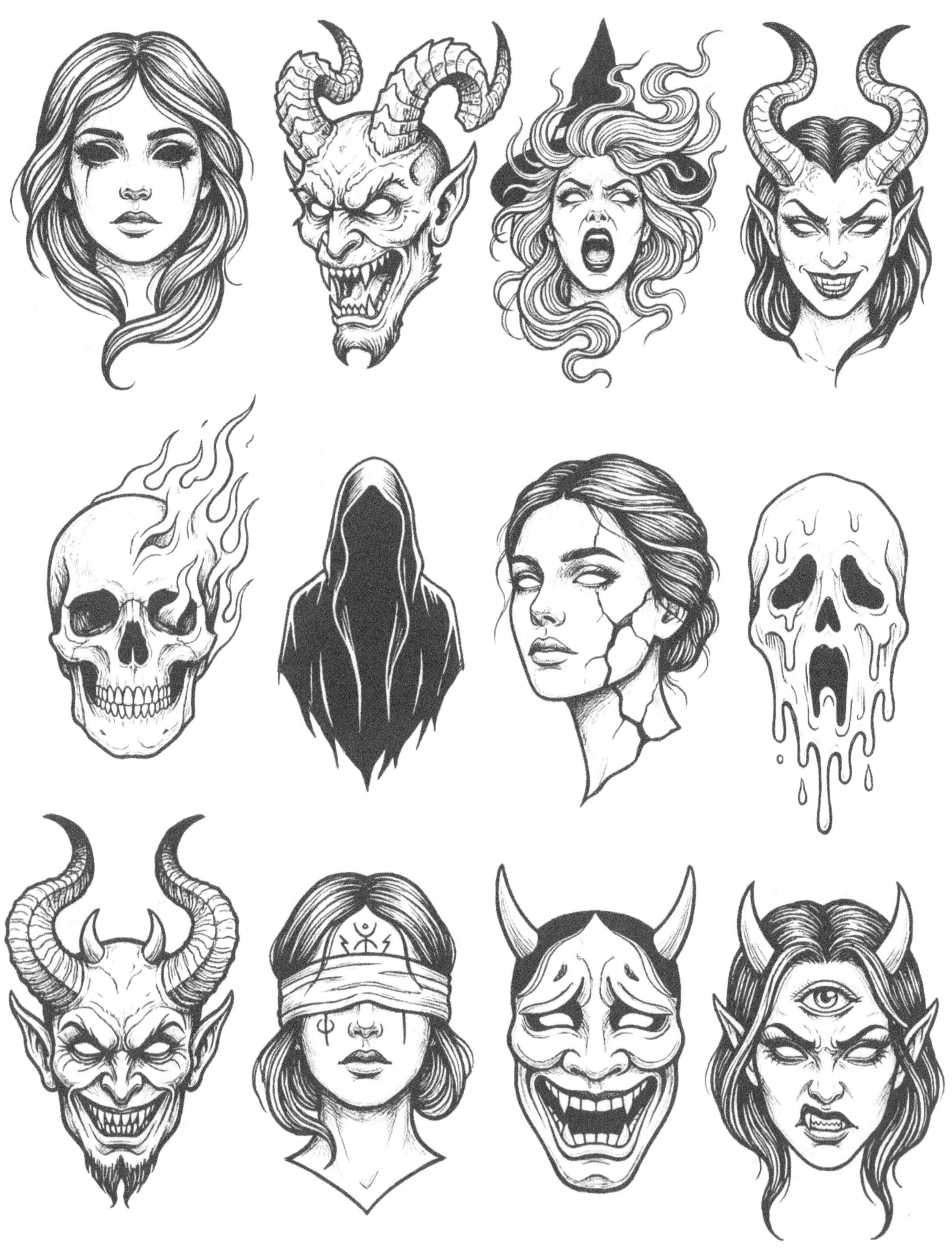

GOTHIC CHURCHES & ARCHITECTURE

Gothic architecture has shaped visual culture for centuries, and in tattoo art it remains one of the most striking sources of atmosphere and mood. Massive arches, towering spires, stained-glass patterns, rose windows, vaulted ceilings and carved stone details all create a language of light and shadow that translates beautifully onto skin.

In tattooing, gothic structures function like monuments of emotion. They can feel sacred, intimidating, mysterious or melancholic. A single architectural element — a pointed arch, a fractured window, a fragment of a cathedral facade — can set the tone for an entire composition. These forms offer rhythm, symmetry, vertical power and a sense of age that blends seamlessly with darker themes, fantasy elements or historic symbolism.

This chapter gathers architectural motifs that can be used as focal points, backgrounds, frames or standalone pieces. Clean silhouettes provide strong structure; intricate ornaments add depth and storytelling; broken stone and shattered windows introduce dramatic contrast. Whether you start from one detail or combine multiple elements, gothic architecture gives you the tools to create scenes that feel timeless and cinematic.

Use these designs as anchors for larger compositions or as inspiration for ornamental linework, atmospheric backgrounds or full sleeve layouts. Let the windows, arches and spires guide your eye toward symmetry, perspective and contrast — key ingredients in powerful tattoo design.

This is the place where stone meets shadow,

where history becomes atmosphere,

and where every line reaches upward.

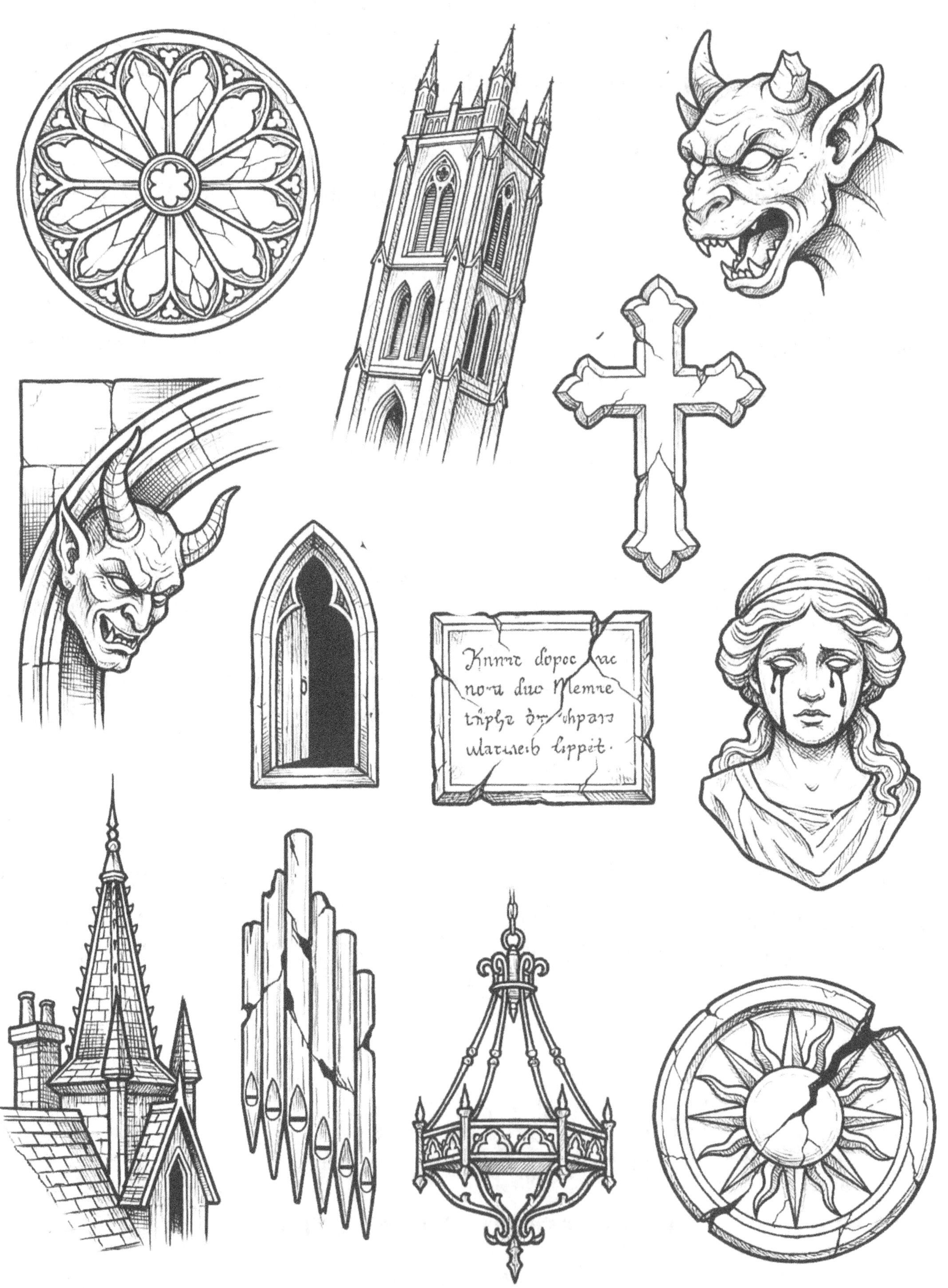

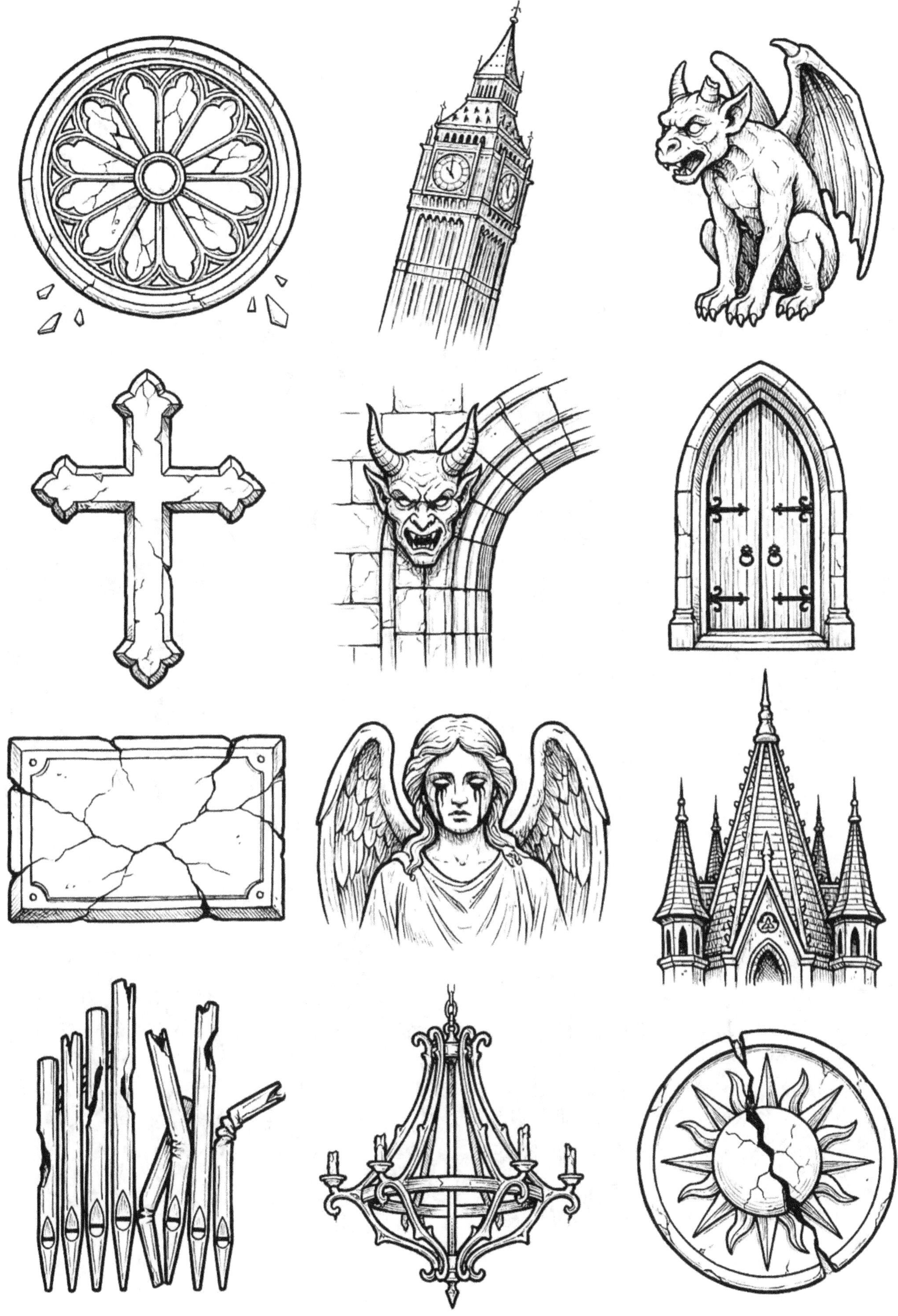

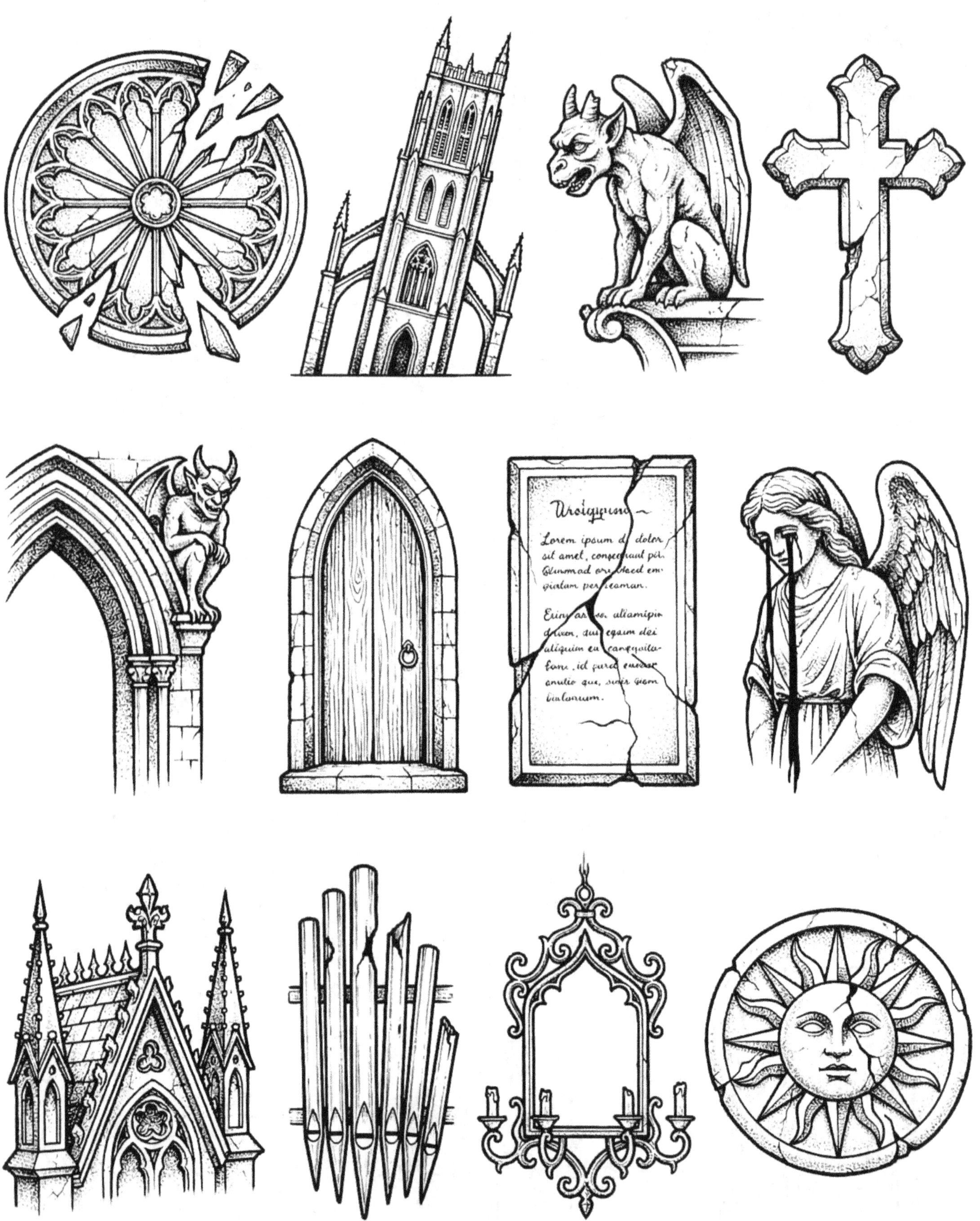

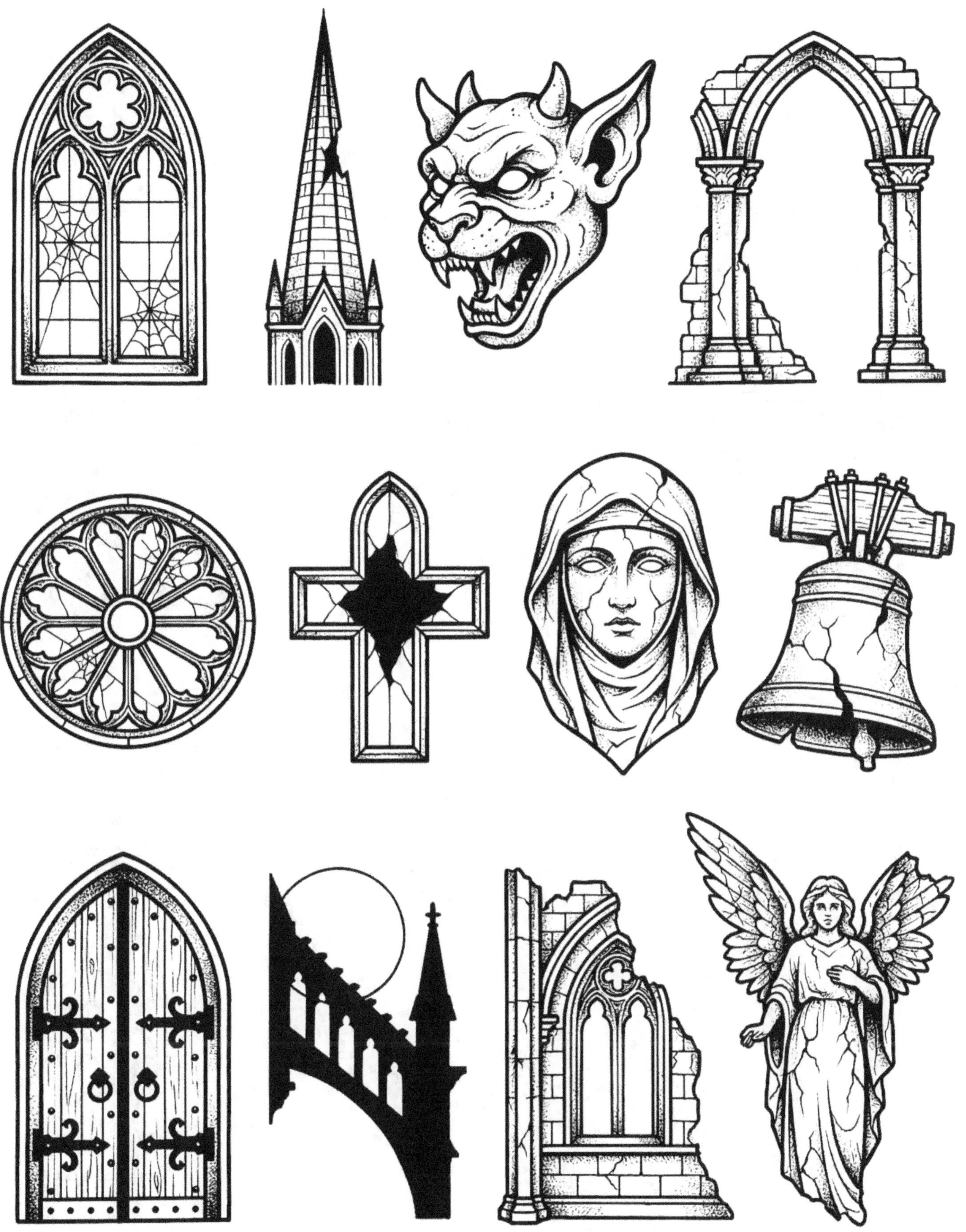

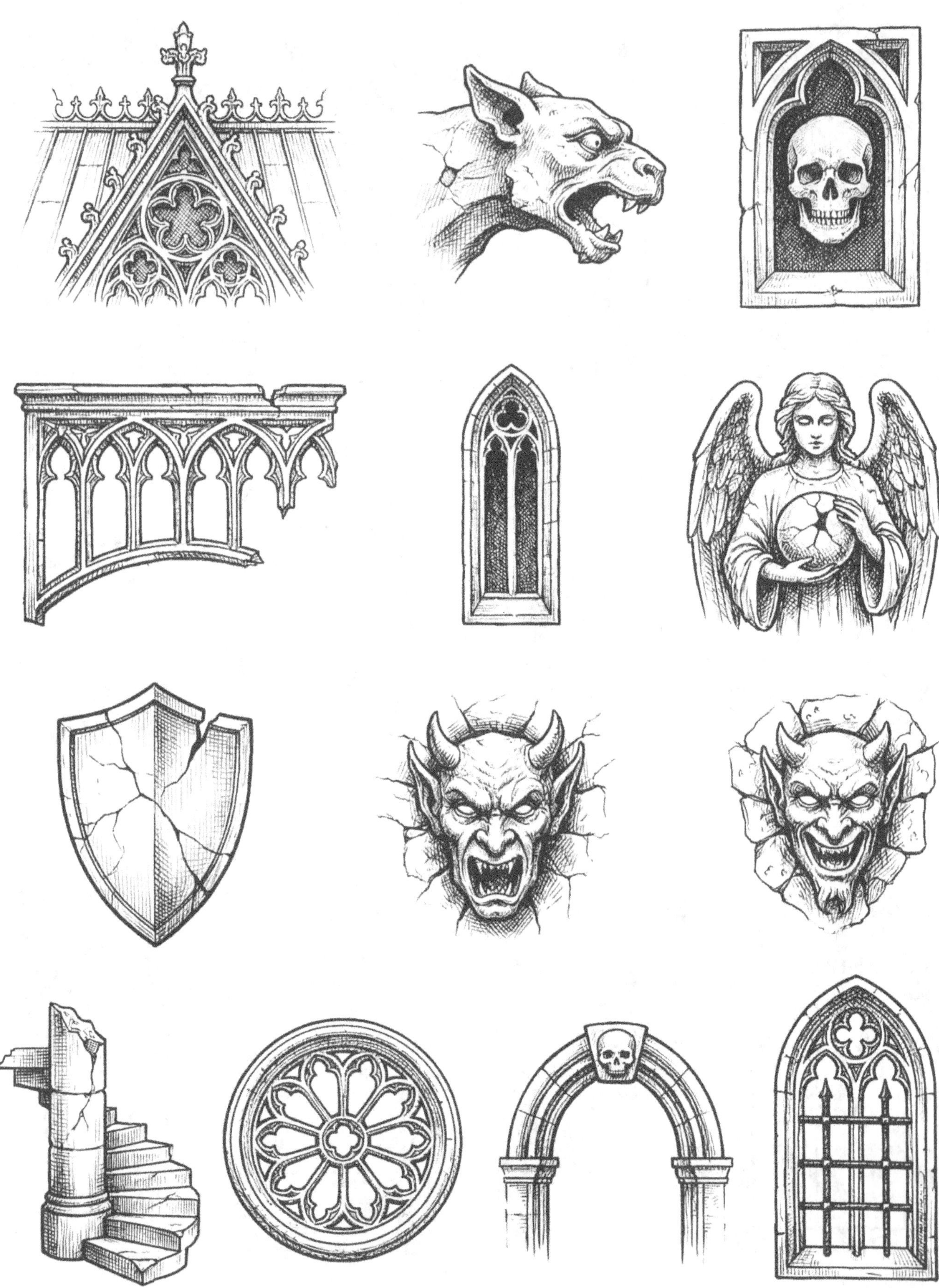

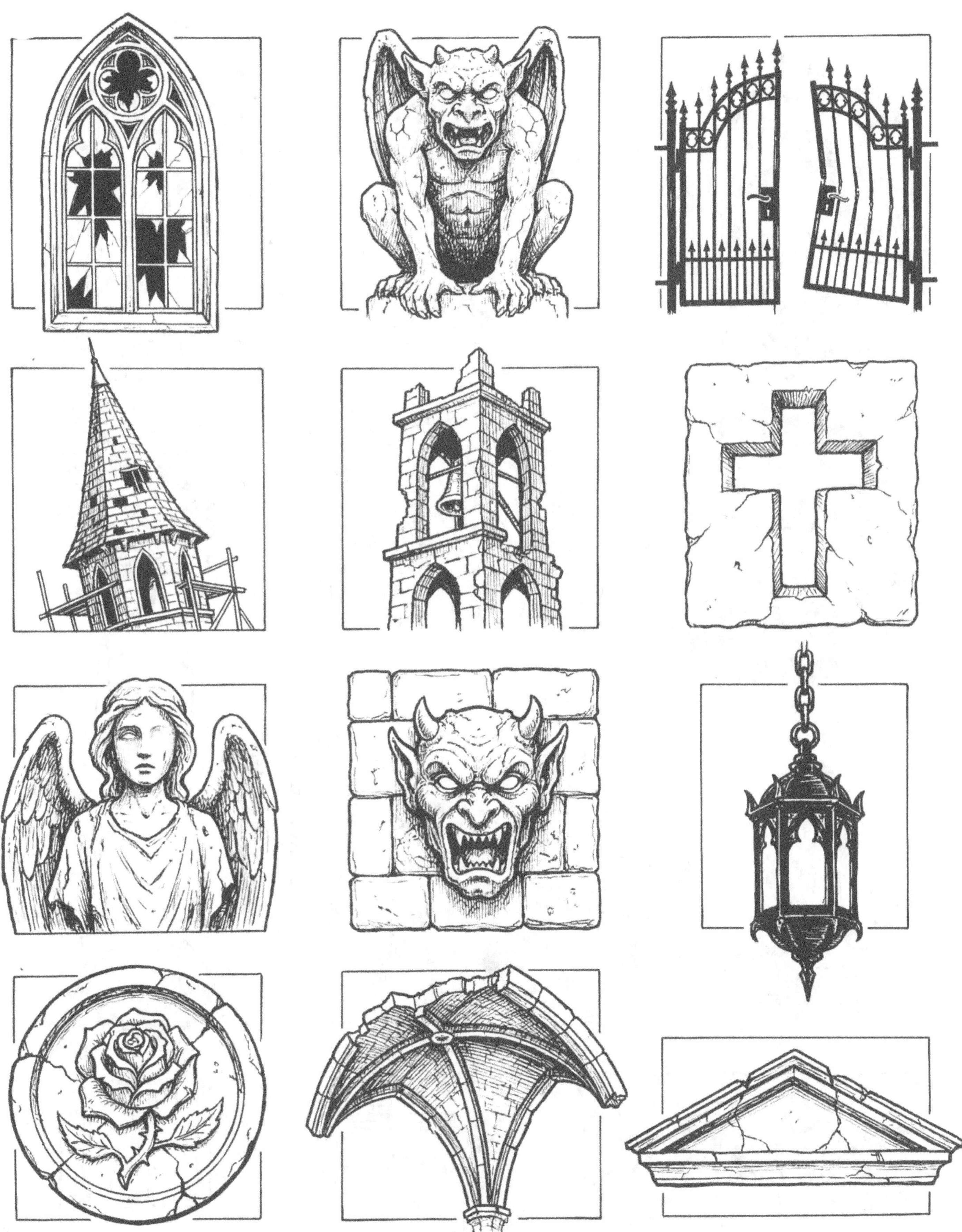

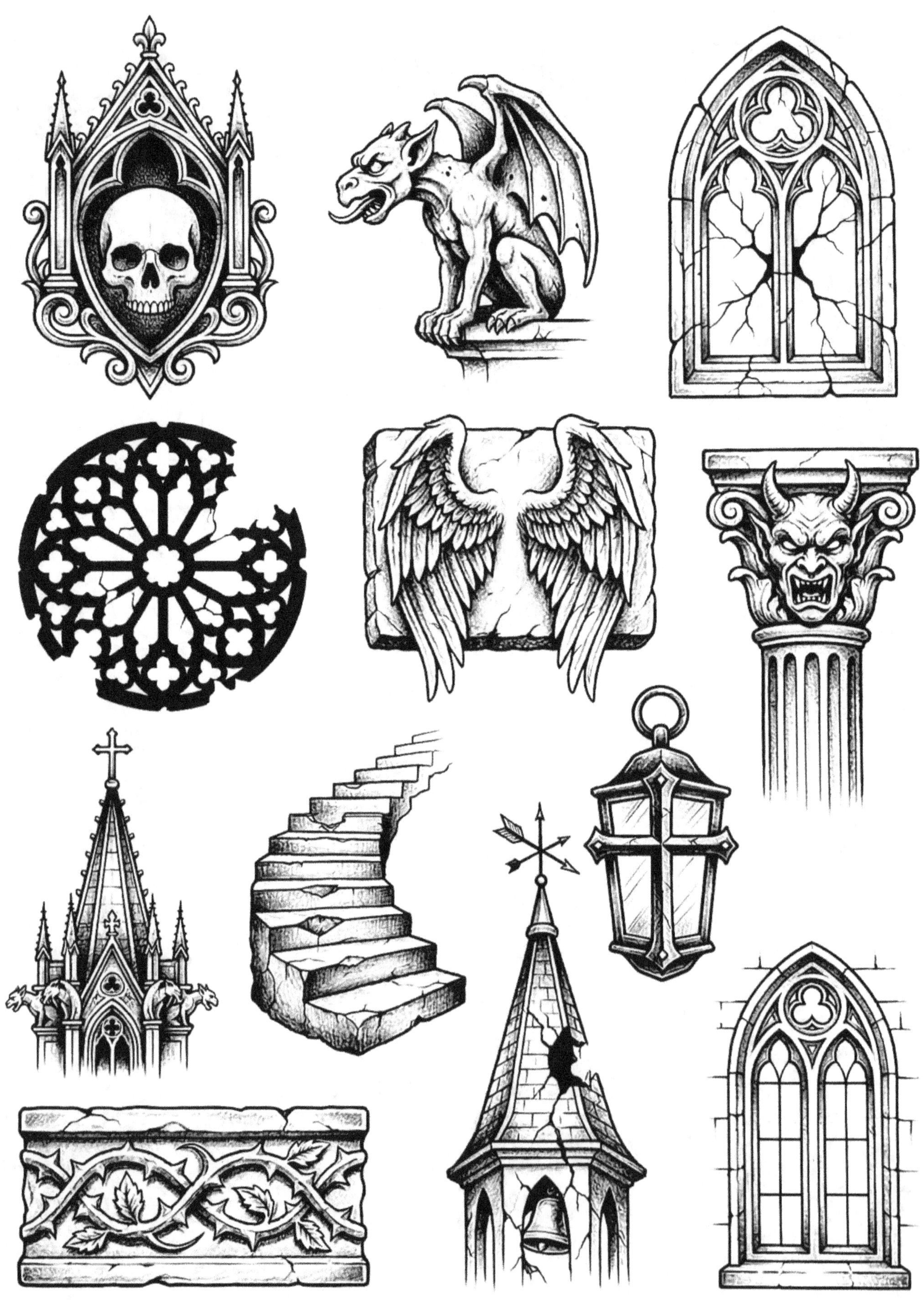

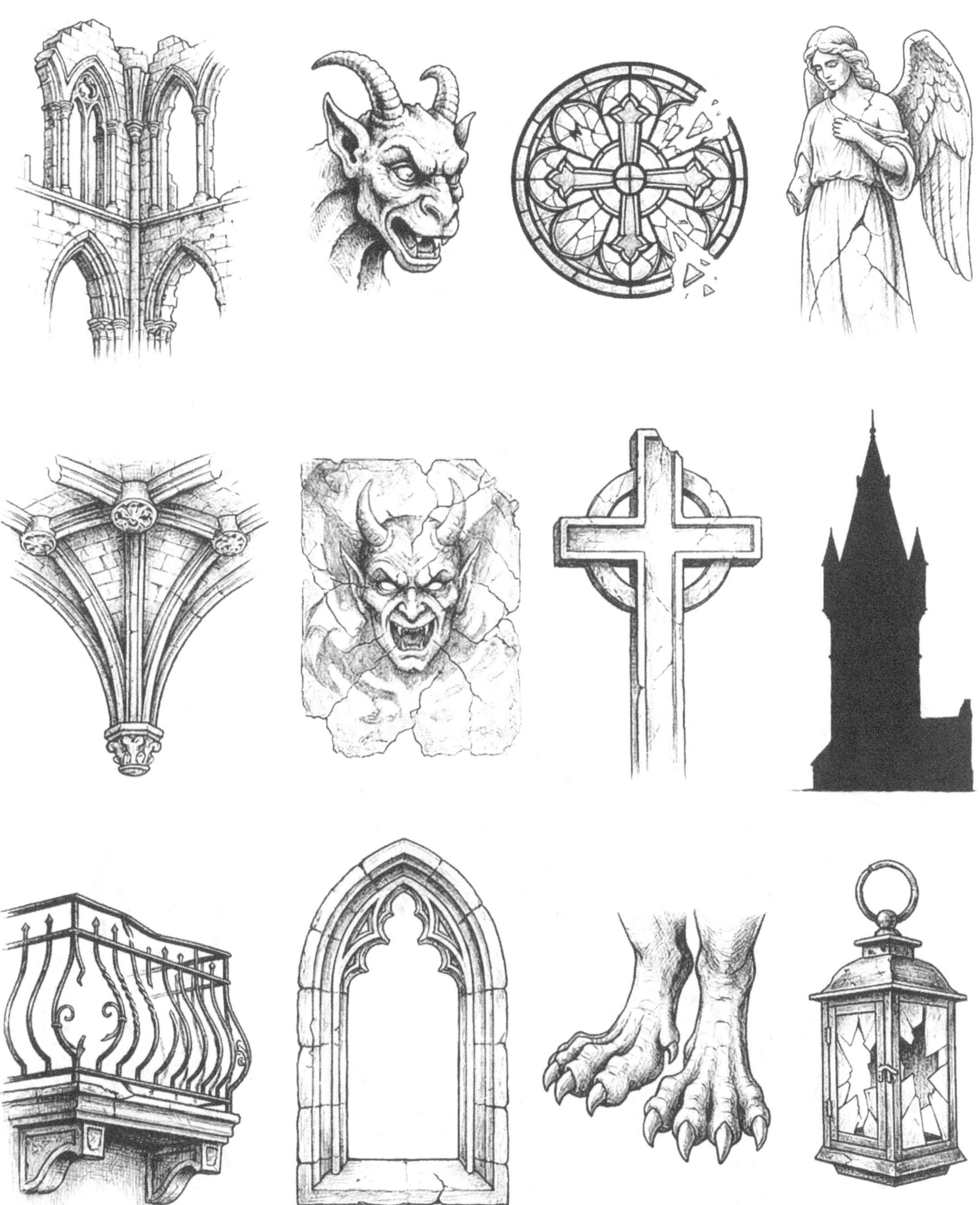

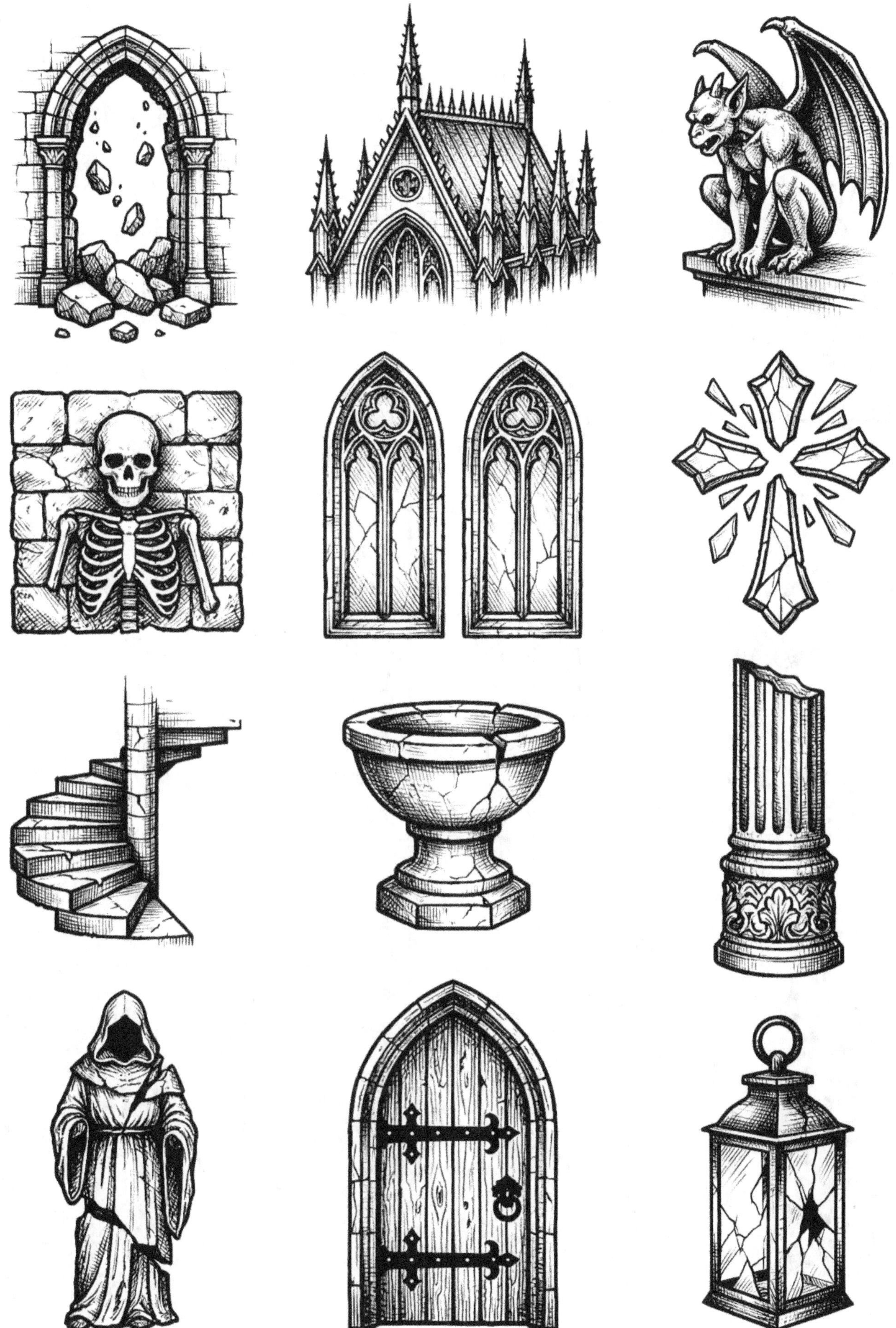

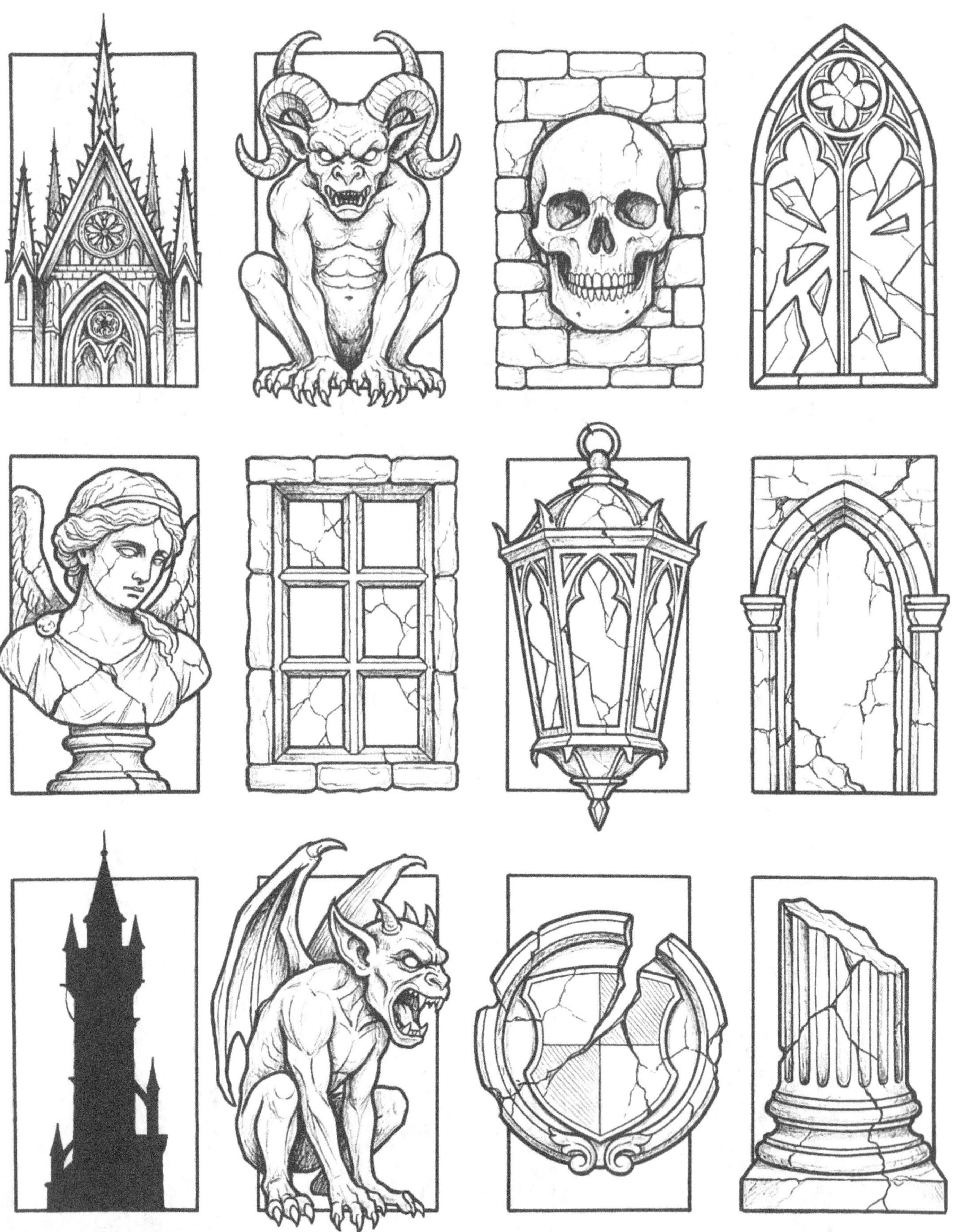

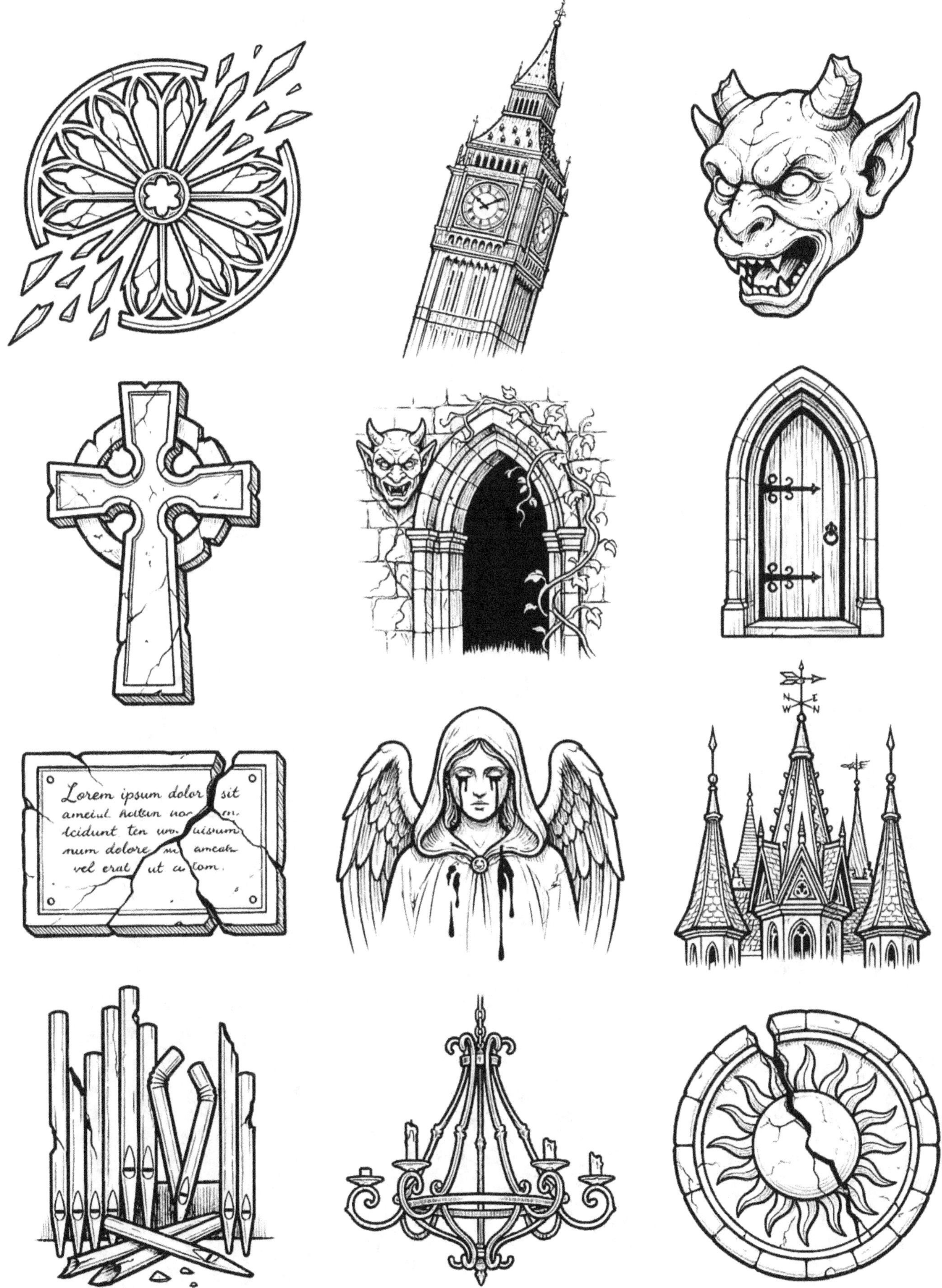

Lorem ipsum dolor sit
ameiul hollin nor m.
lcidunt ten wol uisum
num dolore m amcots
vel erai ut u tom.

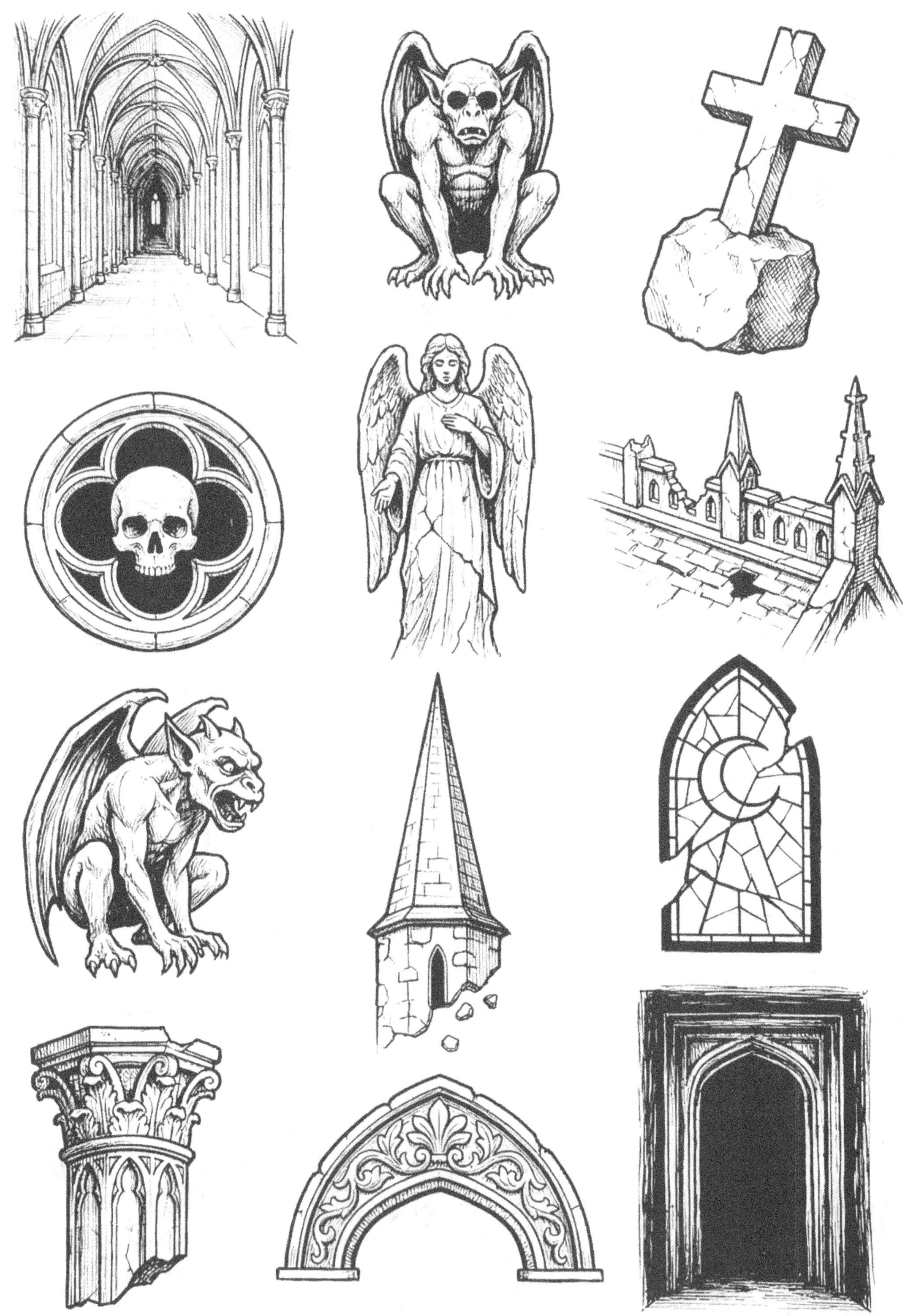

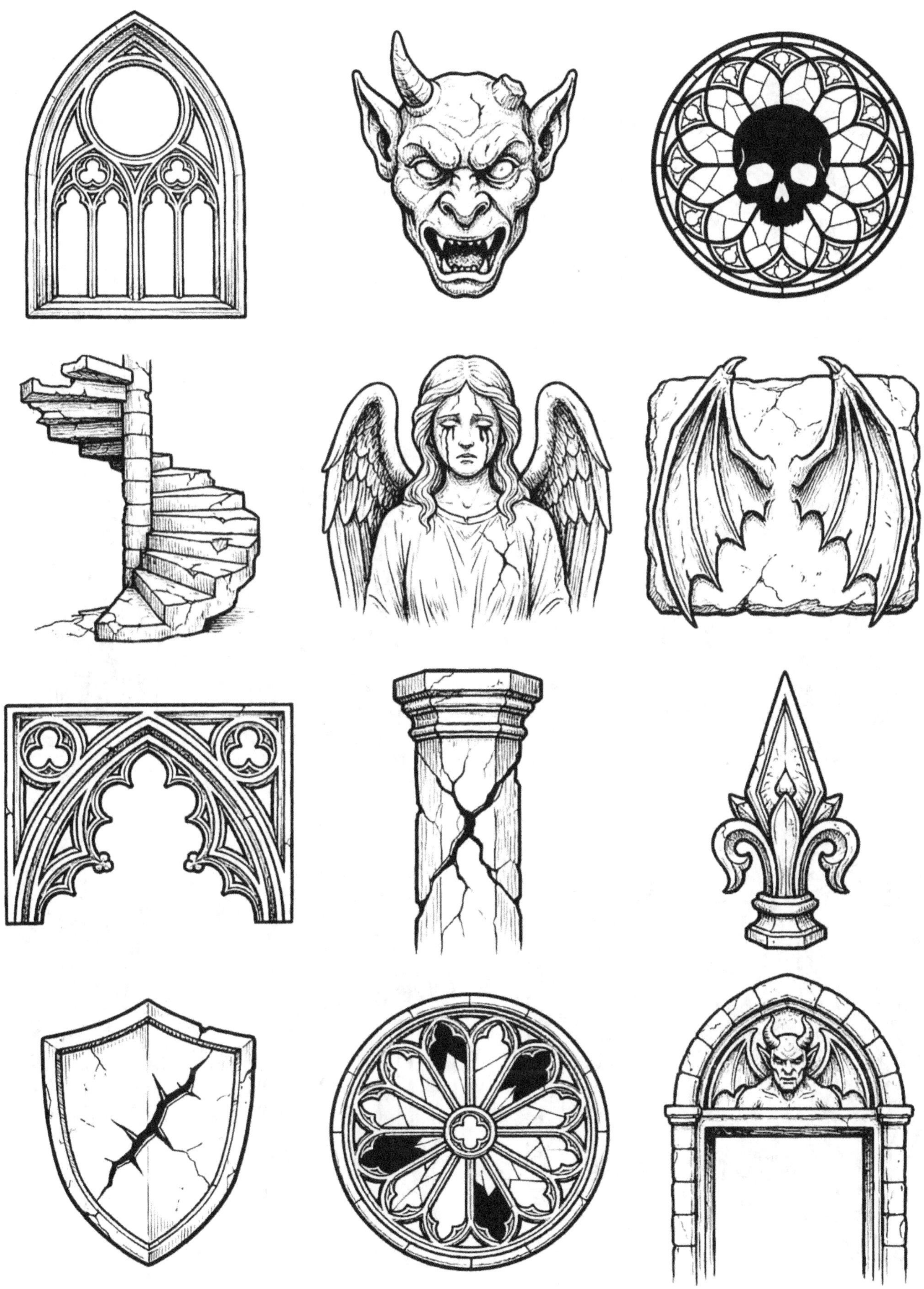

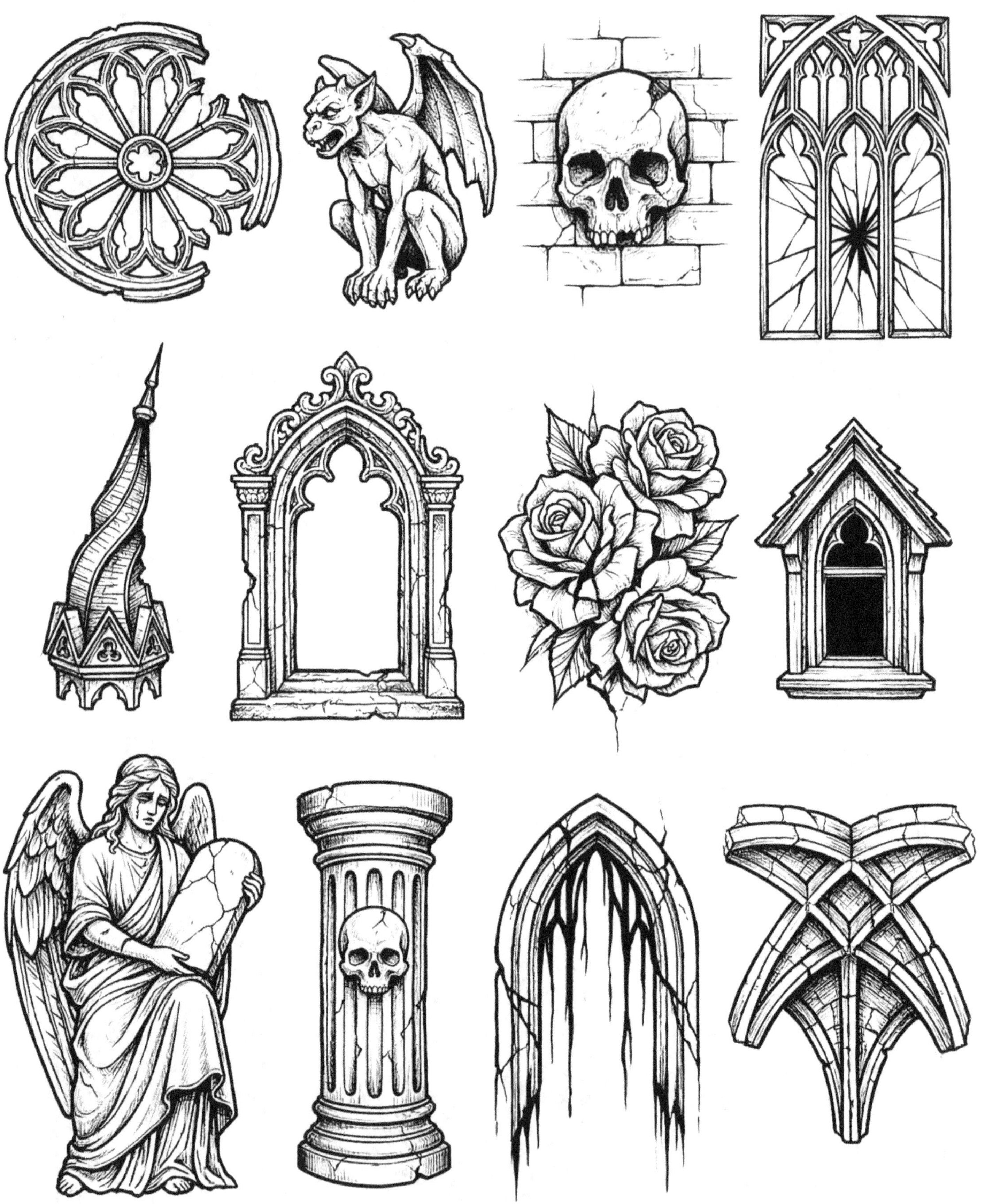

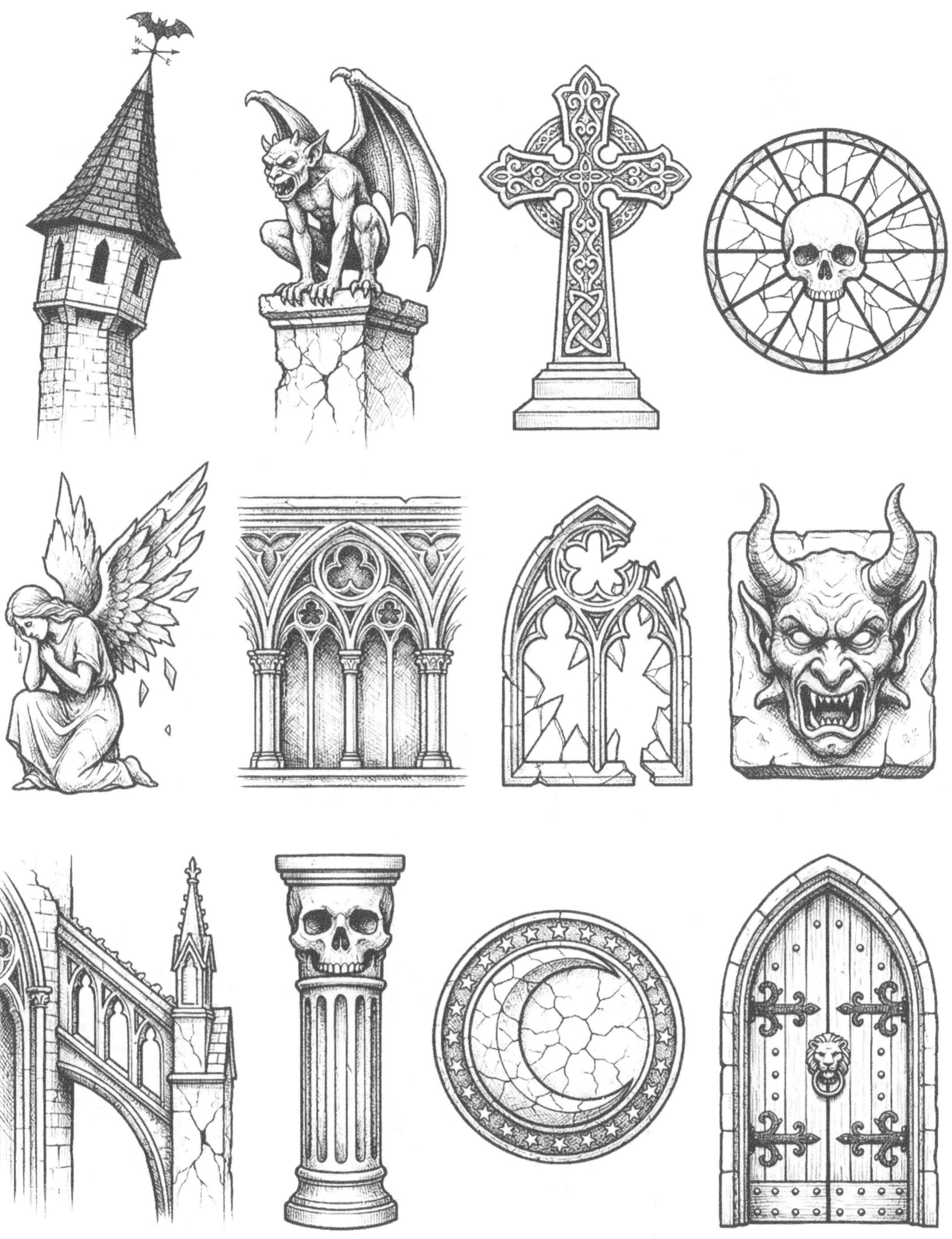

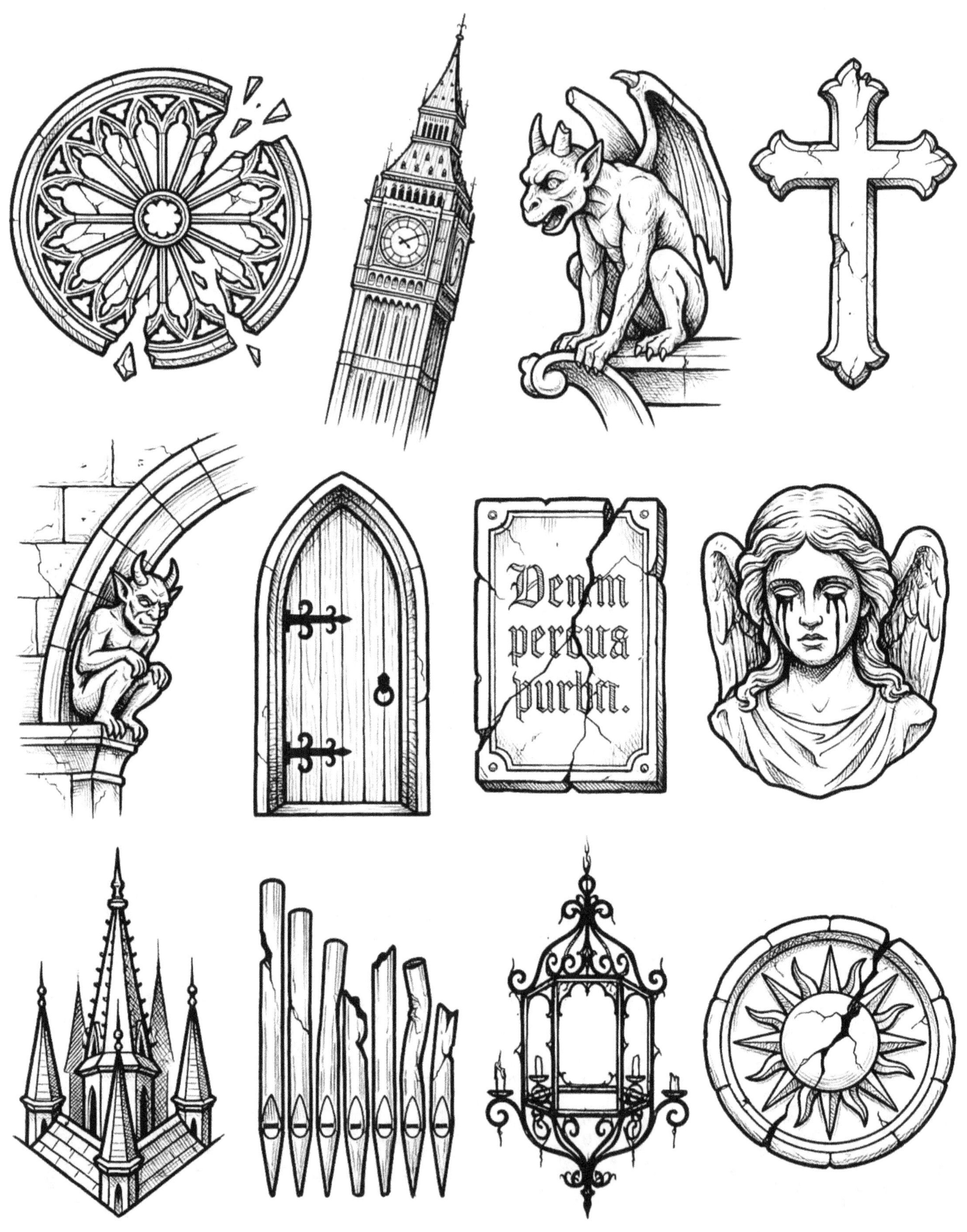

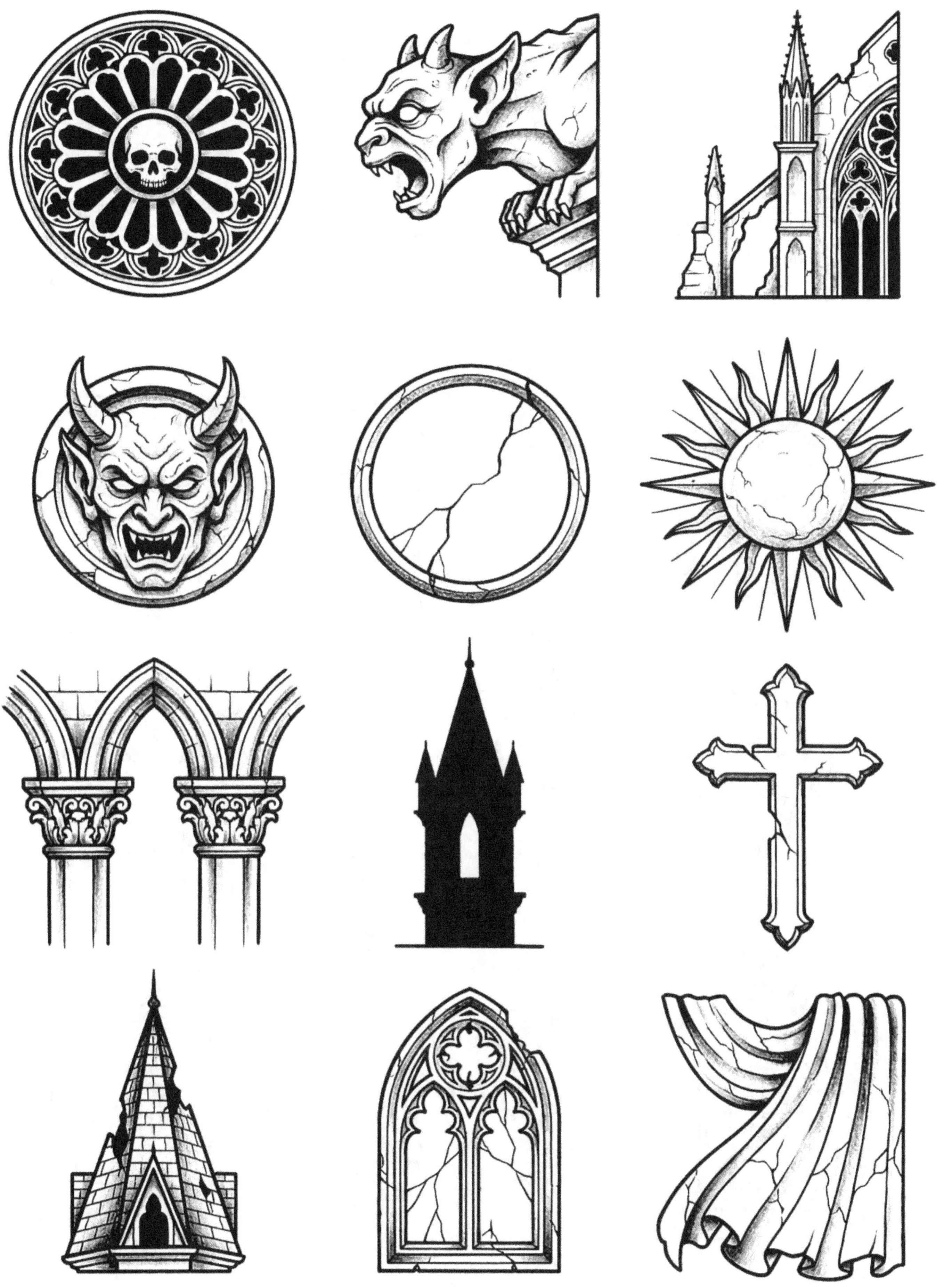

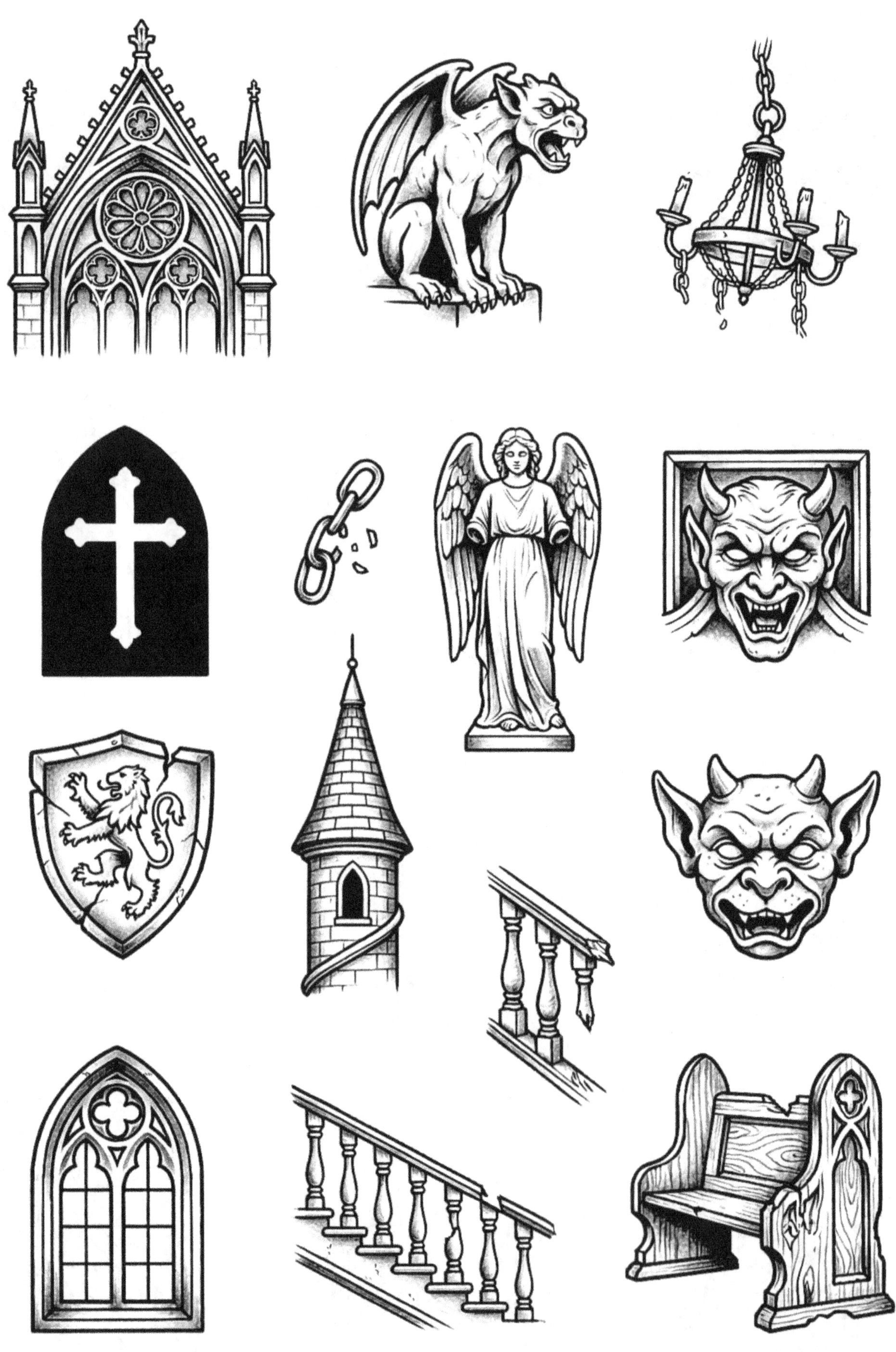

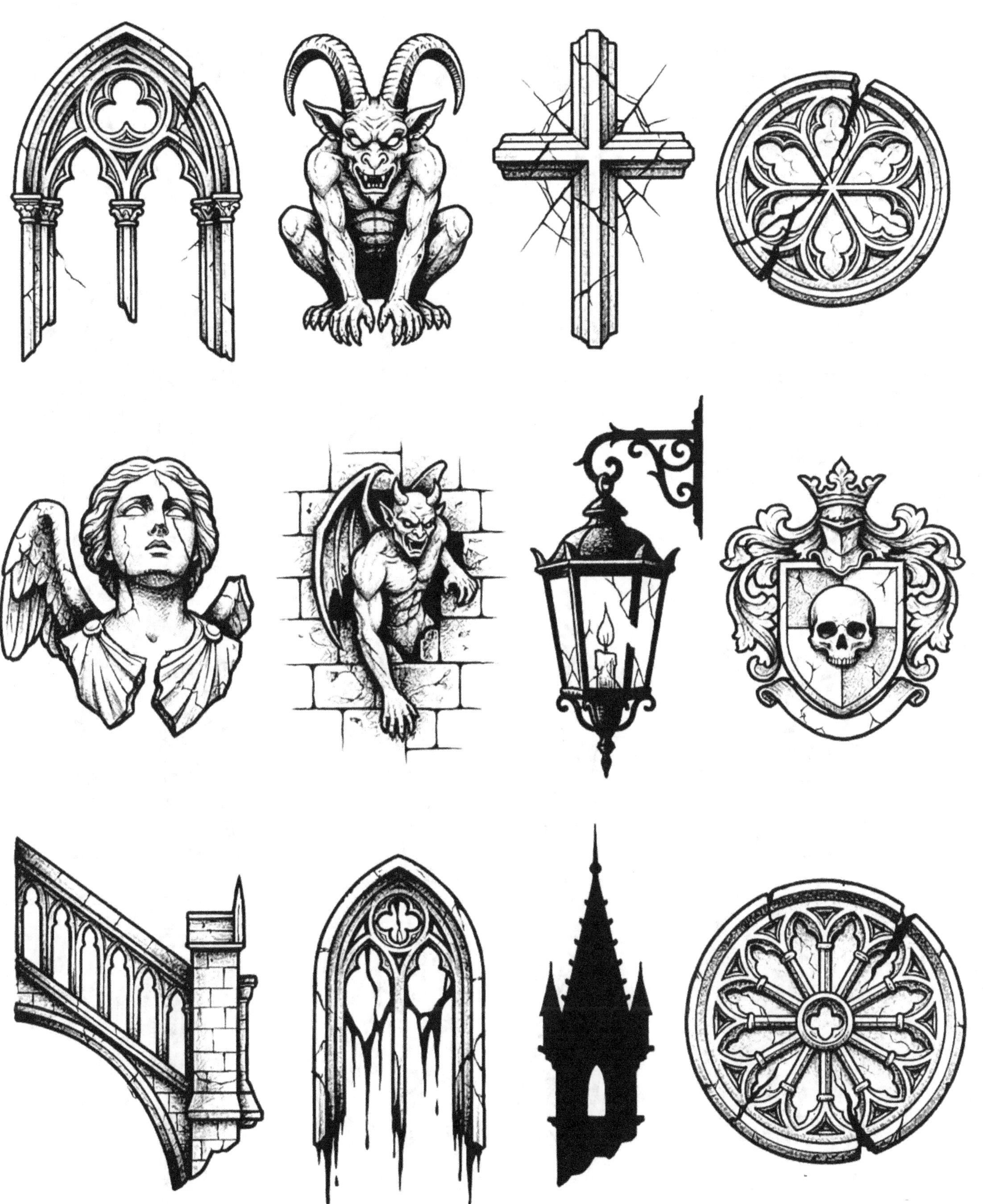

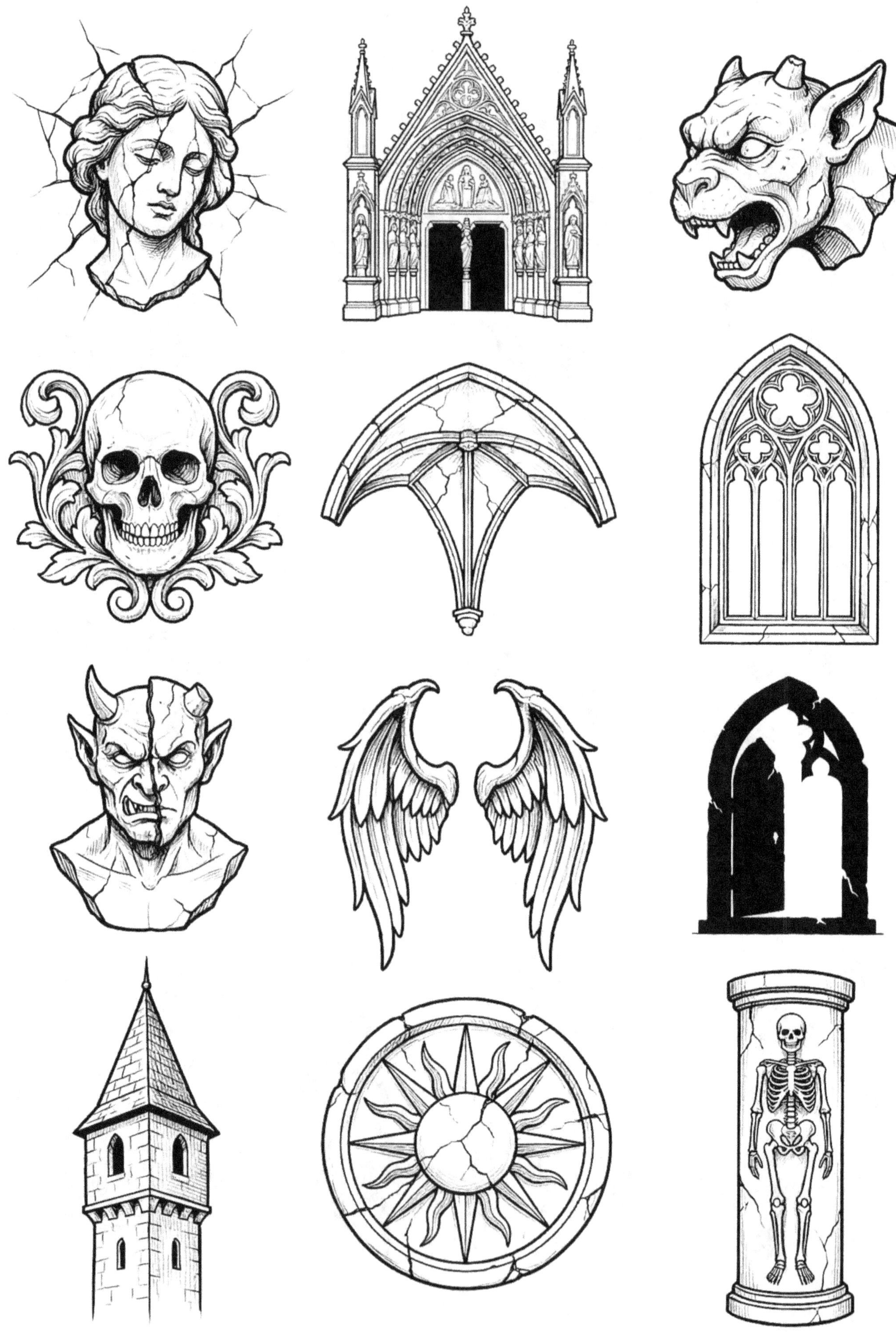

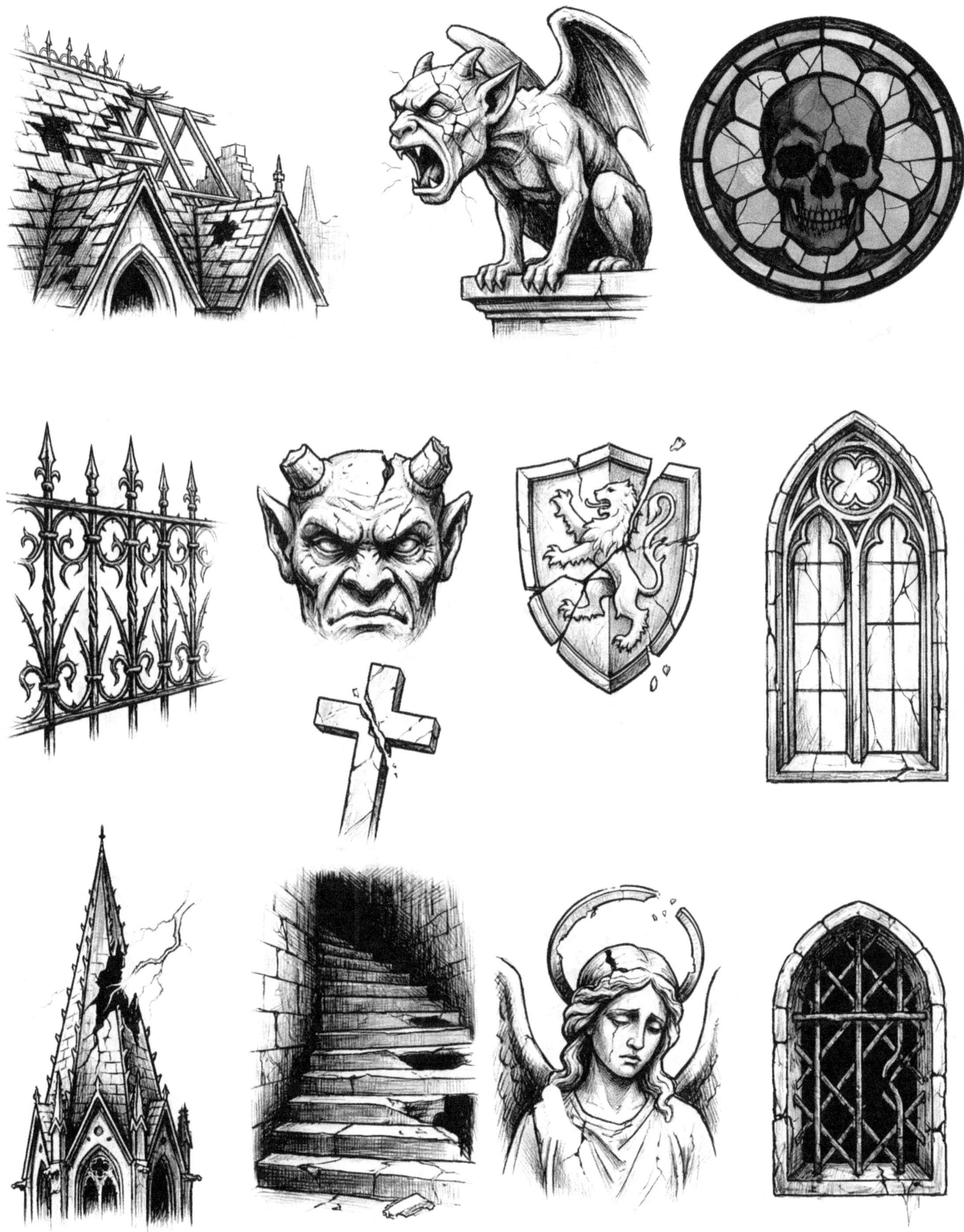

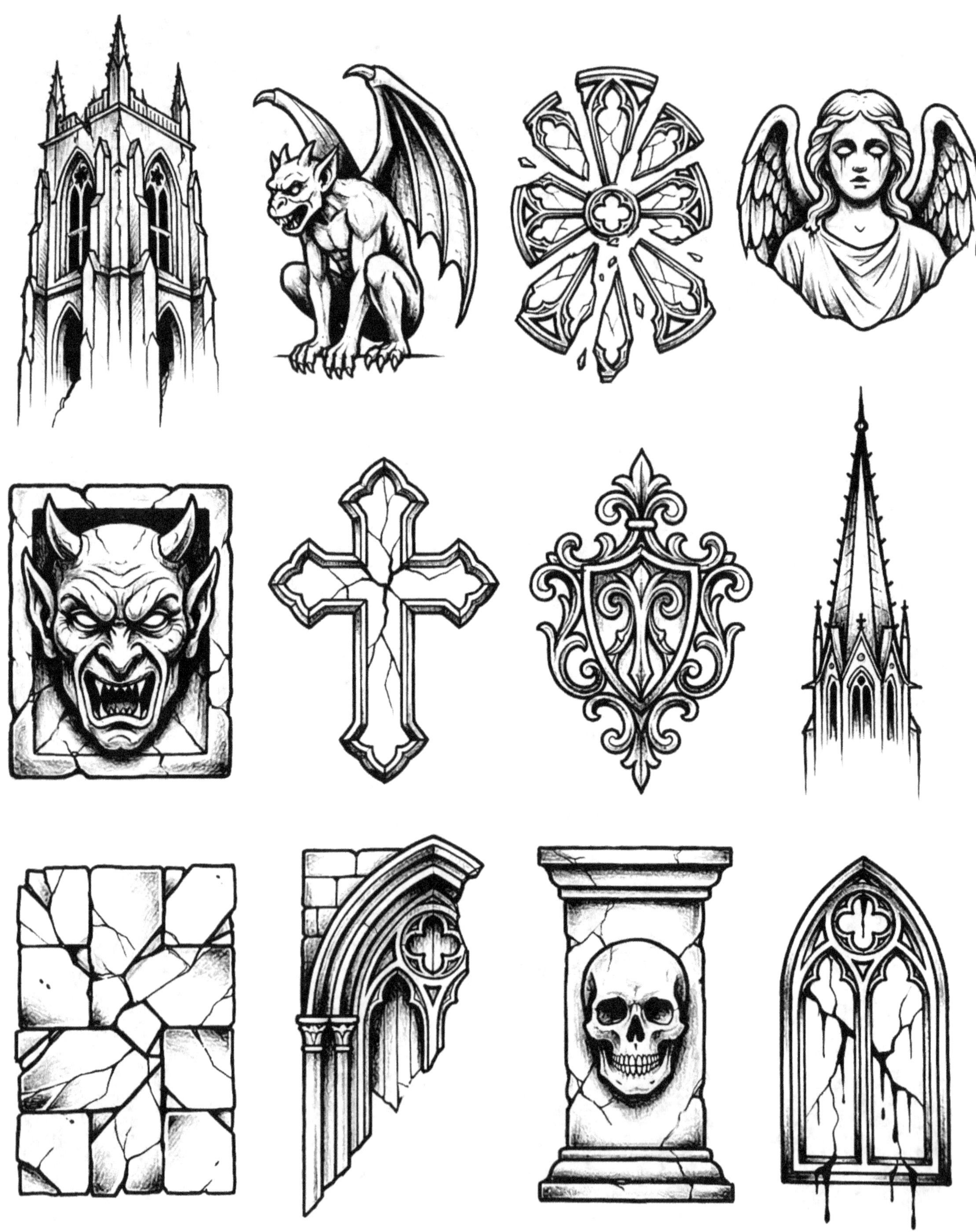

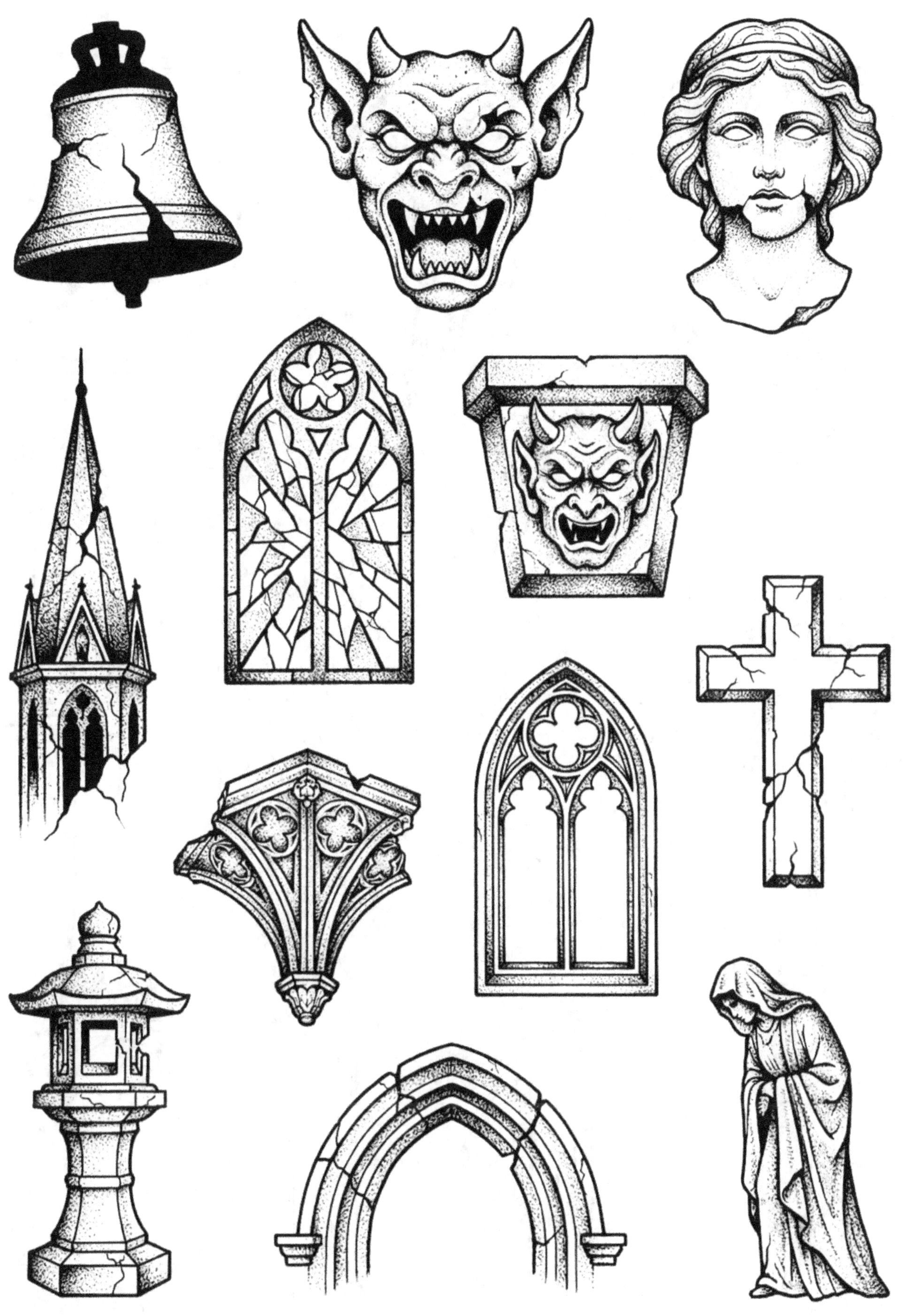

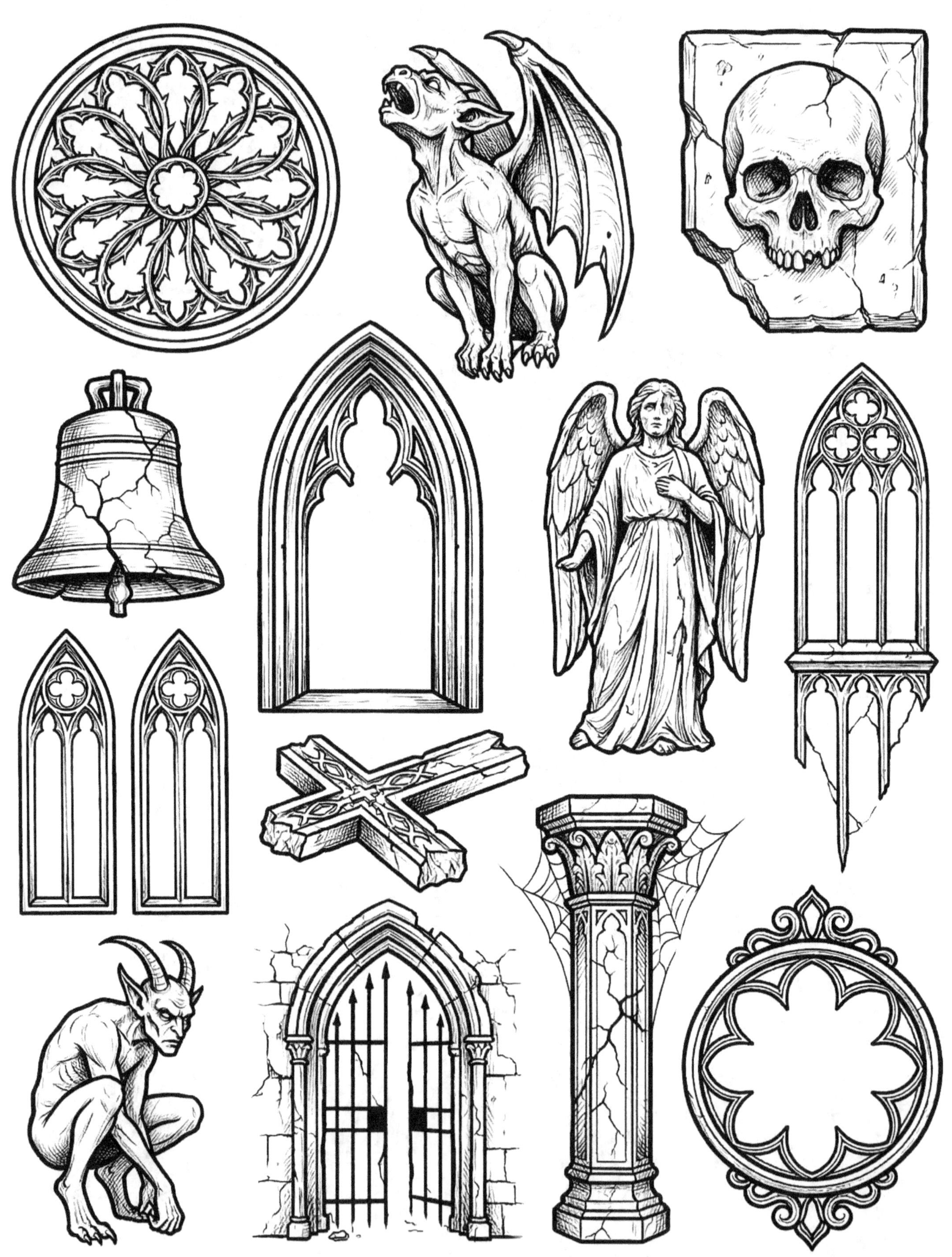

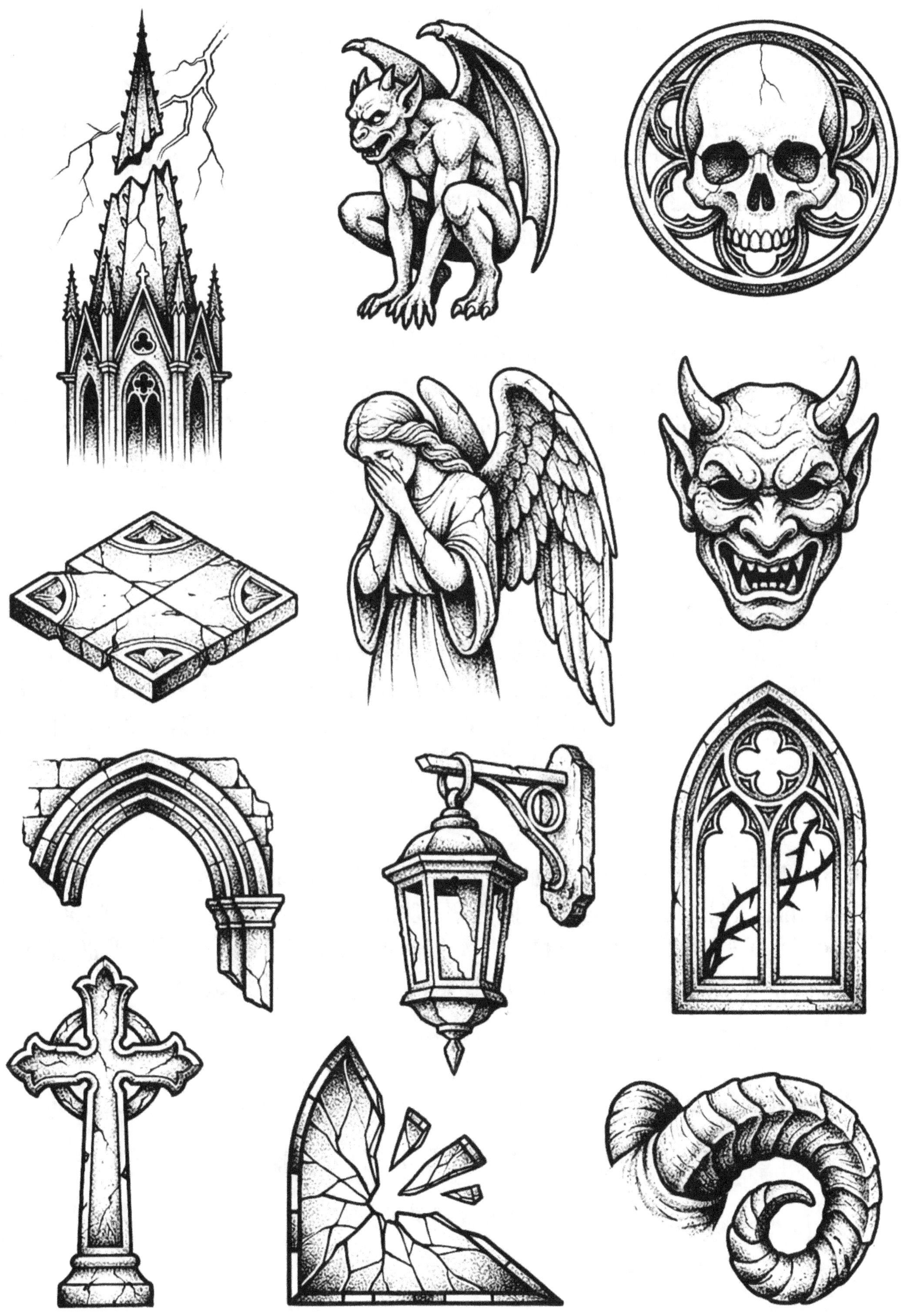

Occult Symbols & Sigils

Occult symbols have always carried a weight far beyond their visual form. They act as codes — marks of belief, fear, intuition, secrecy or personal meaning. A sigil can represent protection, chaos, desire, transformation, memory or inner conflict. Its power lies in the fact, że każdy widzi w nim coś innego. That ambiguity is exactly what makes these motifs so valuable in tattoo art.

In design, occult imagery bridges the worlds of geometry and emotion. Sharp lines, circular structures, runes, alchemical marks, symbols of energy and intention — all of them allow the artist to build meaning without relying on literal storytelling. A simple arrangement of shapes can feel ancient, mystical or ritualistic, depending on how it's composed and how it interacts with the surrounding elements.

This chapter brings together a wide range of sigils and symbolic forms that can be used as focal points, supporting motifs or repeating patterns within a larger composition. Some designs are sharp and aggressive; others are subtle and meditative. Together they create a vocabulary you can adapt to different styles — from dark fantasy and witchcraft themes to minimalist geometric pieces.

Use these symbols to construct your own meanings. Combine them, distort them, break them, refine them. A sigil can stand alone on the skin as a powerful mark, or it can serve as the backbone of a sleeve, chest piece or ritual-inspired composition. The strength of occult imagery comes from its ability to suggest something unseen and unspoken.

This chapter invites you into a world of intention, secrecy and interpretation —

a space where lines become language

and symbols become identity.

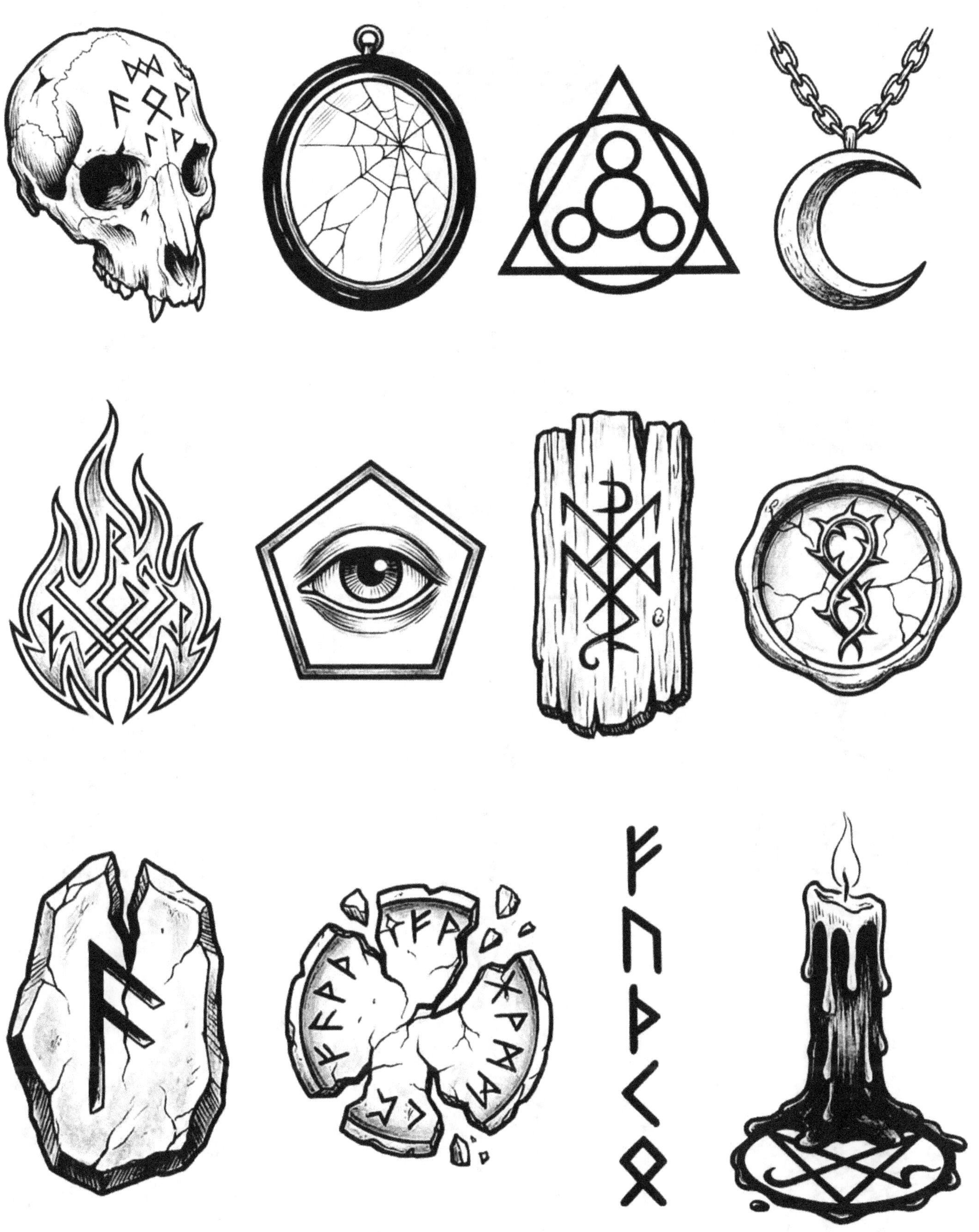

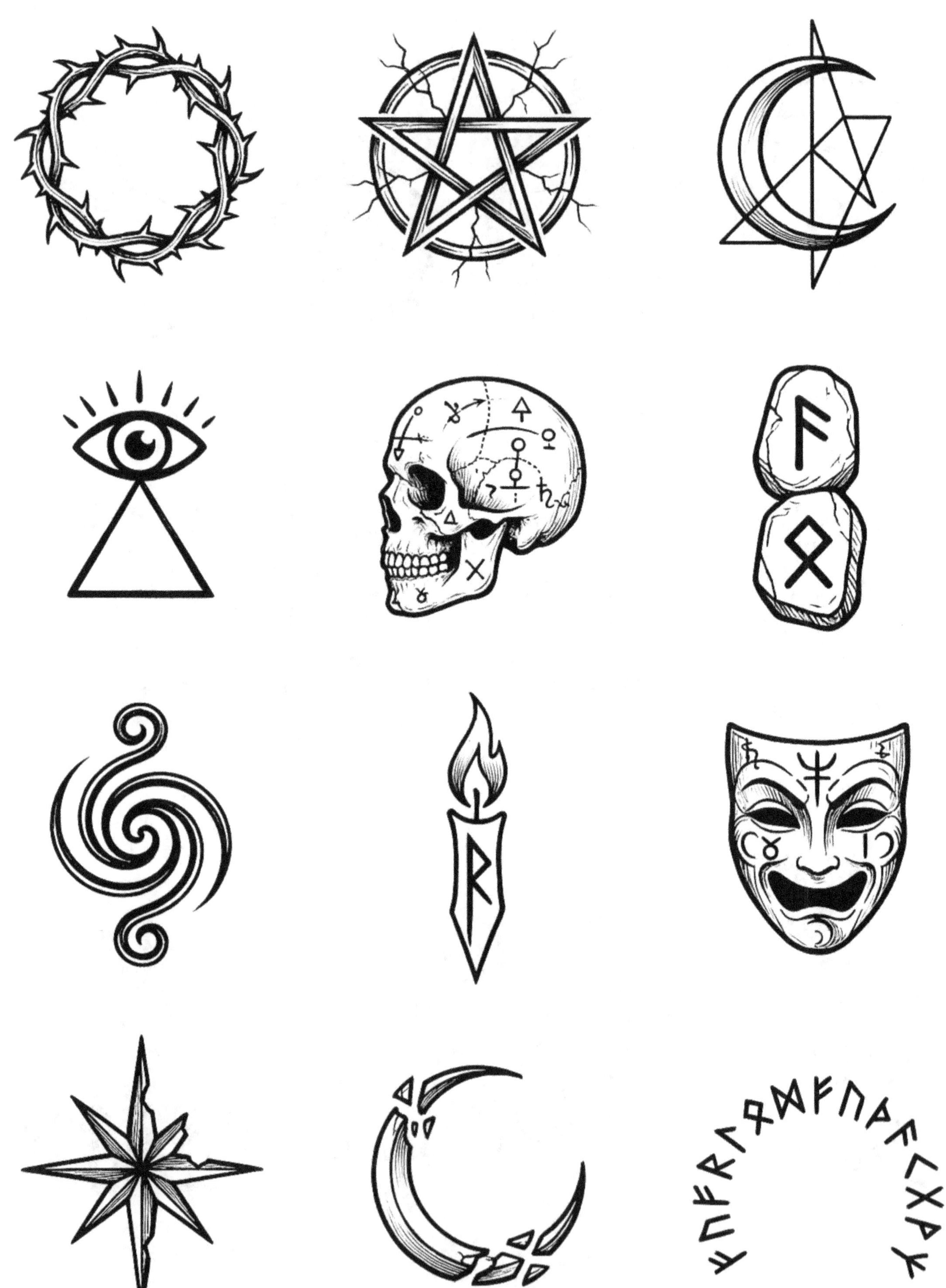

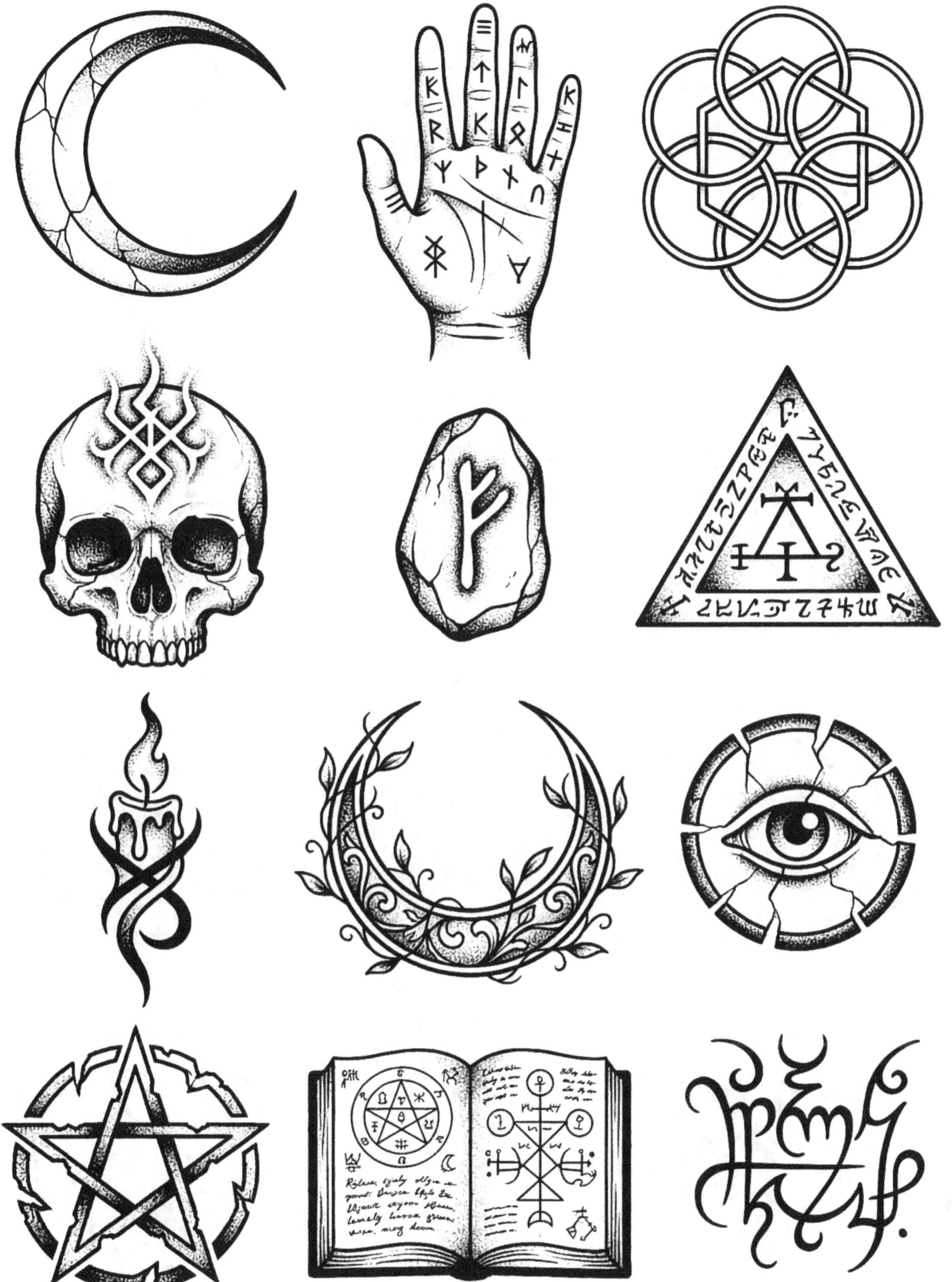

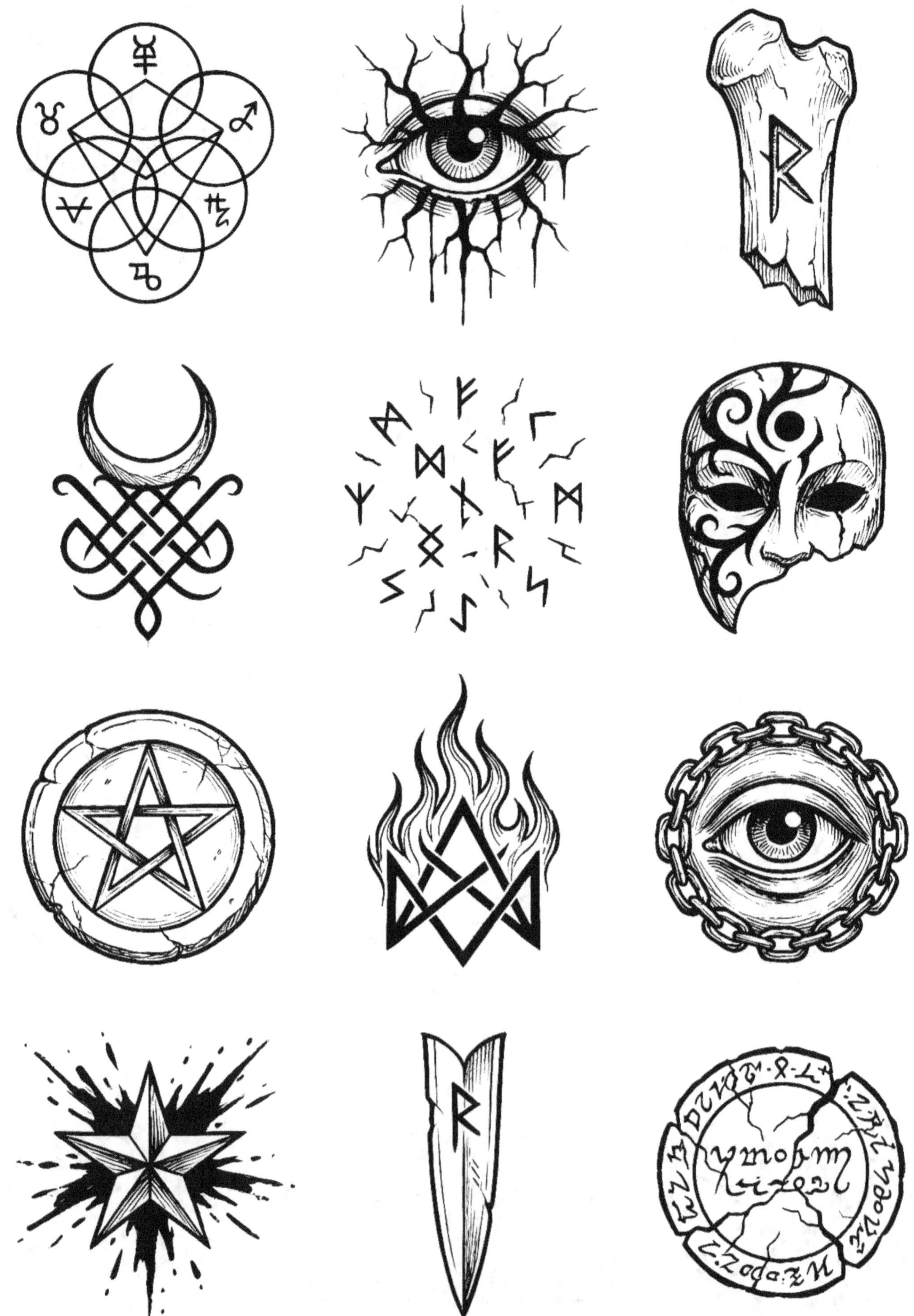

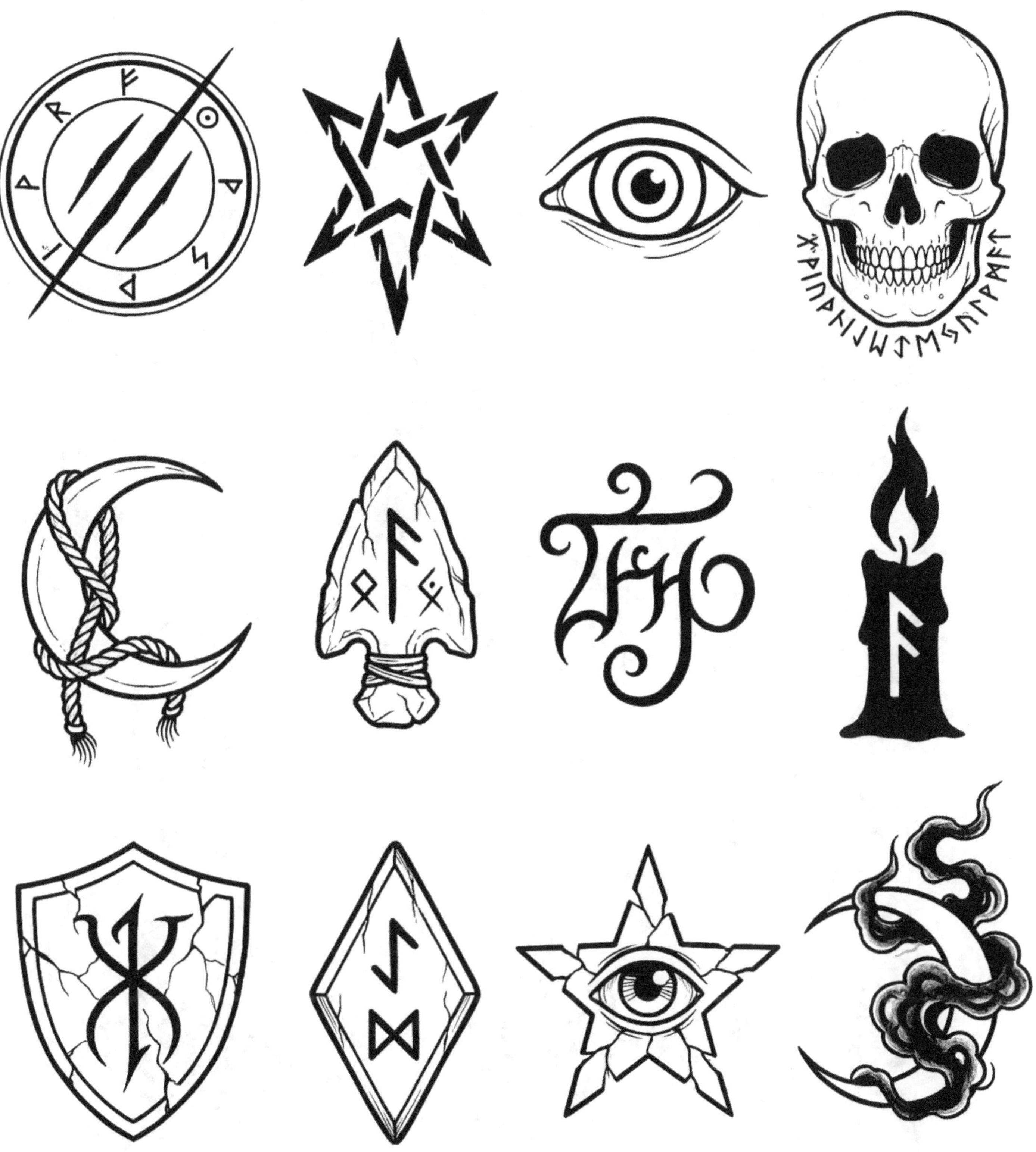

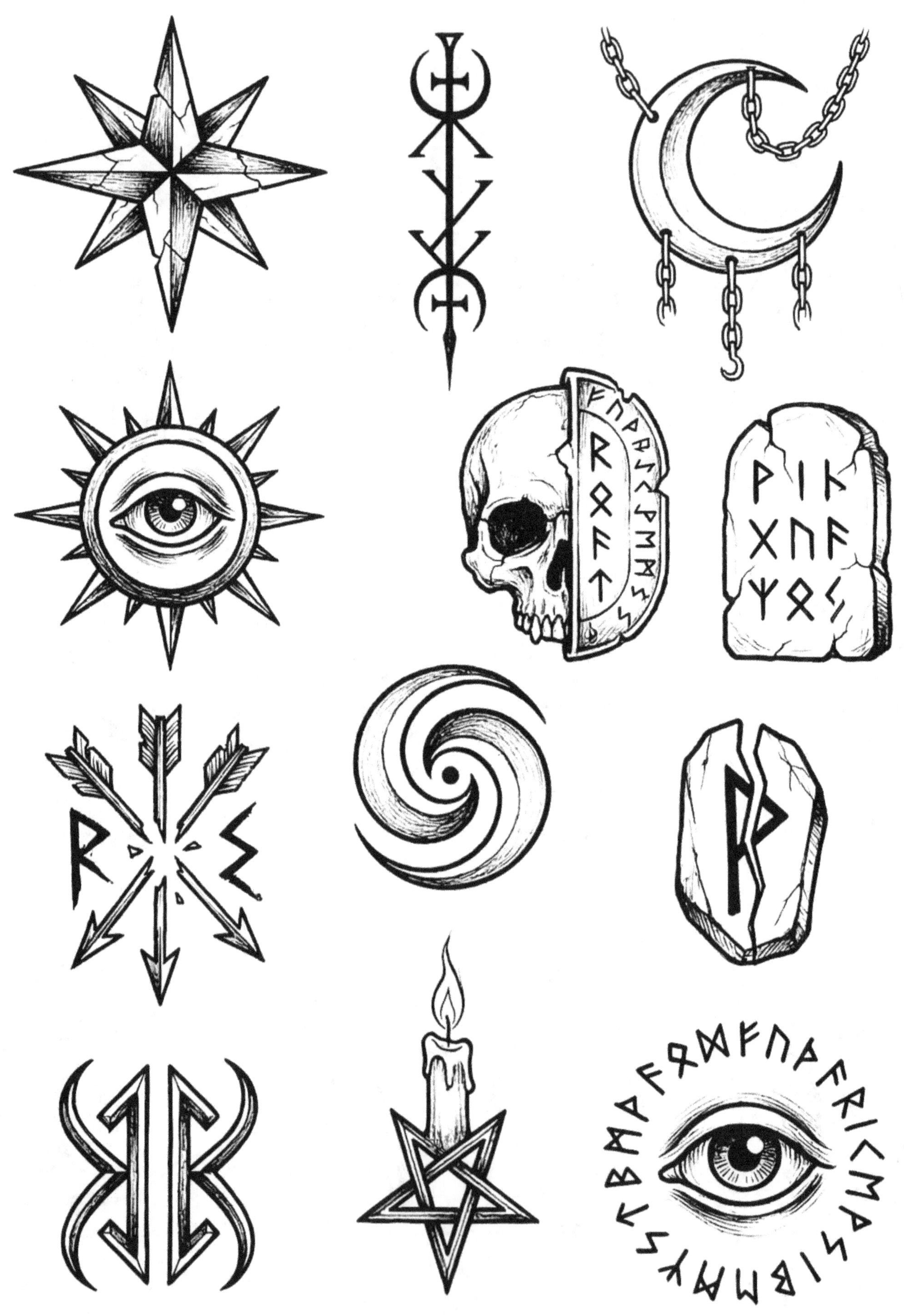

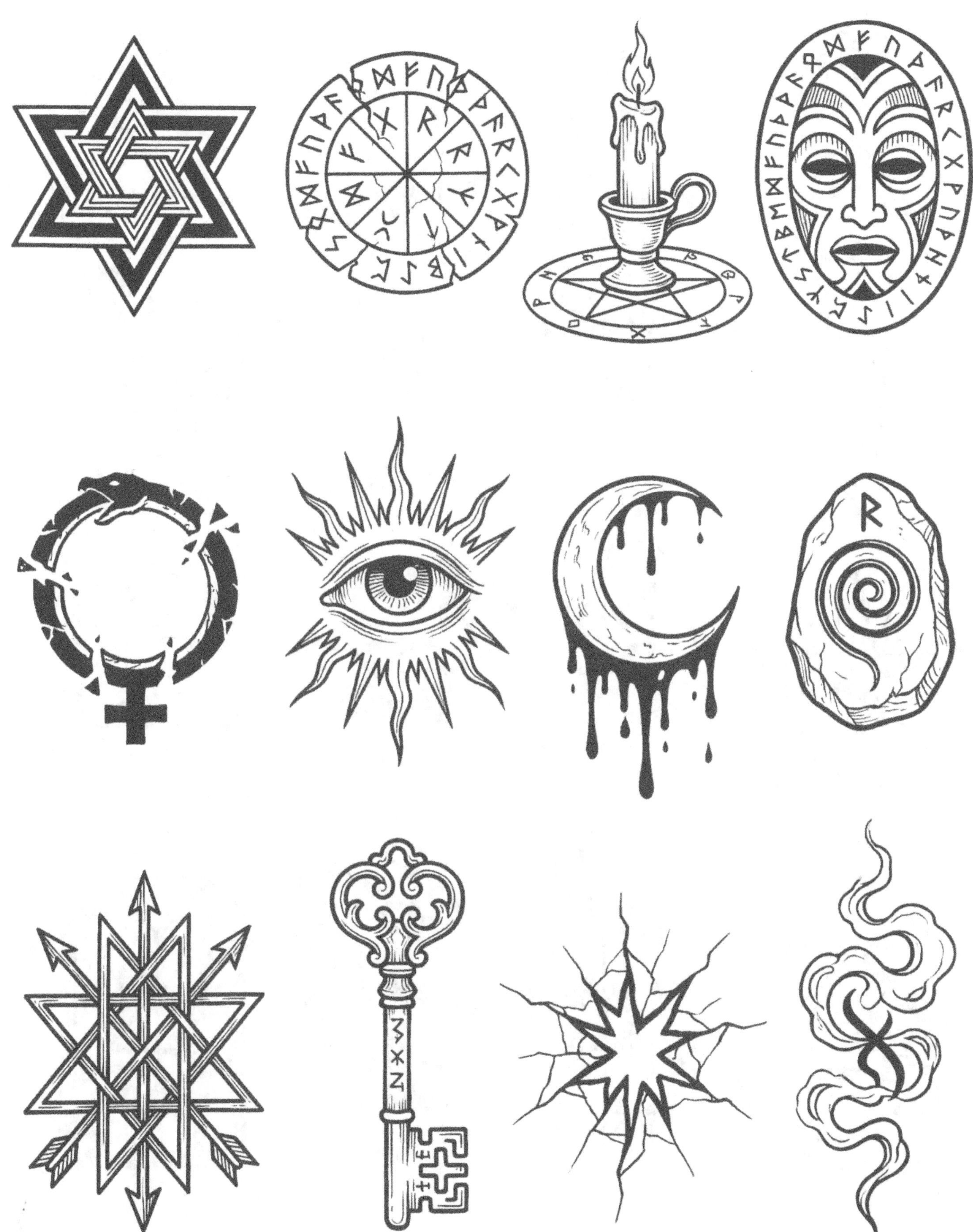

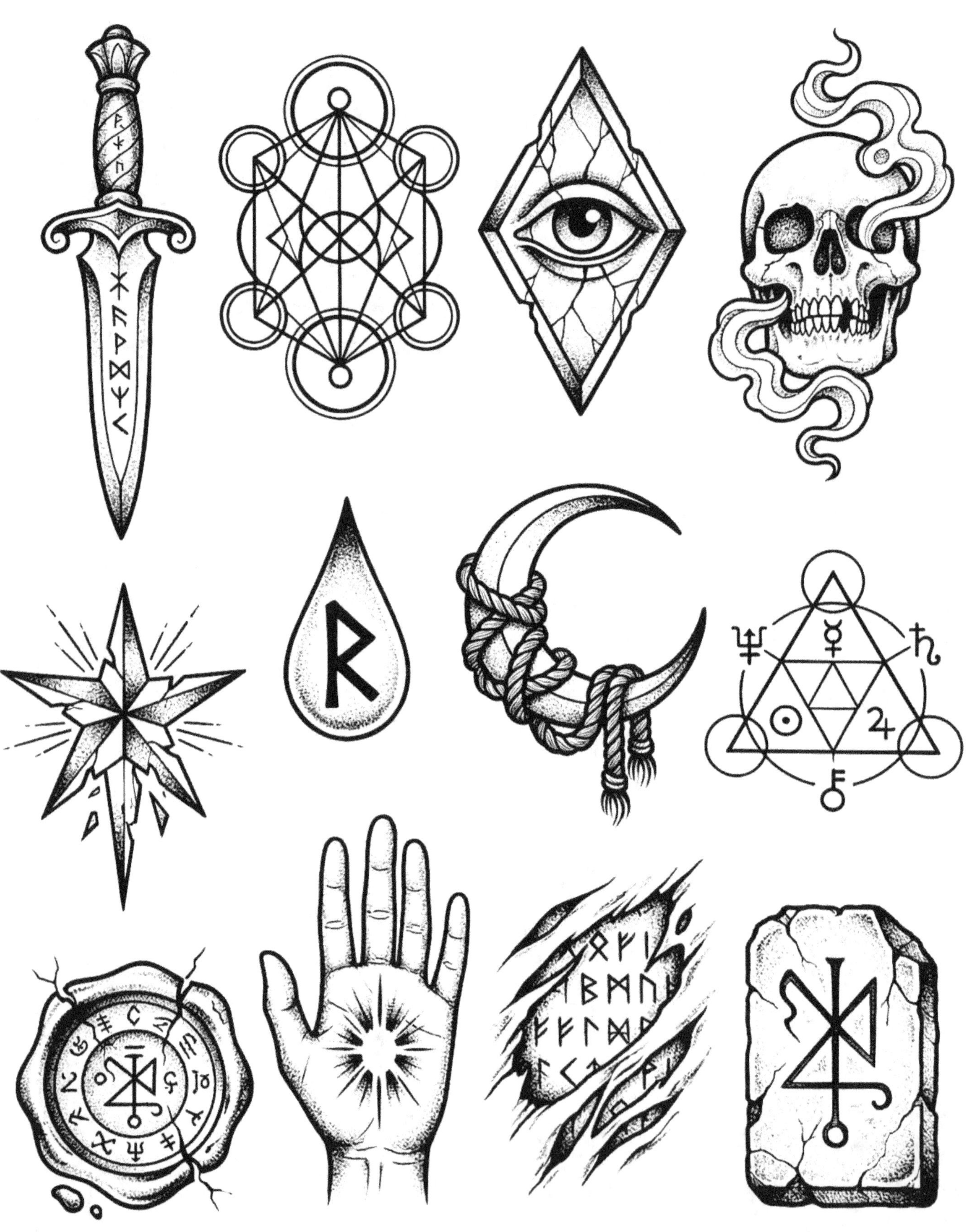

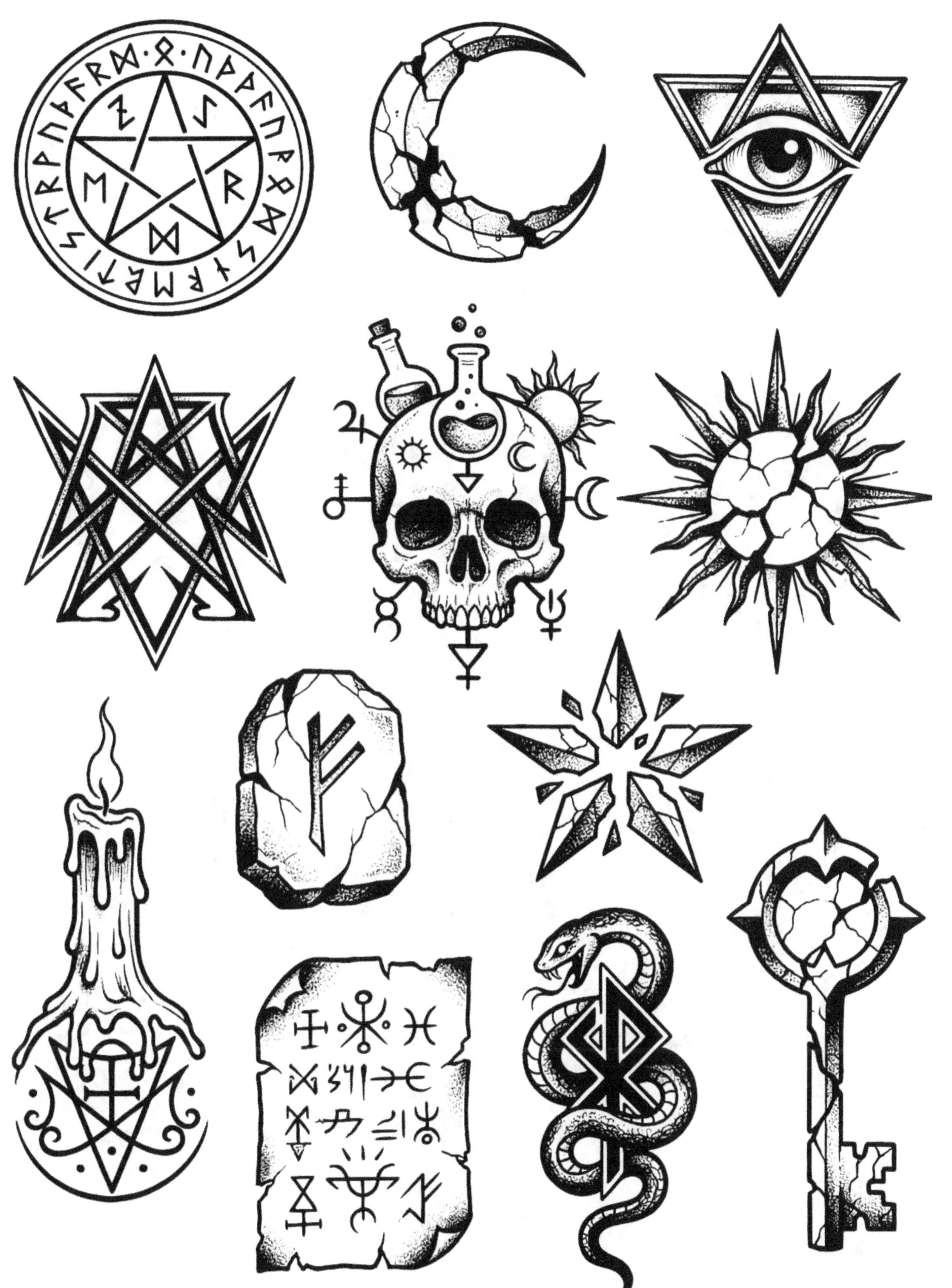

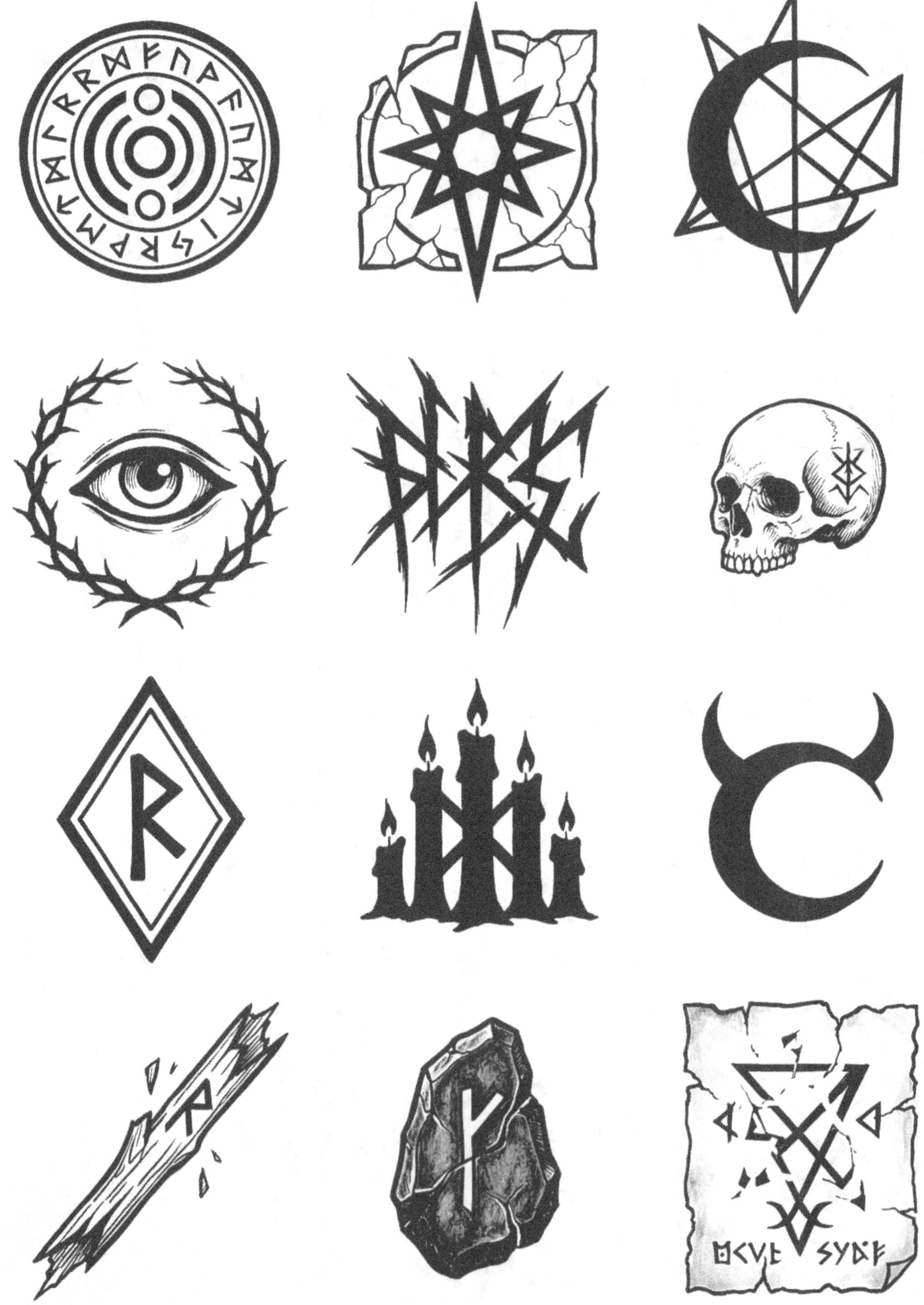

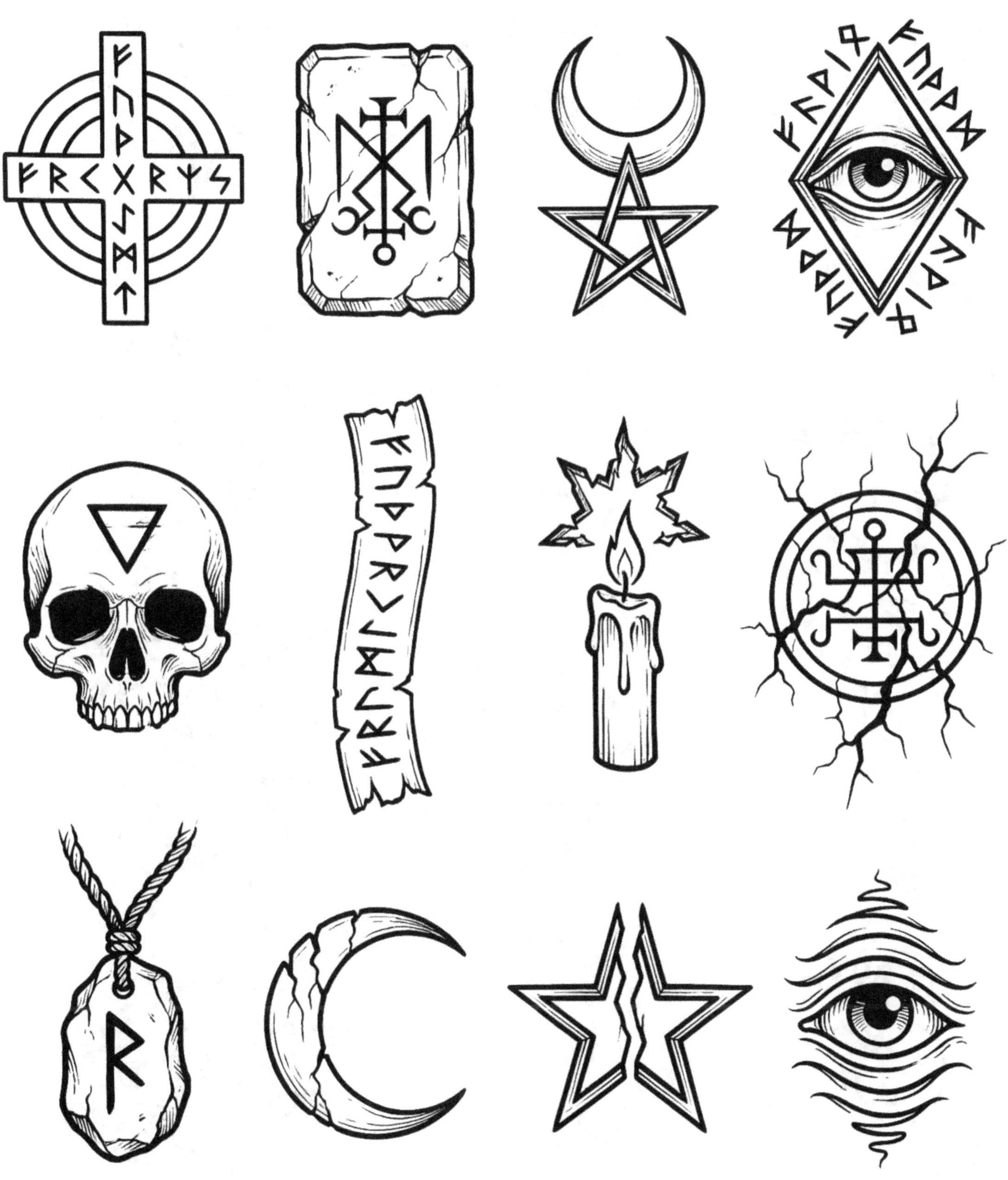

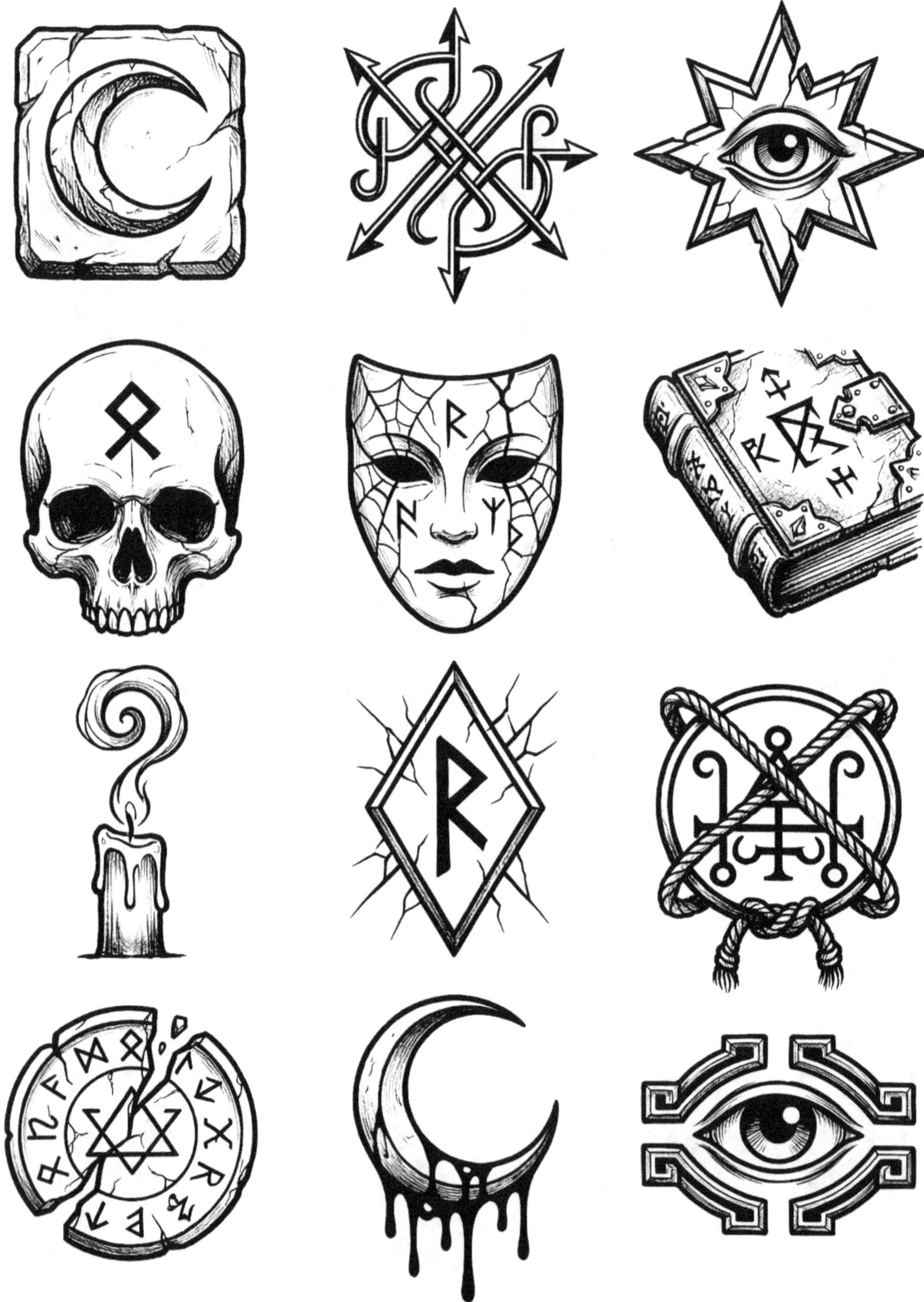

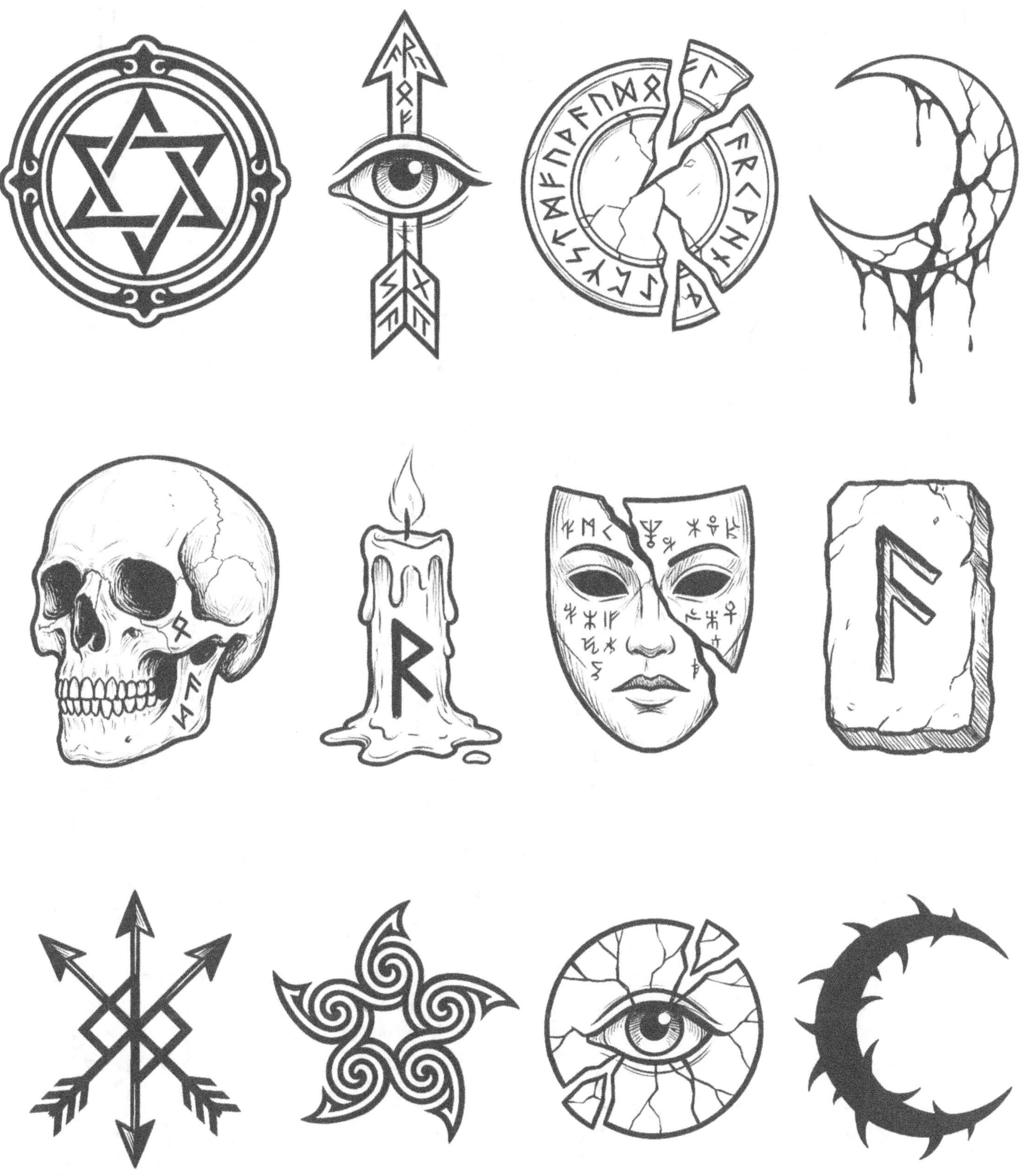

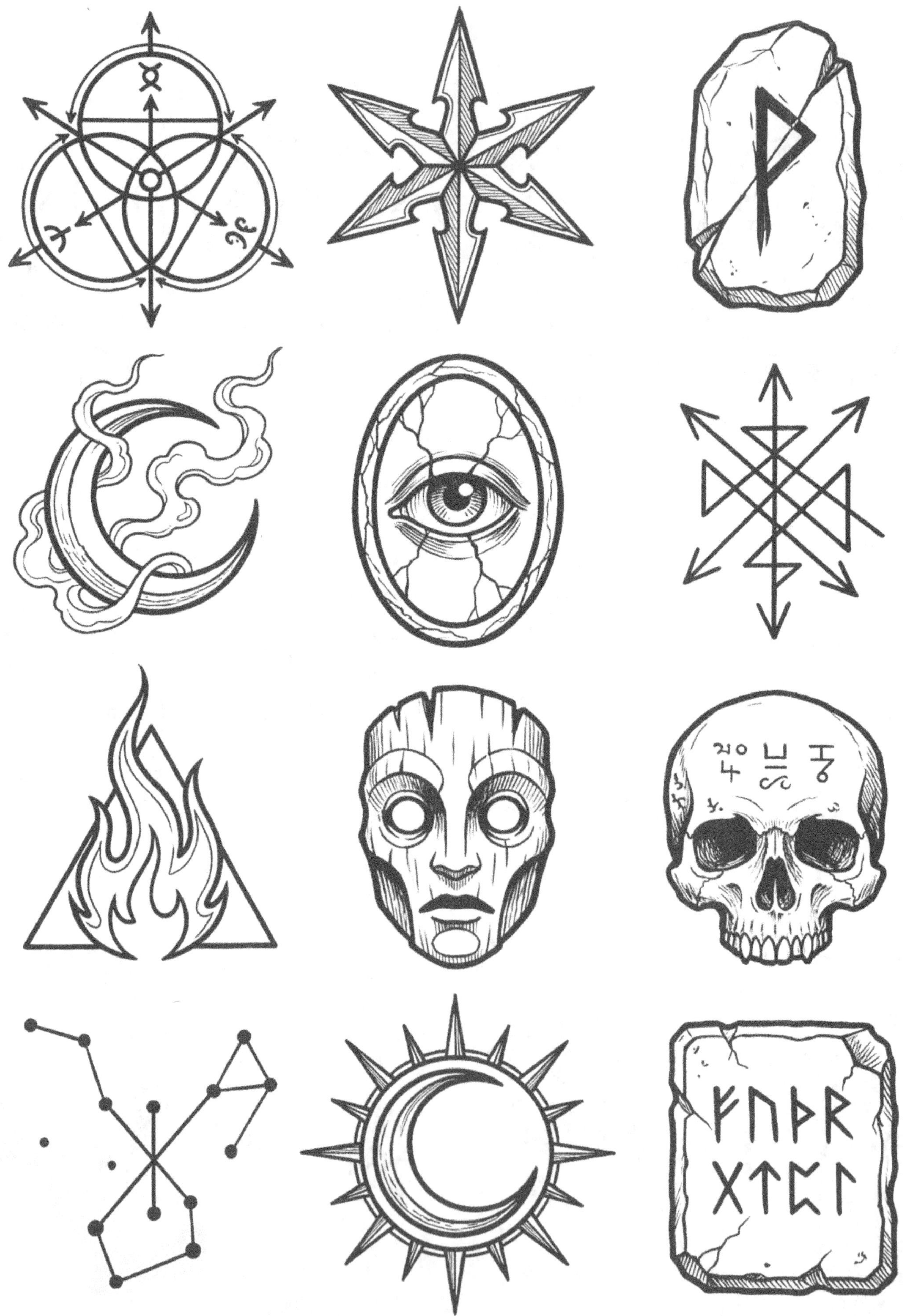

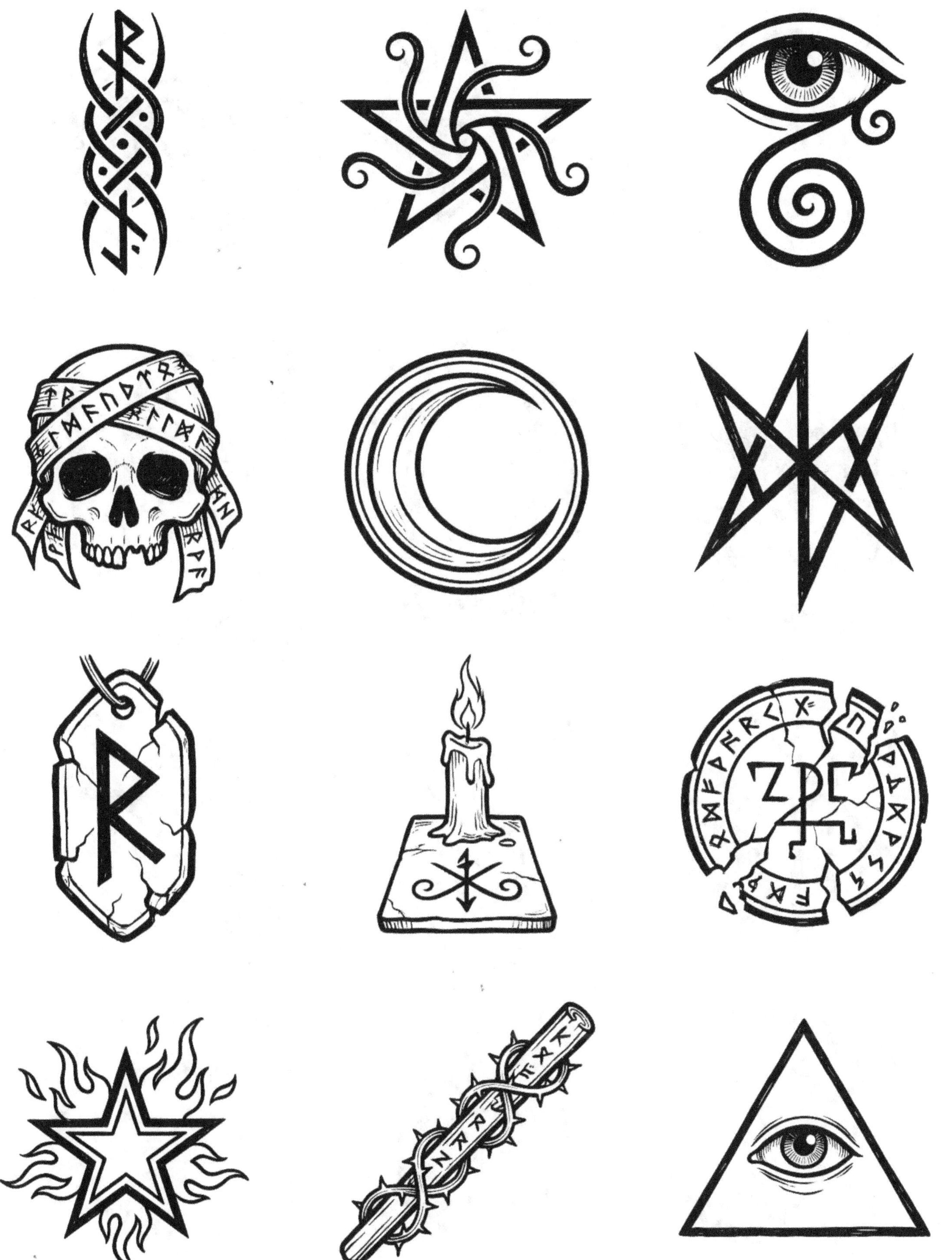

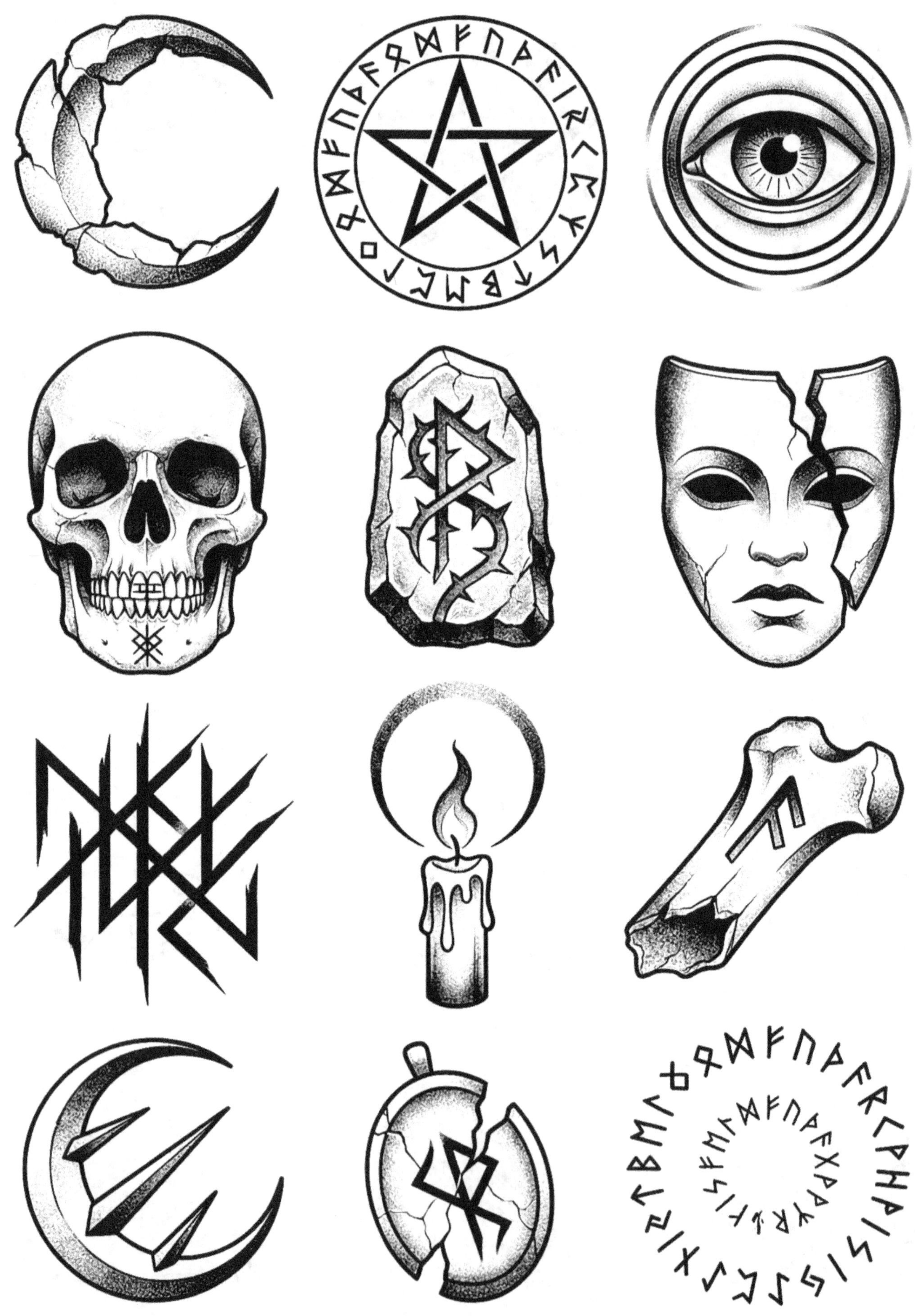

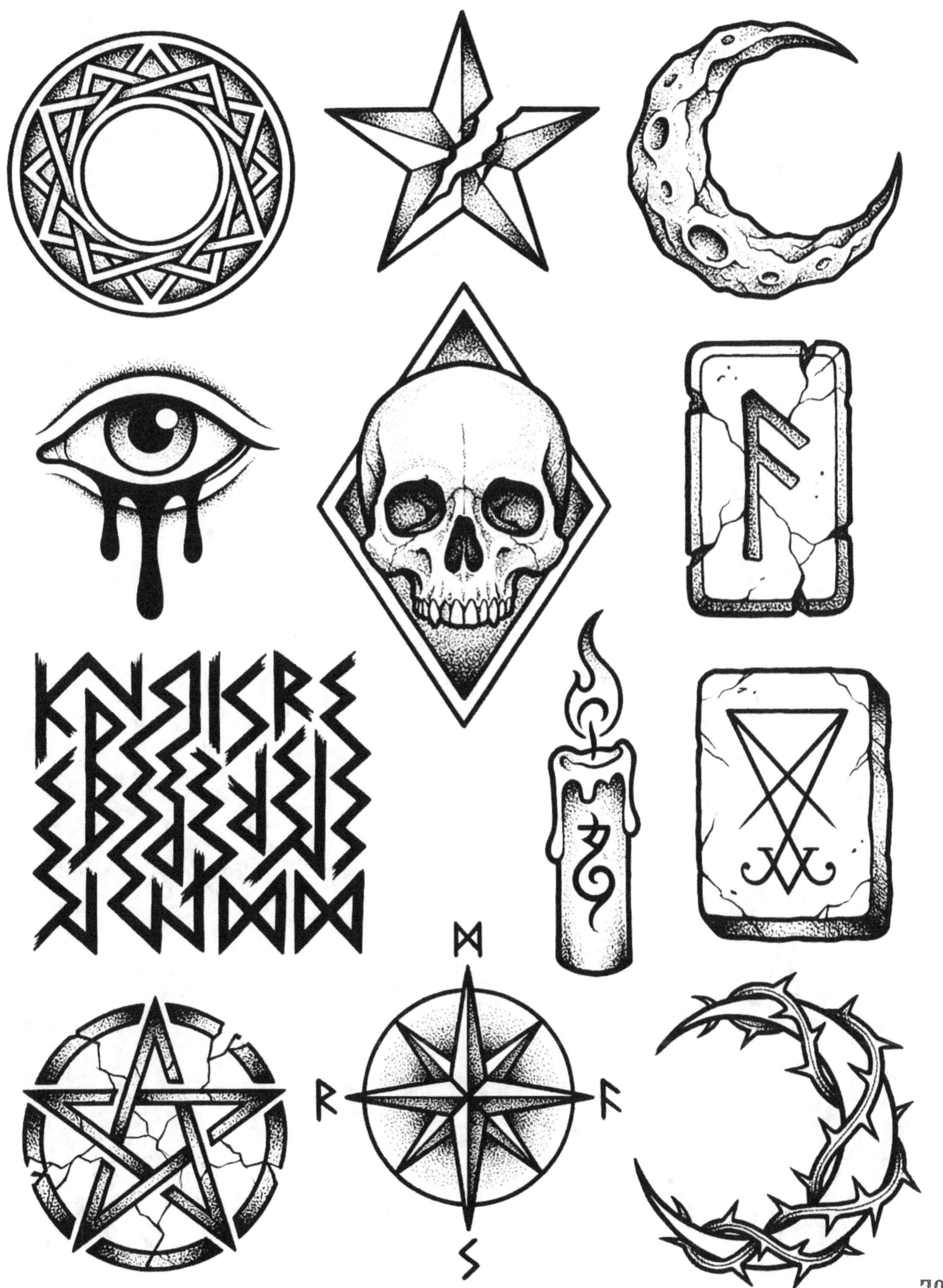

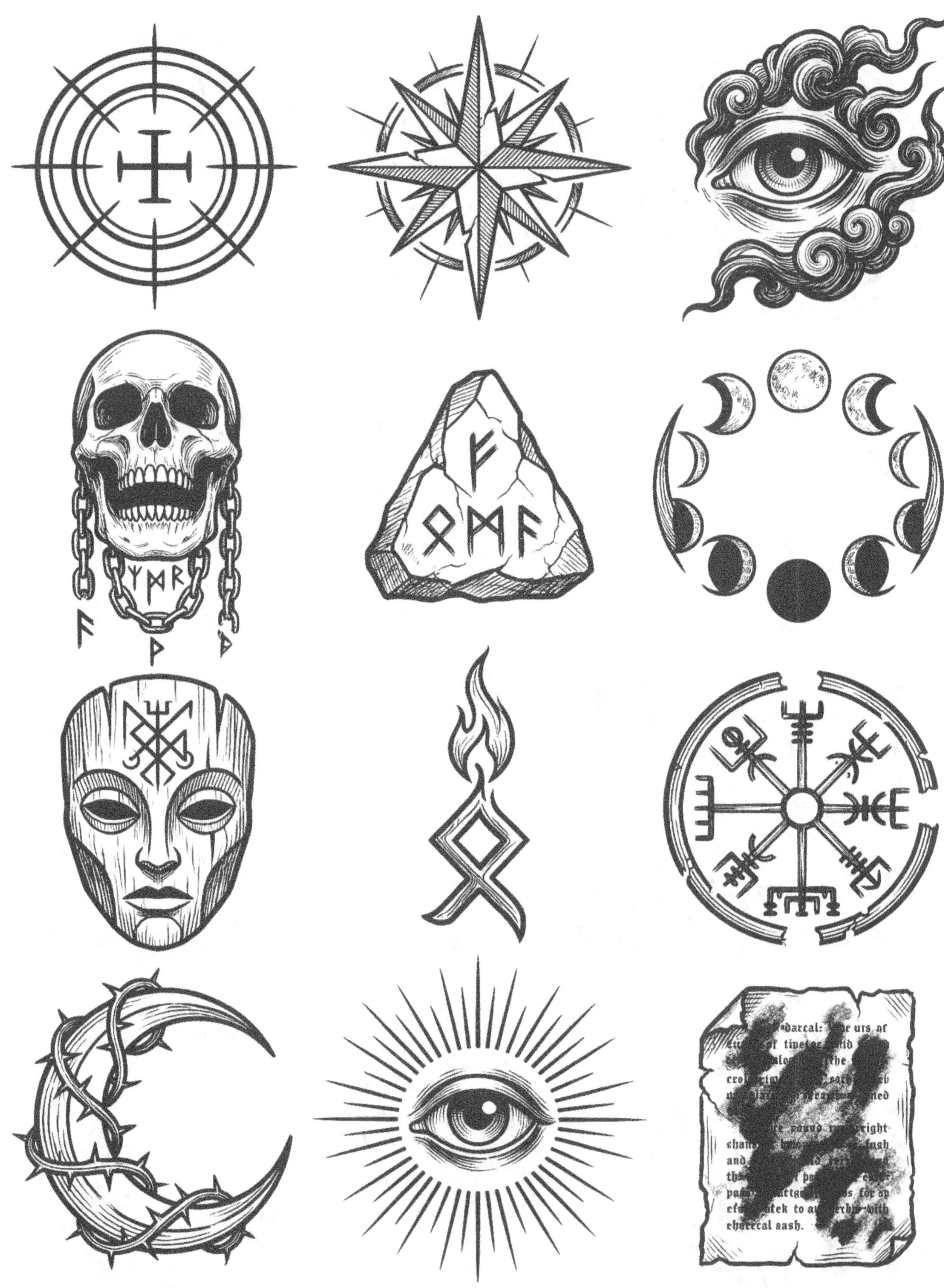

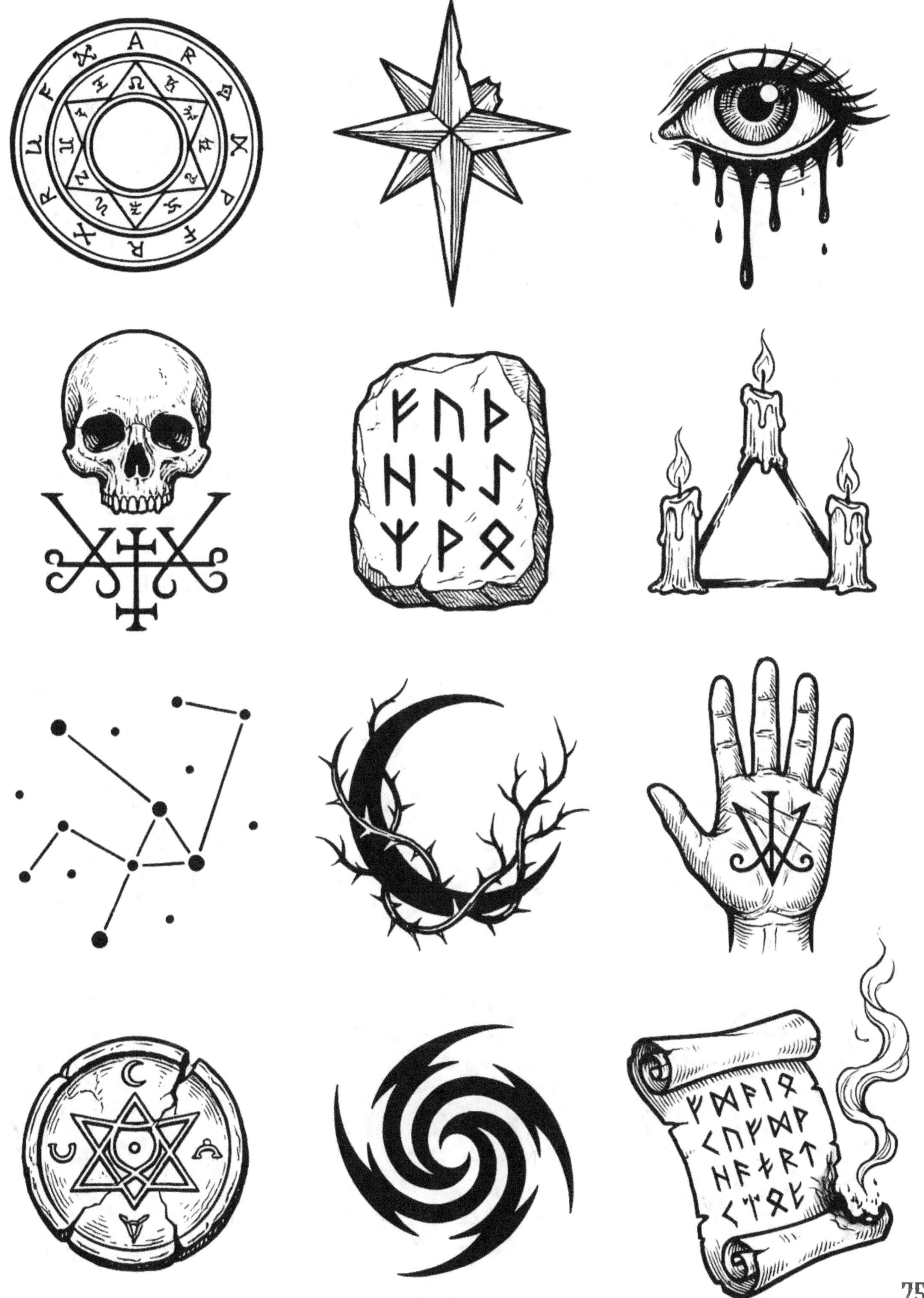

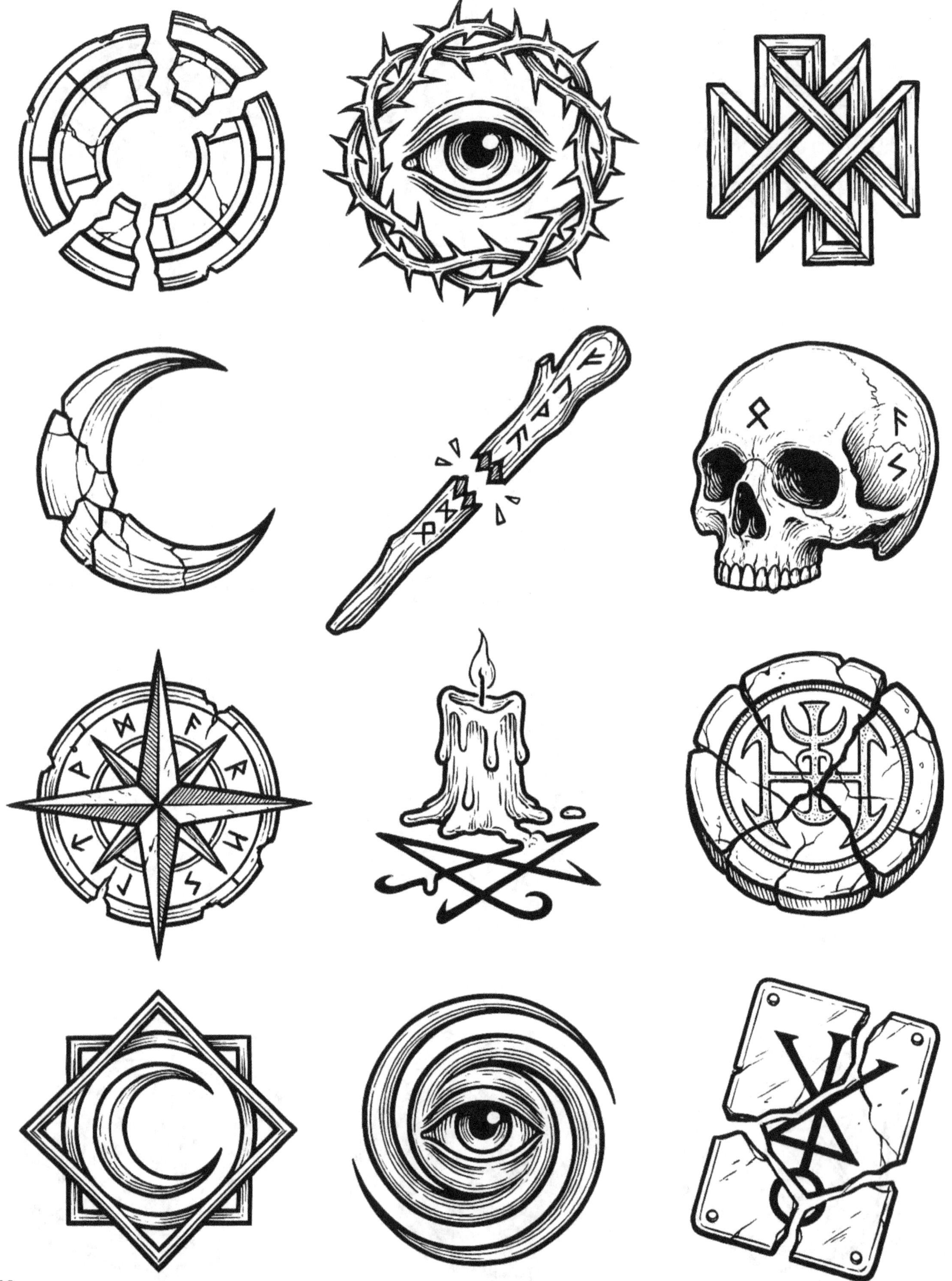

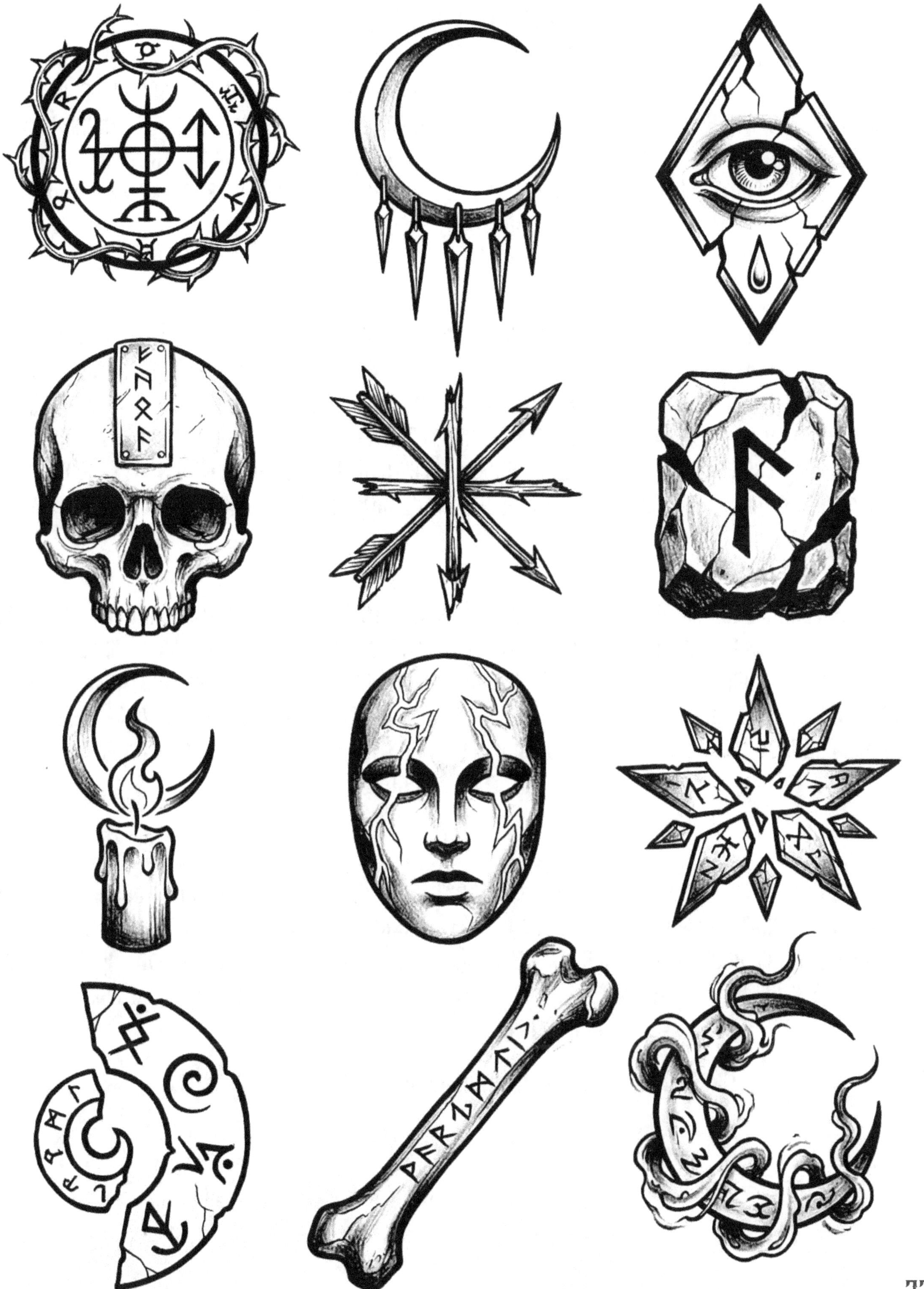

DARK FANTASY CREATURES

DARK FANTASY LIVES IN THE SPACE BETWEEN REALITY AND IMAGINATION — A WORLD WHERE FEAR, BEAUTY, MYTHOLOGY AND CHAOS INTERTWINE. CREATURES BORN FROM THIS REALM ARE NEVER JUST MONSTERS. THEY ARE SYMBOLS OF INSTINCT, TRANSFORMATION, CONFLICT AND THE SUBCONSCIOUS. THEY CAN BE FIERCE, TRAGIC, ELEGANT, GROTESQUE OR OTHERWORLDLY, BUT THEY ALWAYS CARRY A PRESENCE THAT MAKES THEM UNFORGETTABLE.

IN TATTOO ART, DARK FANTASY CREATURES OFFER LIMITLESS CREATIVE POTENTIAL. THEIR FORMS ARE NOT BOUND BY ANATOMY OR REALISM, WHICH ALLOWS THE ARTIST TO PUSH PROPORTIONS, TEXTURES AND EXPRESSIONS FAR BEYOND THE HUMAN SHAPE. HORNS, WINGS, DISTORTED SILHOUETTES, GLOWING EYES, ELONGATED LIMBS — EVERY DETAIL ADDS PERSONALITY AND MOOD. THESE CREATURES DON'T RELY ON LITERAL REPRESENTATION; THEY RELY ON FEELING. THEY CAN BE BUILT FROM FRAGMENTS OF ANIMALS, SPIRITS, DEMONS, SHADOWS OR FOLKLORE, AND STILL COMMUNICATE THEIR ESSENCE INSTANTLY.

THIS CHAPTER BRINGS TOGETHER A WIDE RANGE OF DESIGNS MEANT TO SPARK IMAGINATION. SOME OF THE CREATURES APPEAR POWERFUL AND PREDATORY, OTHERS SPECTRAL AND HOLLOW, AND SOME FEEL ALMOST RITUALISTIC IN THEIR PRESENCE. EACH OFFERS OPPORTUNITIES FOR STRIKING COMPOSITIONS, WHETHER YOU'RE CREATING A STANDALONE PIECE, A SLEEVE BACKGROUND, OR A FULL NARRATIVE SCENE. THE FREEDOM OF DARK FANTASY ALLOWS YOU TO DEFINE YOUR OWN VISUAL RULES AND EXPLORE WHAT LIES BEYOND THE EDGES OF THE NATURAL WORLD.

USE THESE DESIGNS TO EXPERIMENT WITH CONTRAST, SILHOUETTE AND EMOTIONAL TONE. NOTICE HOW SUBTLE DEVIATIONS FROM ANATOMY CAN CREATE TENSION, HOW EXAGGERATED FEATURES SHAPE PERSONALITY, AND HOW THE BALANCE BETWEEN SHADOW AND HIGHLIGHT SETS THE MOOD. DARK FANTASY THRIVES ON DISTORTION AND WONDER — LET THESE CREATURES HELP YOU BUILD TATTOOS THAT FEEL ALIVE, DRAMATIC AND FILLED WITH STORY.

THIS IS THE REALM WHERE IMAGINATION SHAPES THE IMPOSSIBLE,

WHERE MYTH BREATHES THROUGH INK,

AND WHERE EVERY CREATURE TELLS A STORY BEYOND WORDS.

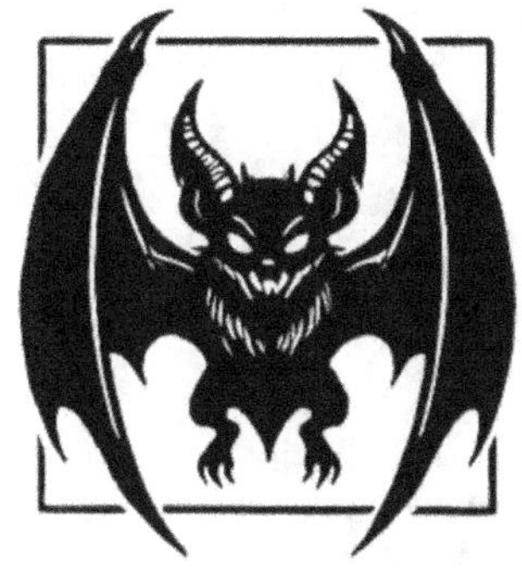
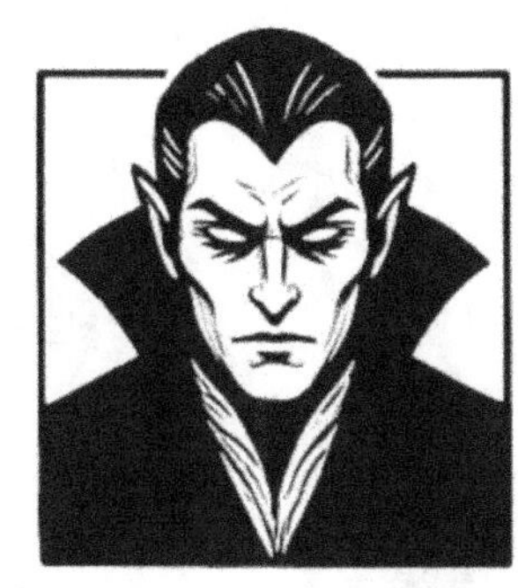
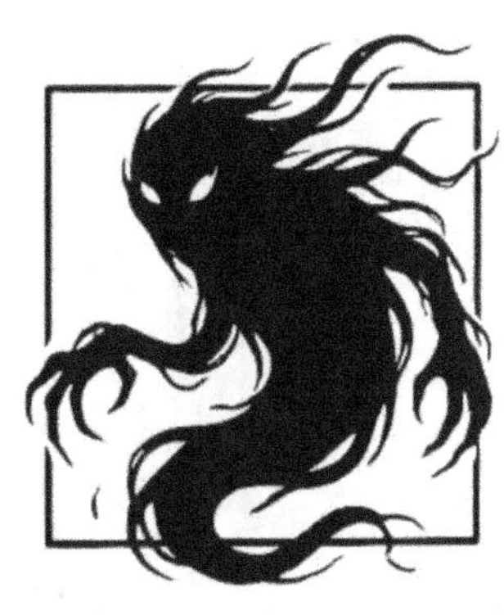
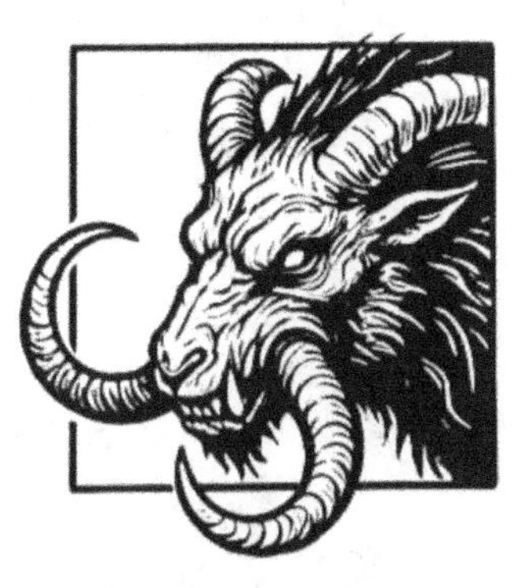
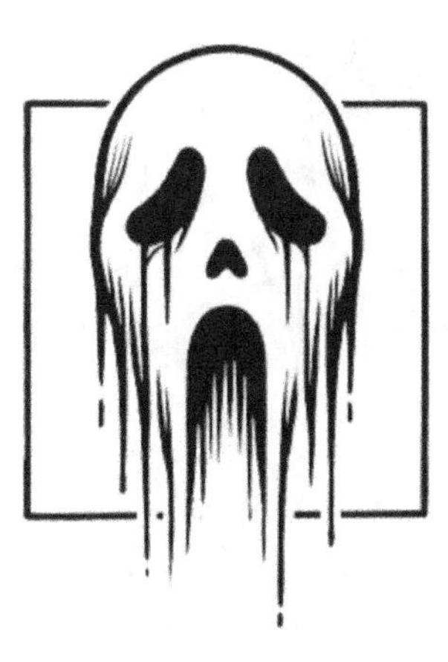
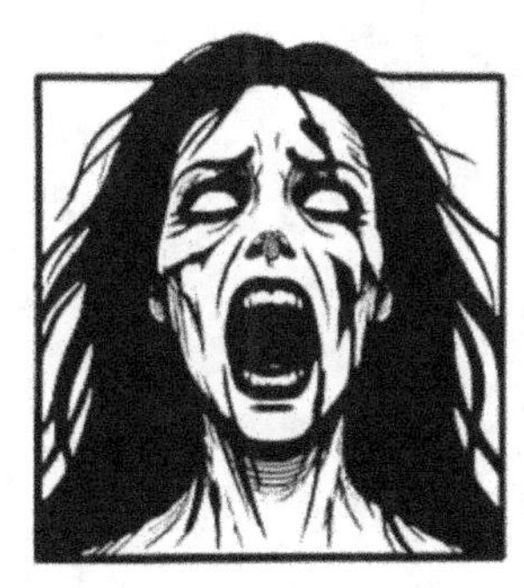
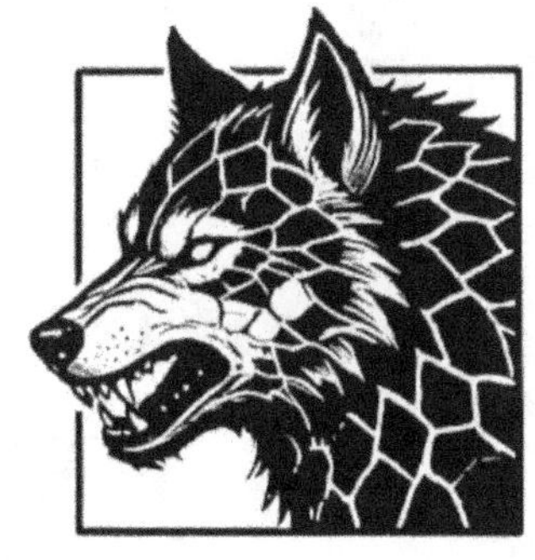
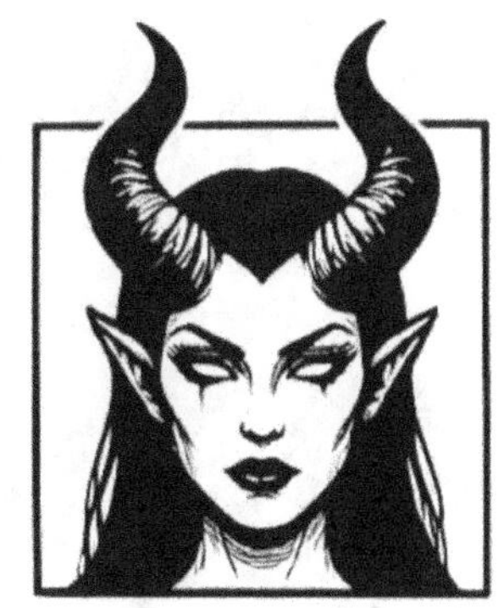
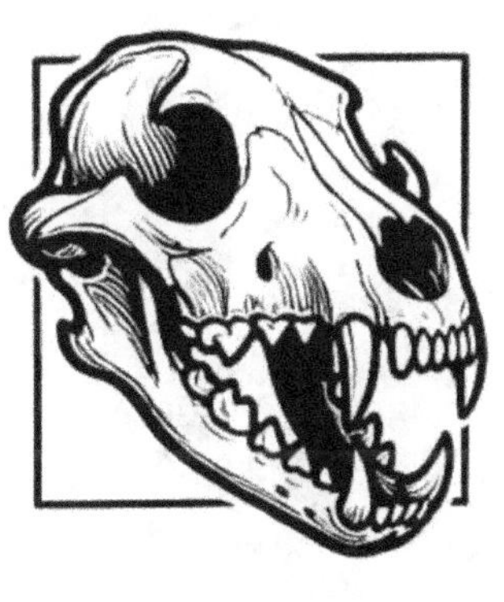
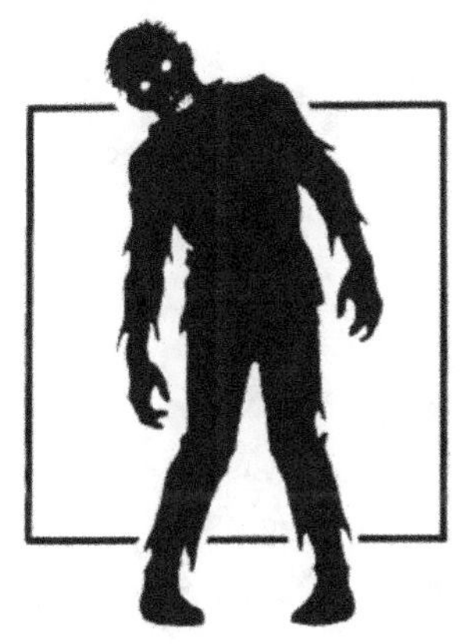
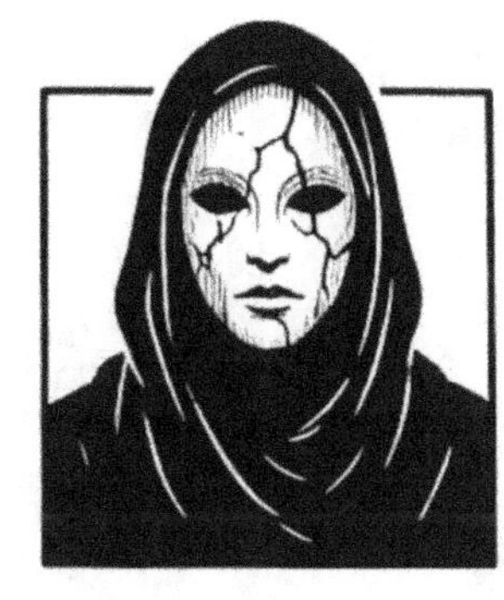
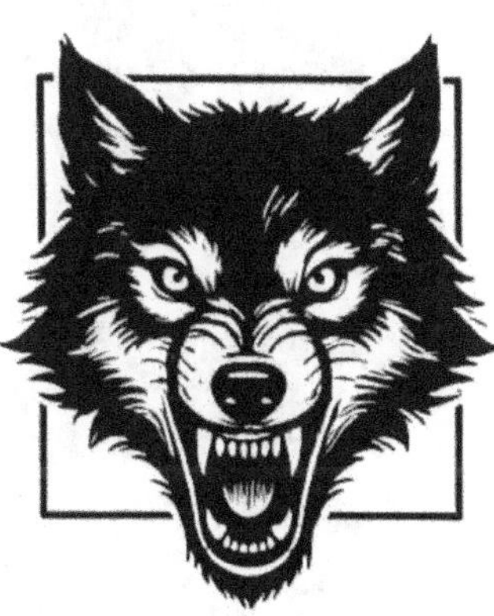

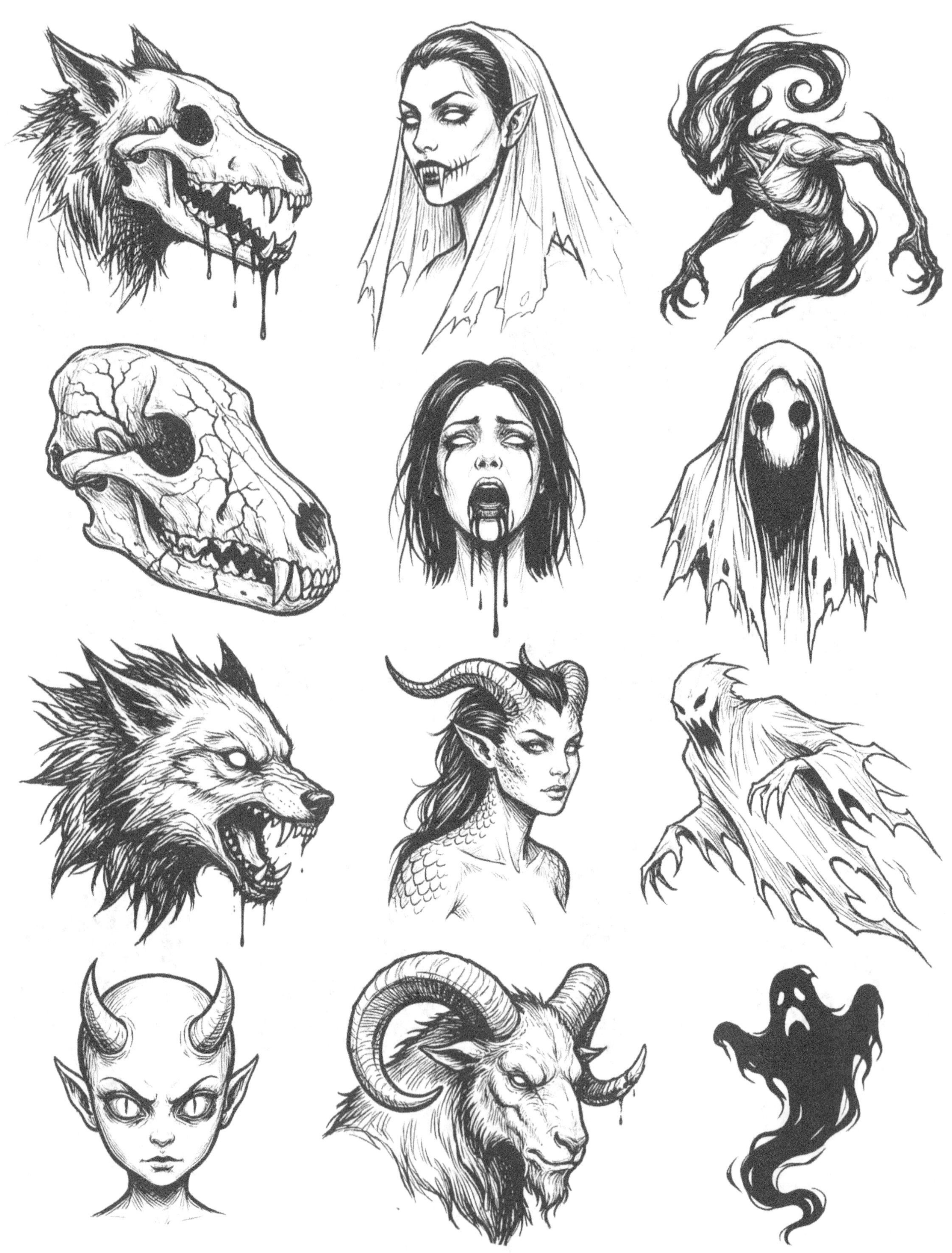

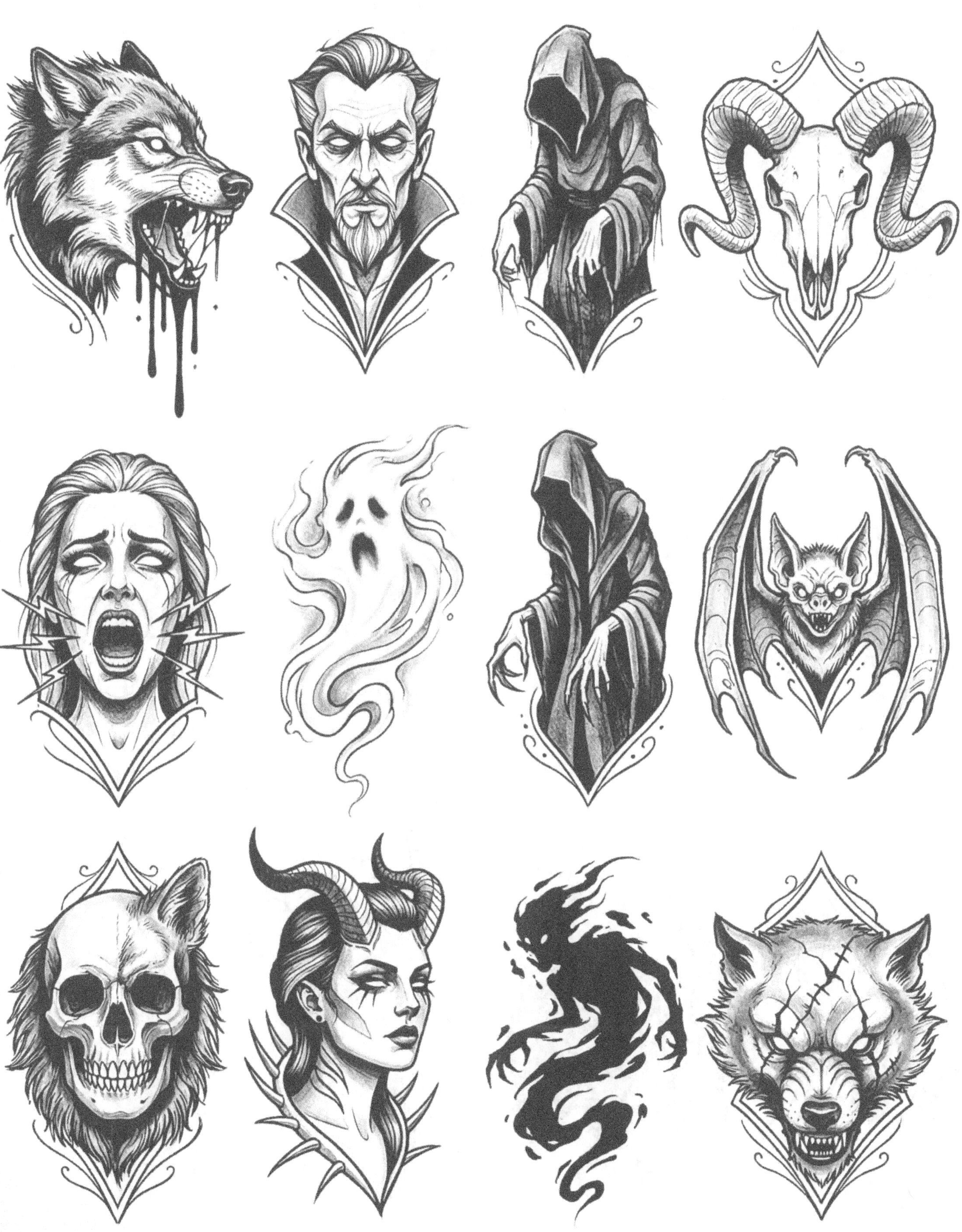

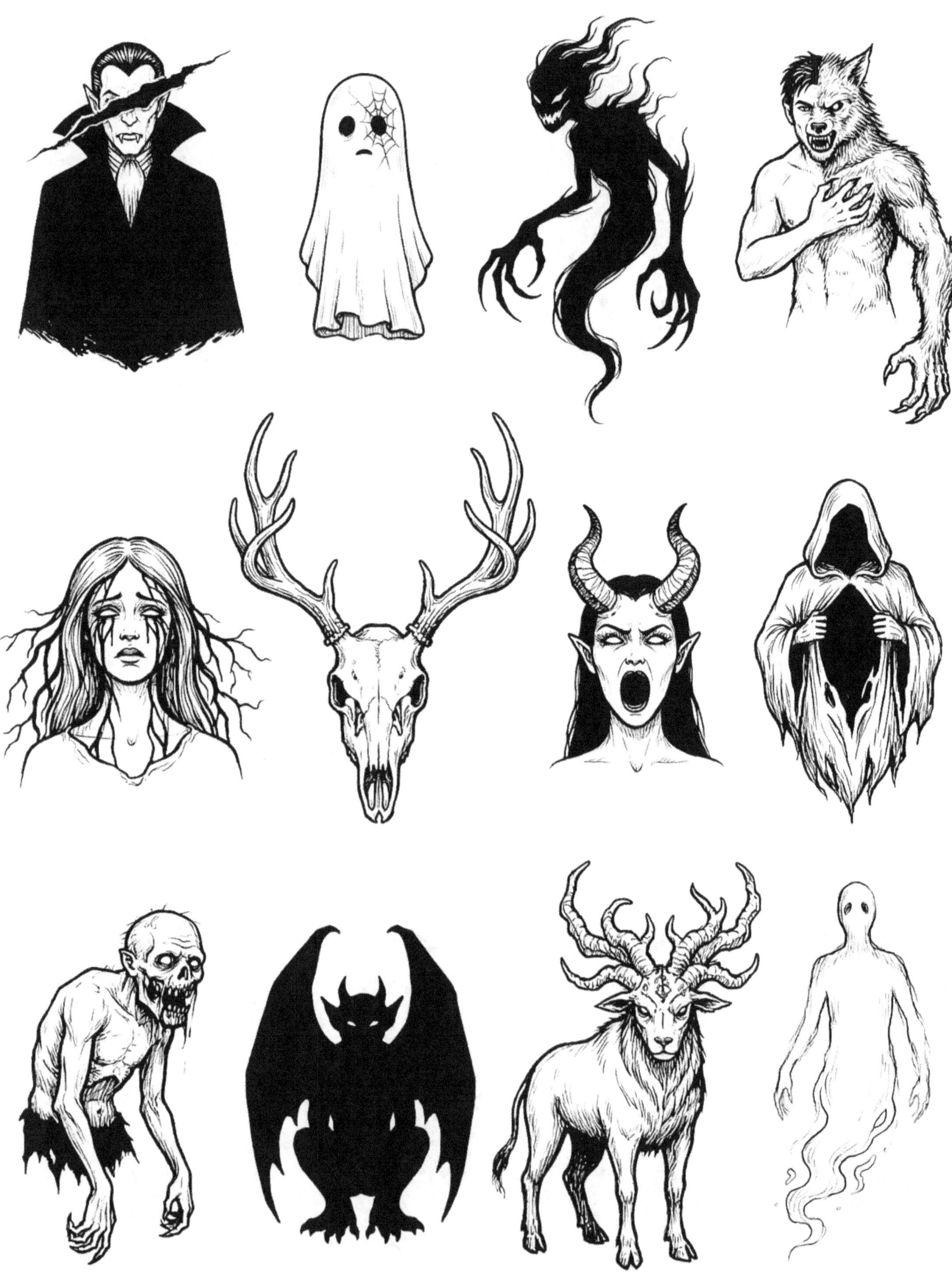

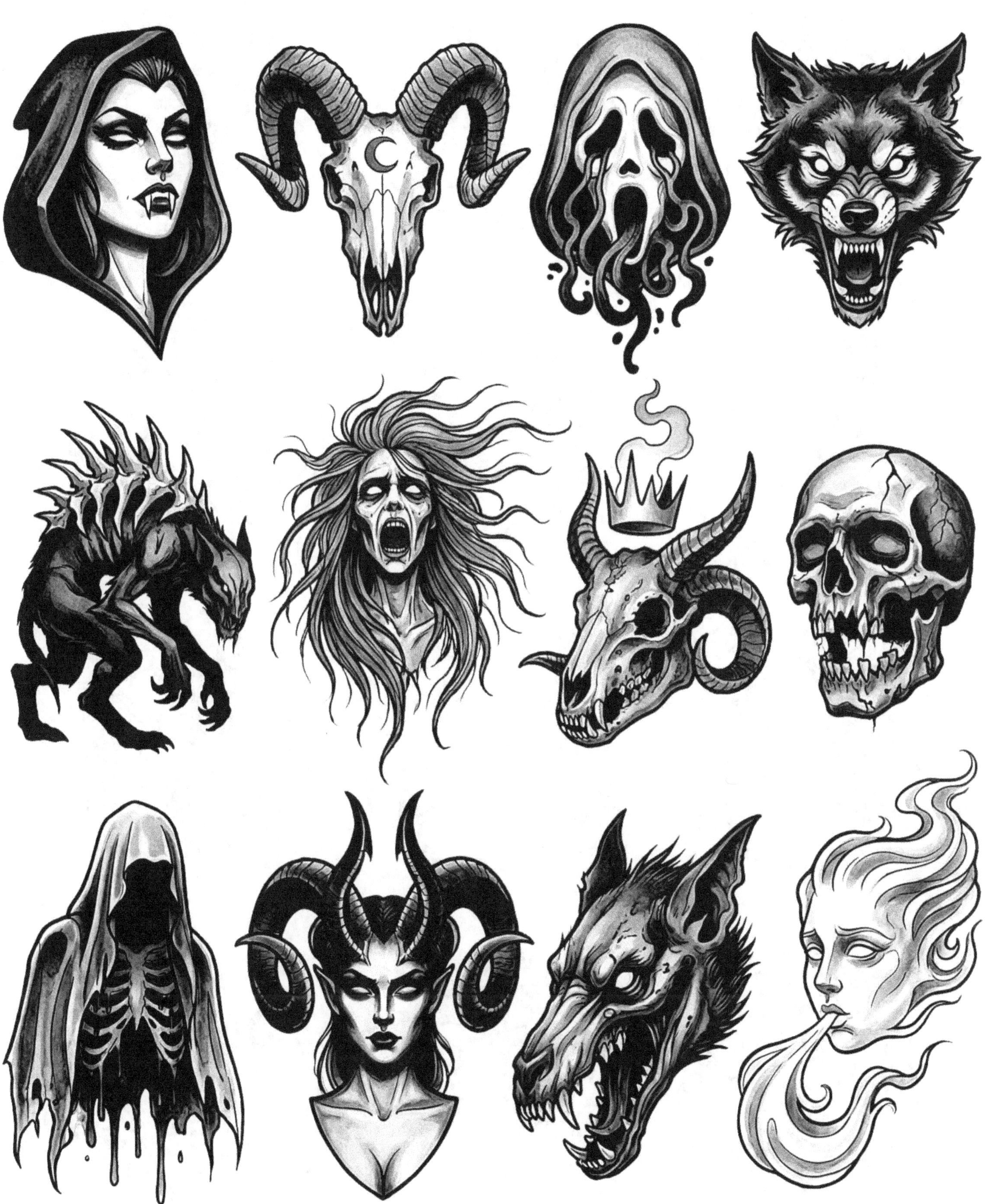

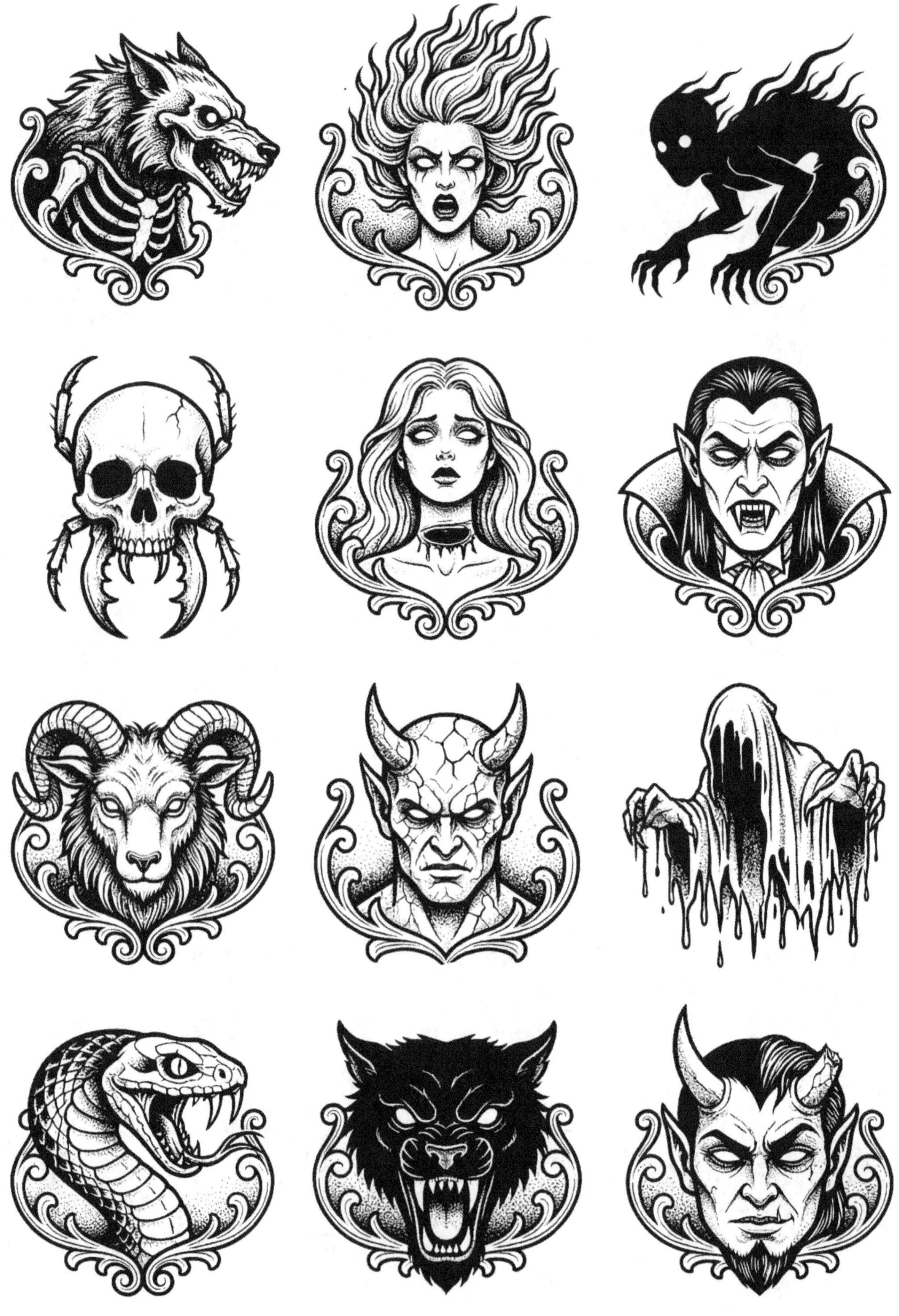

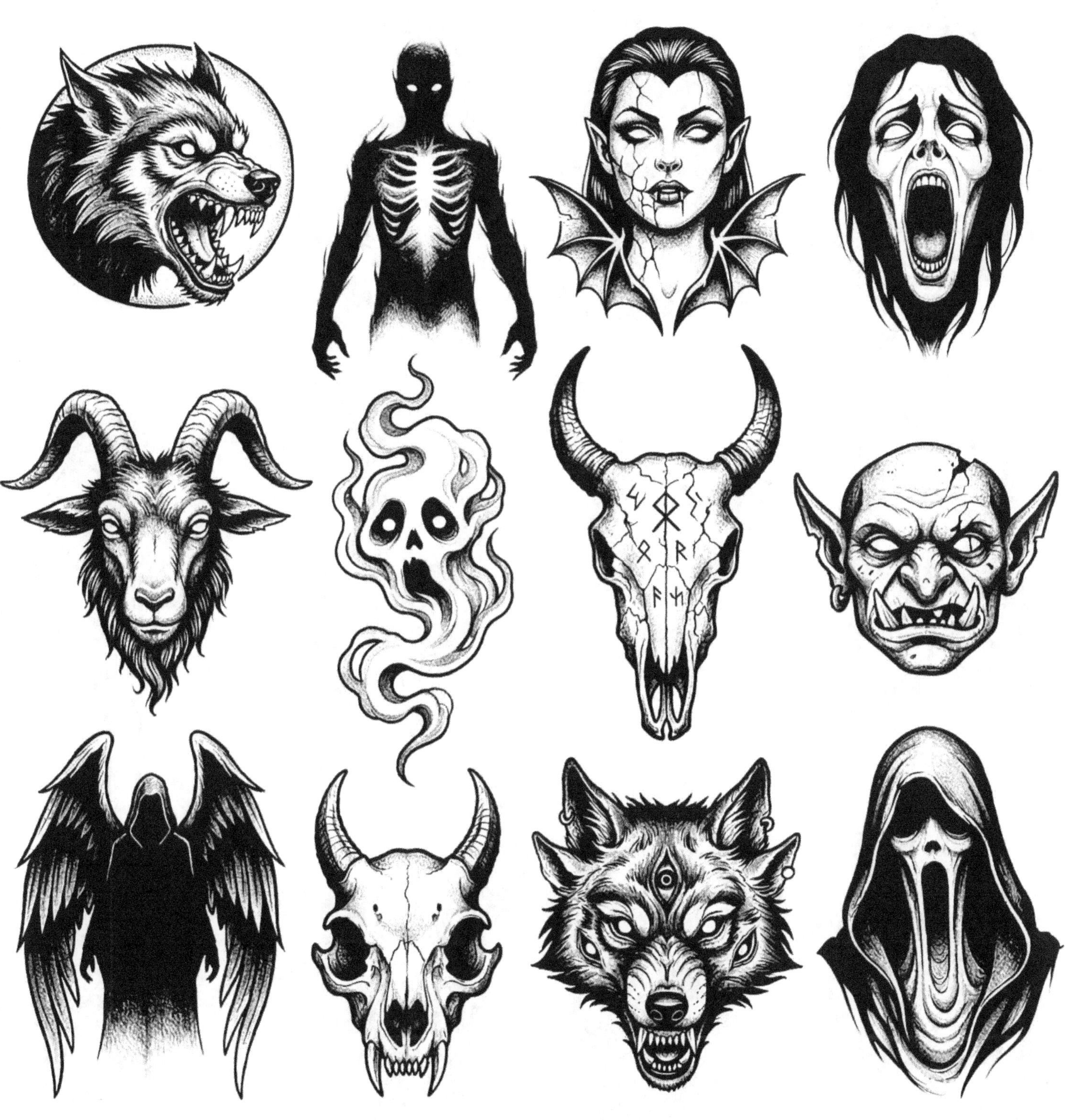

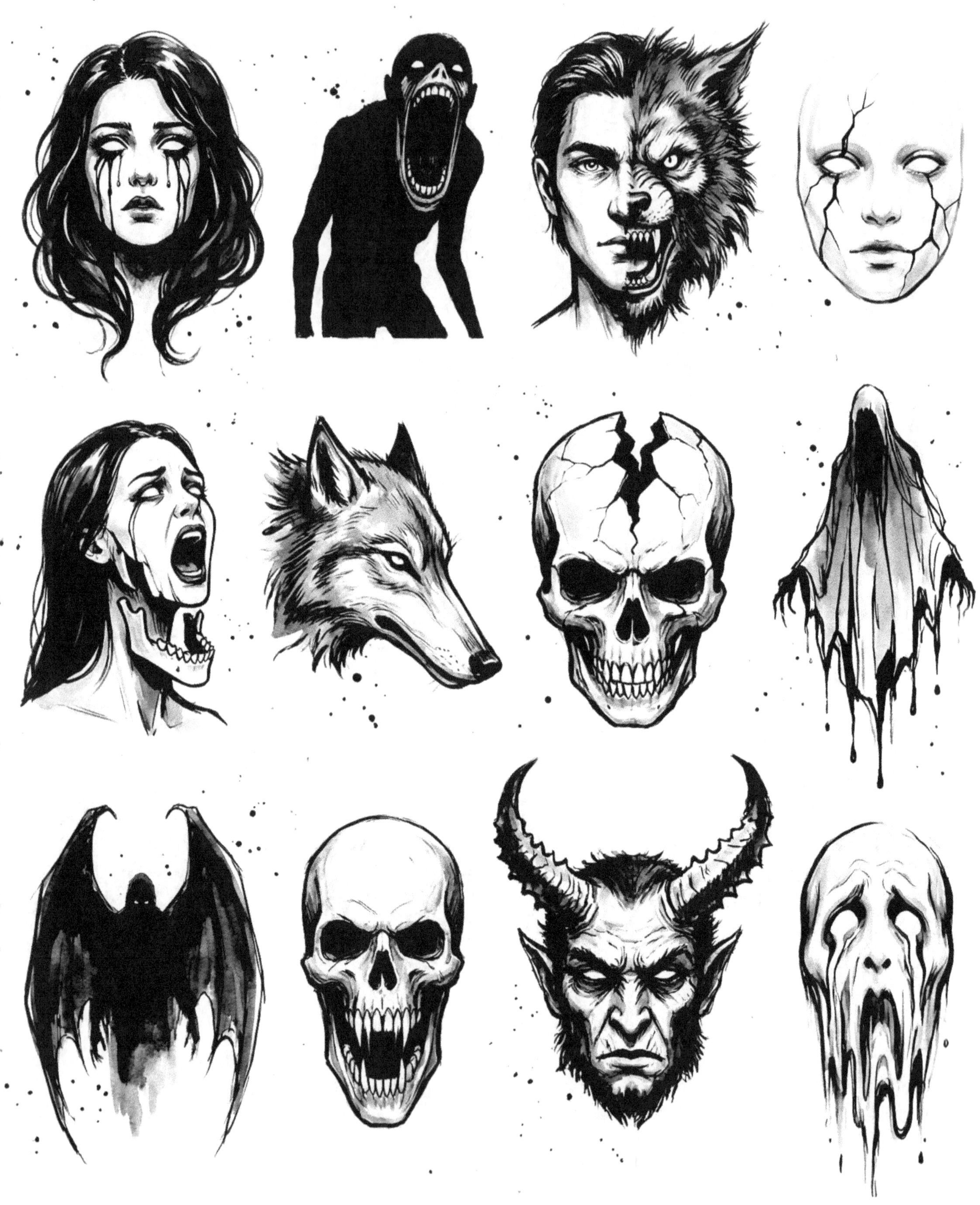

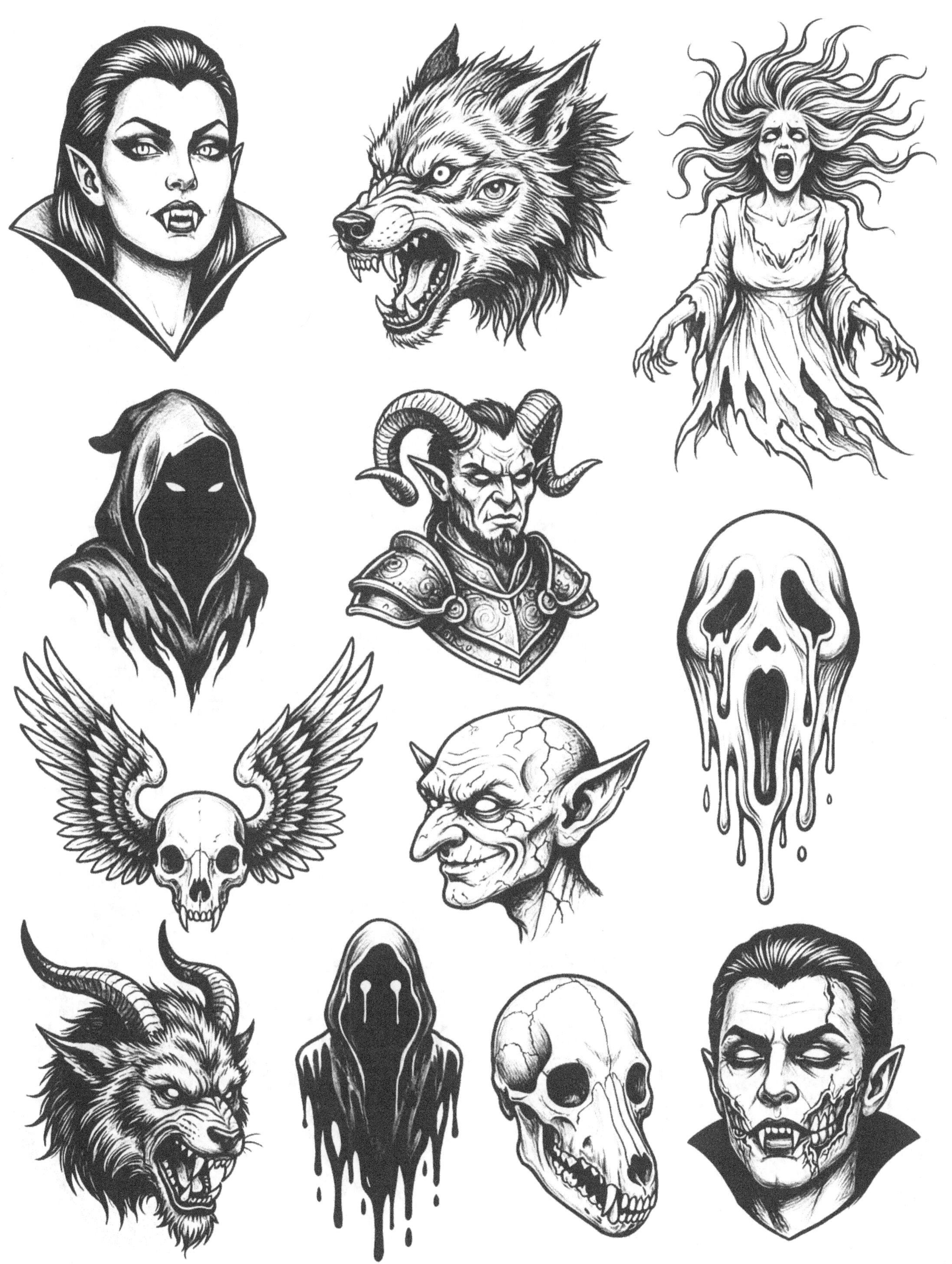

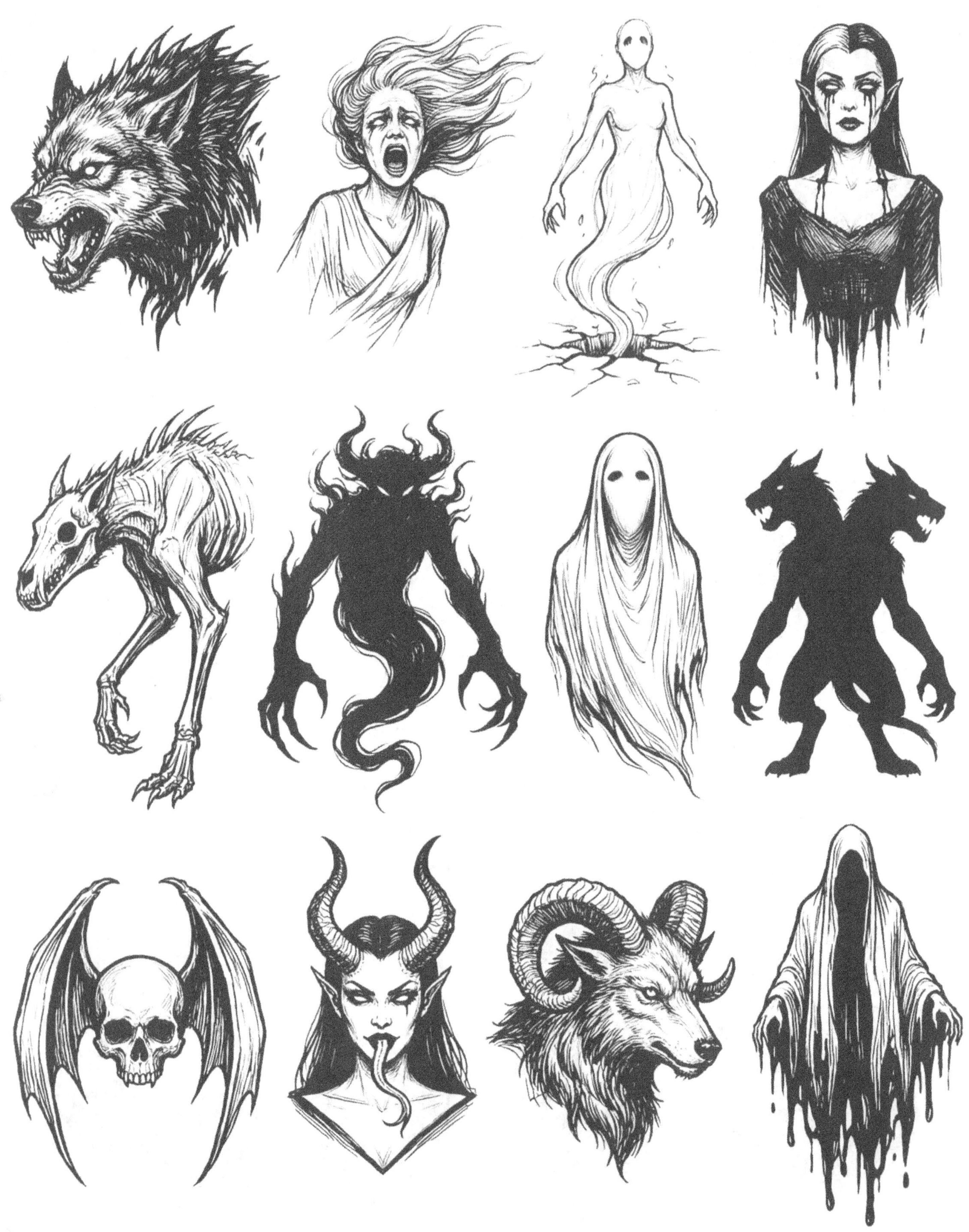

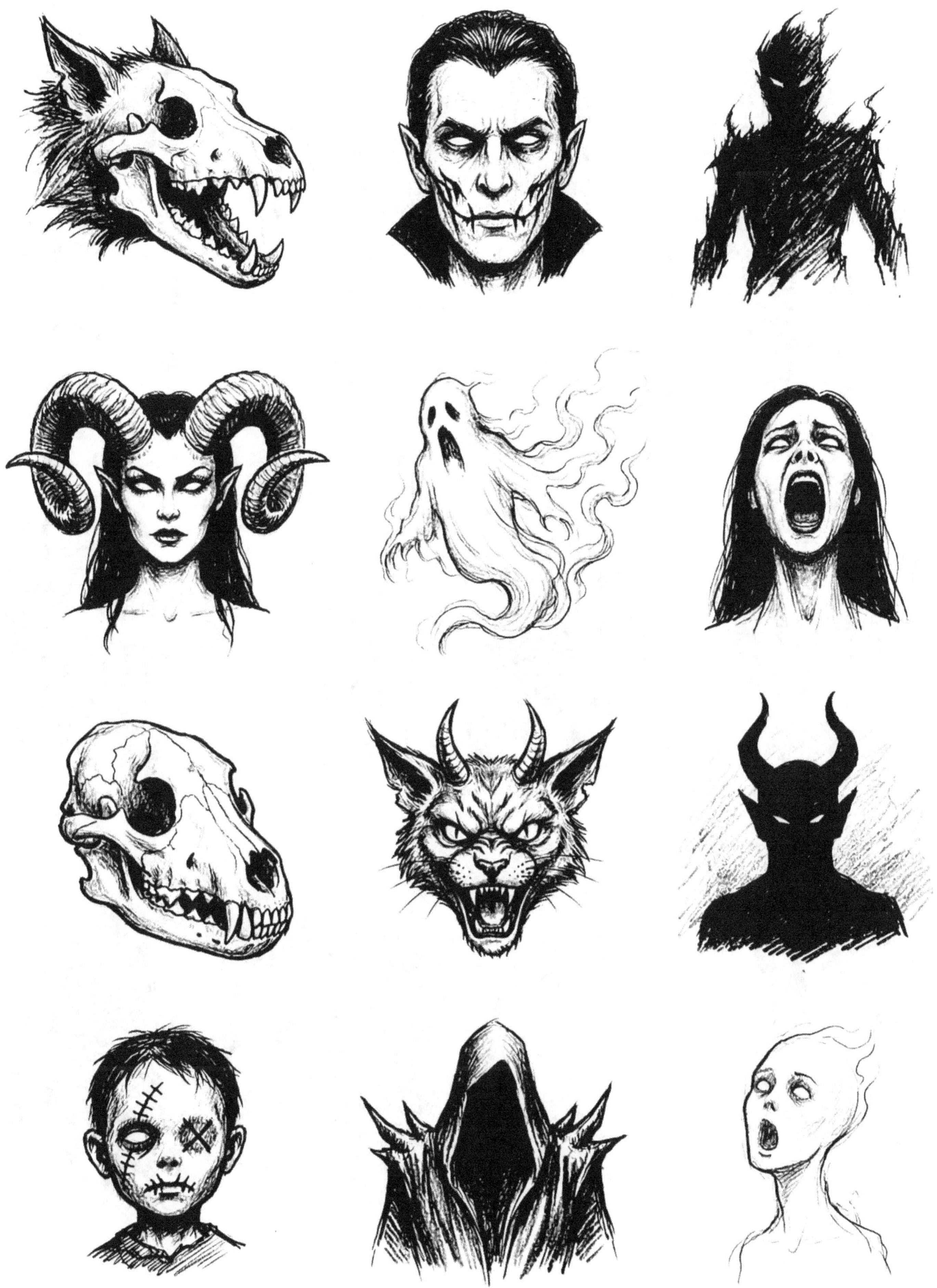

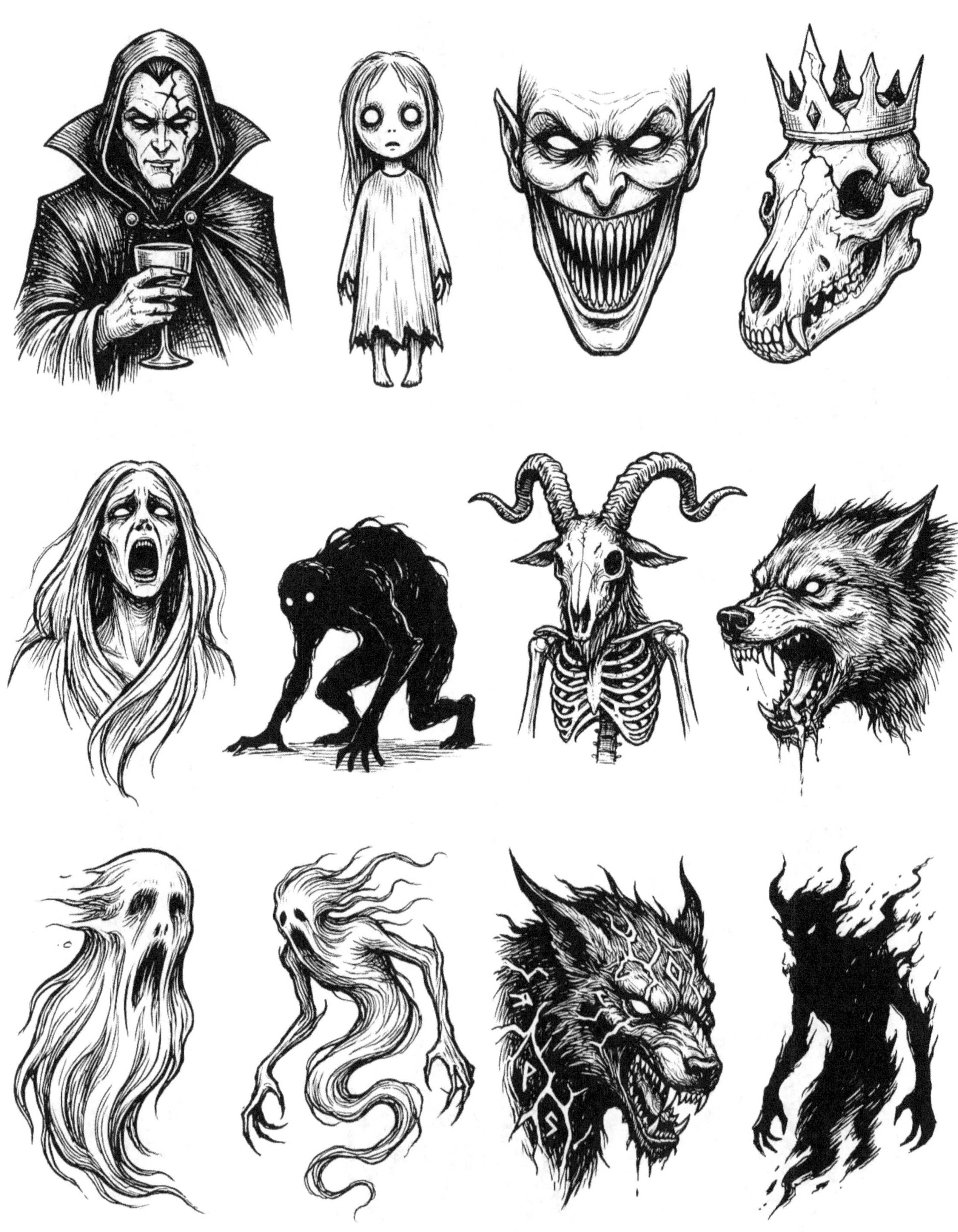

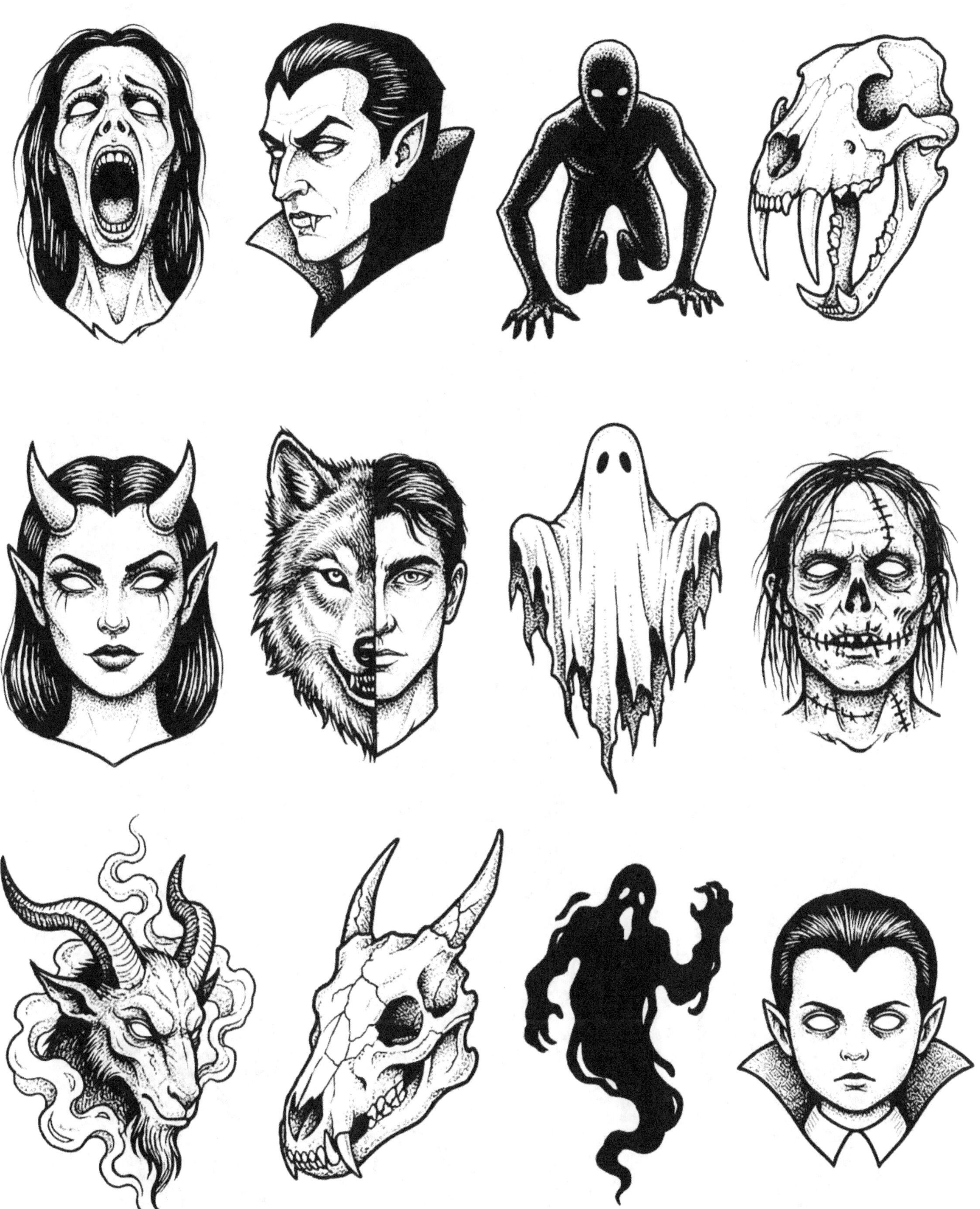

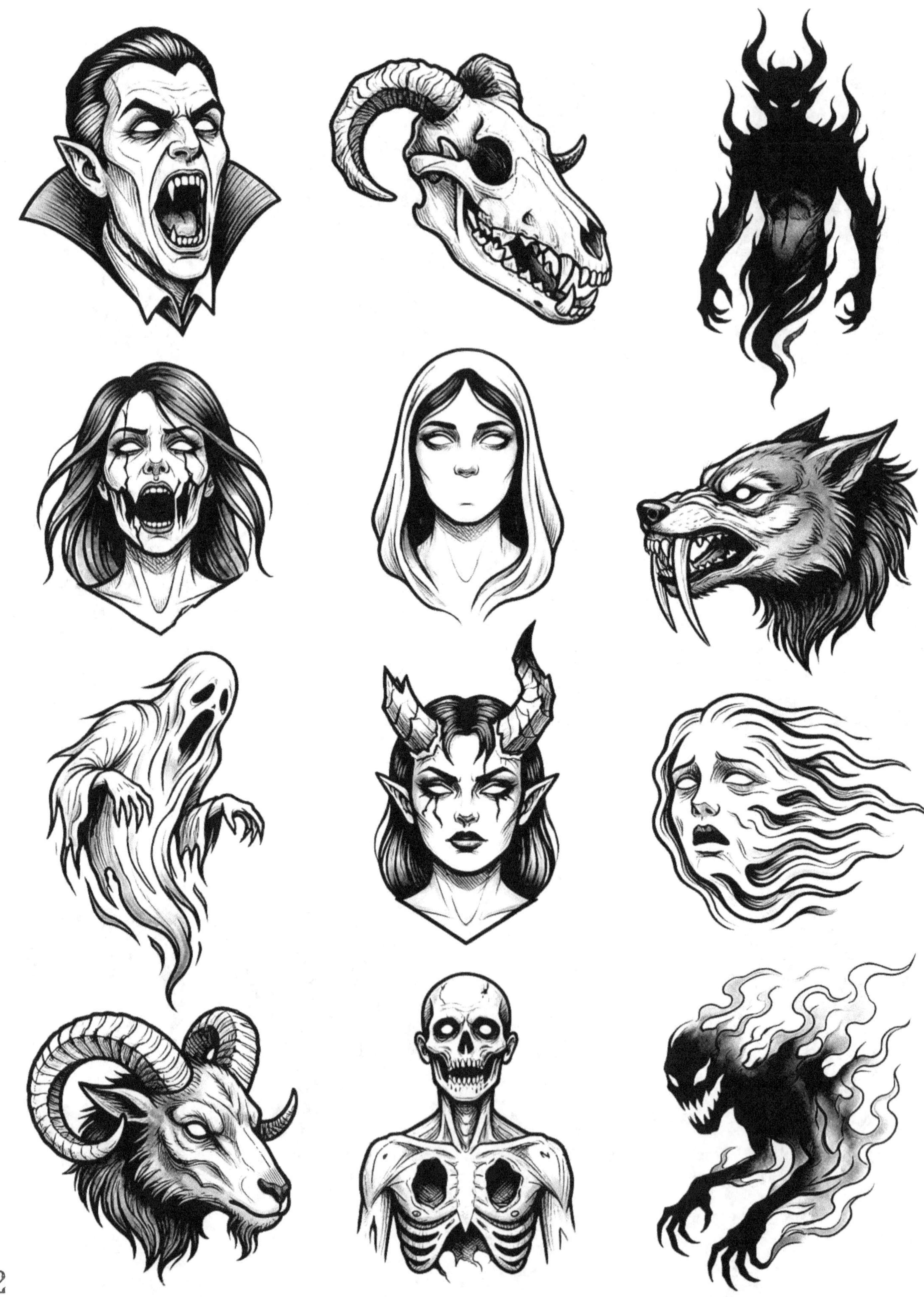

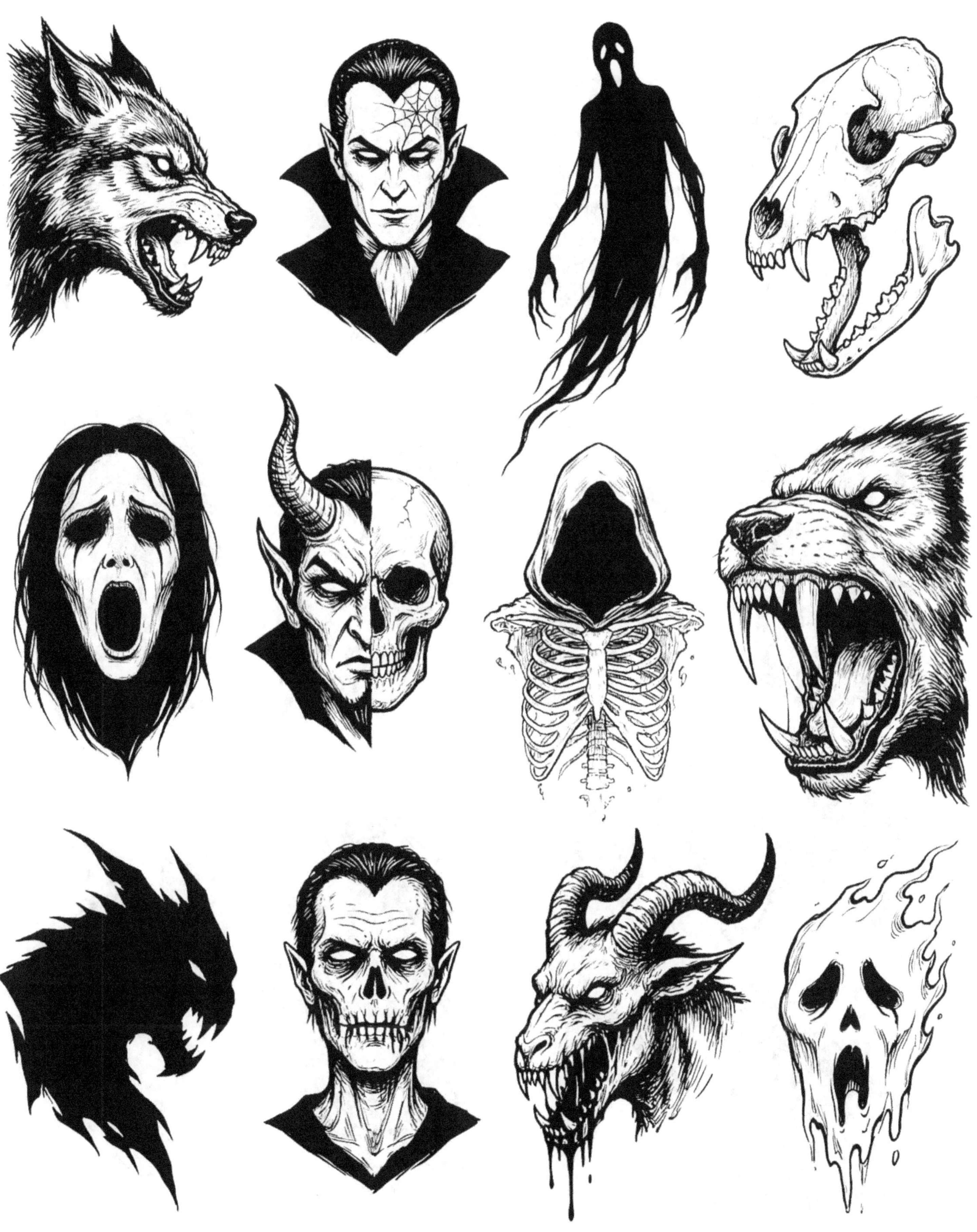

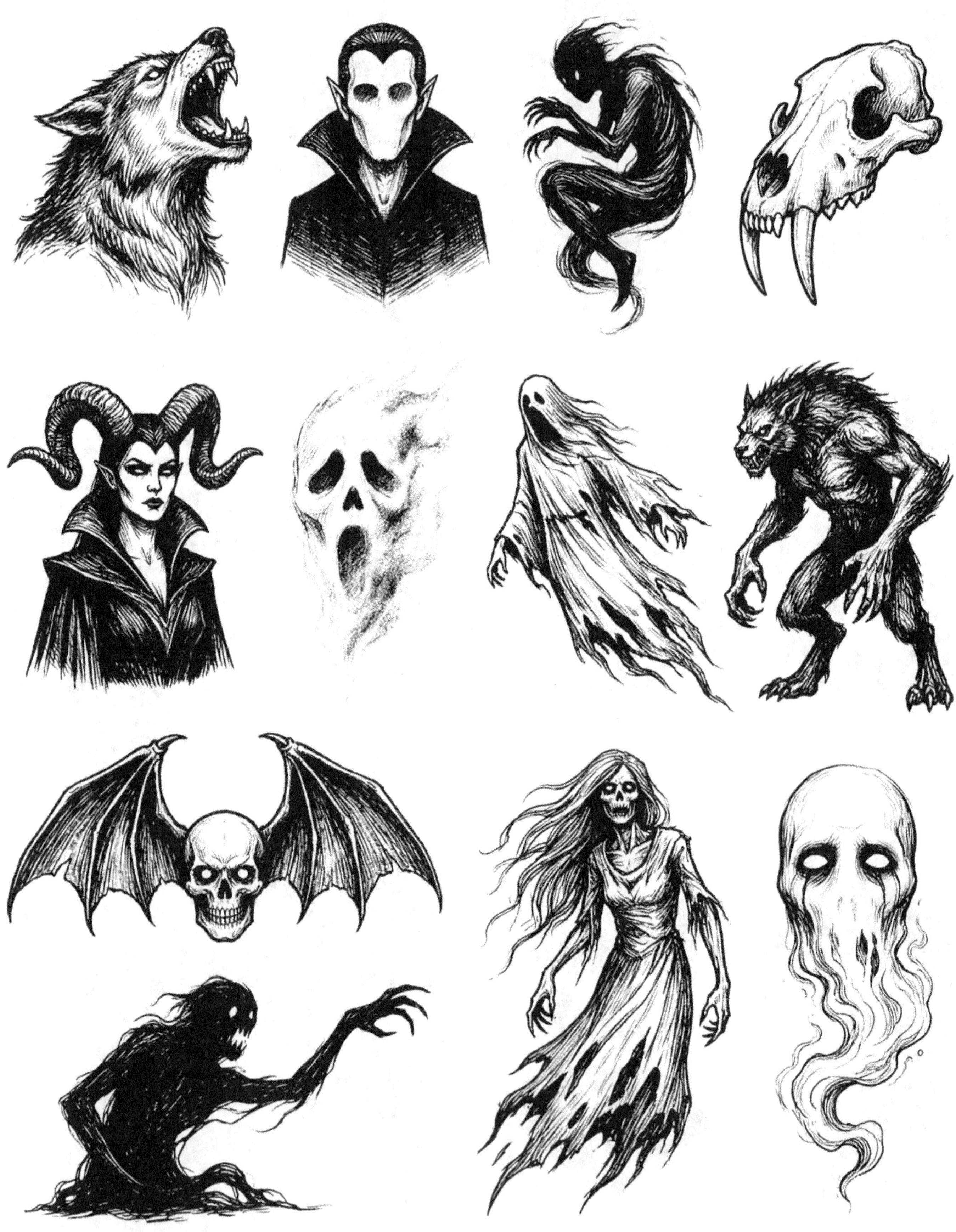

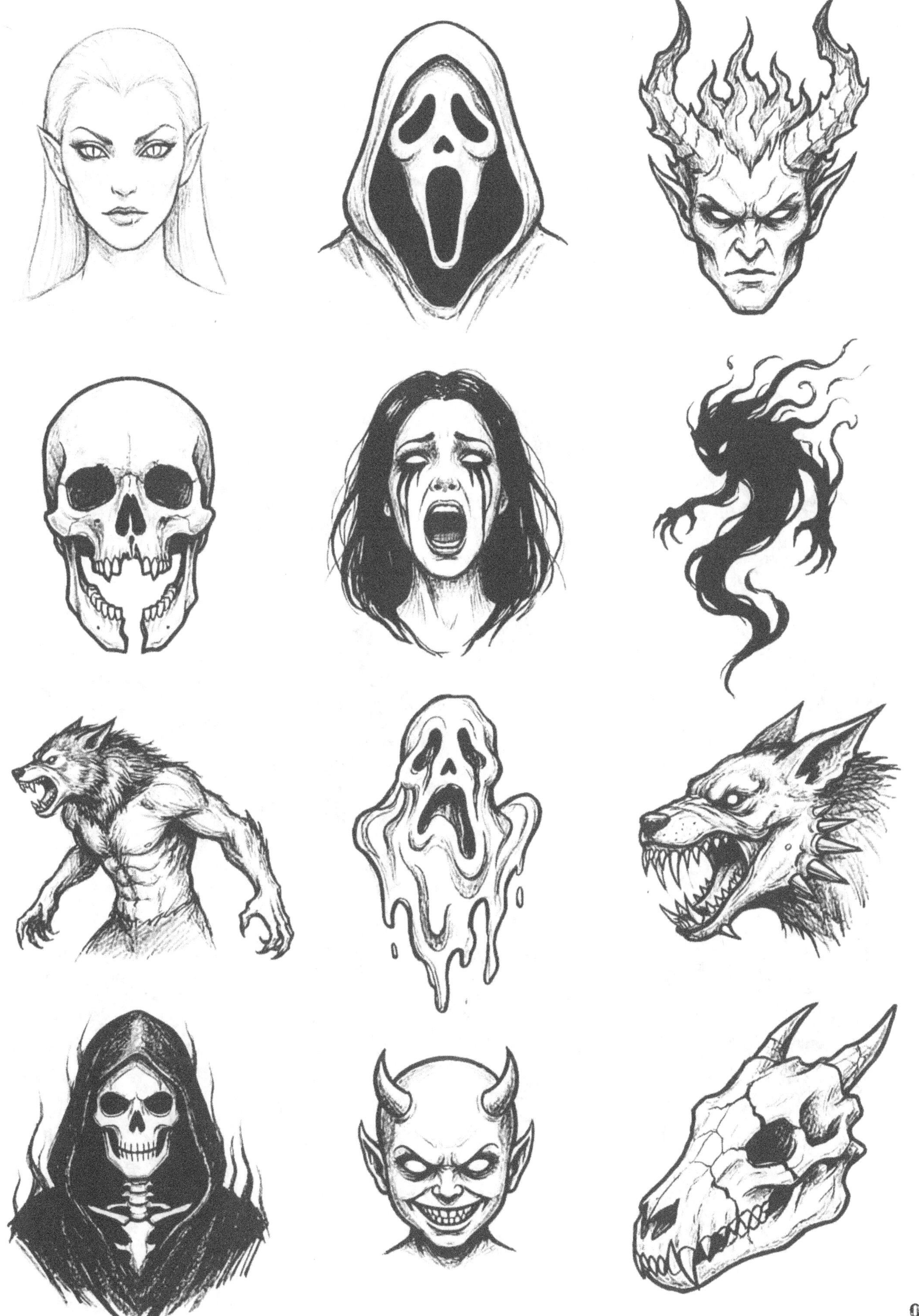

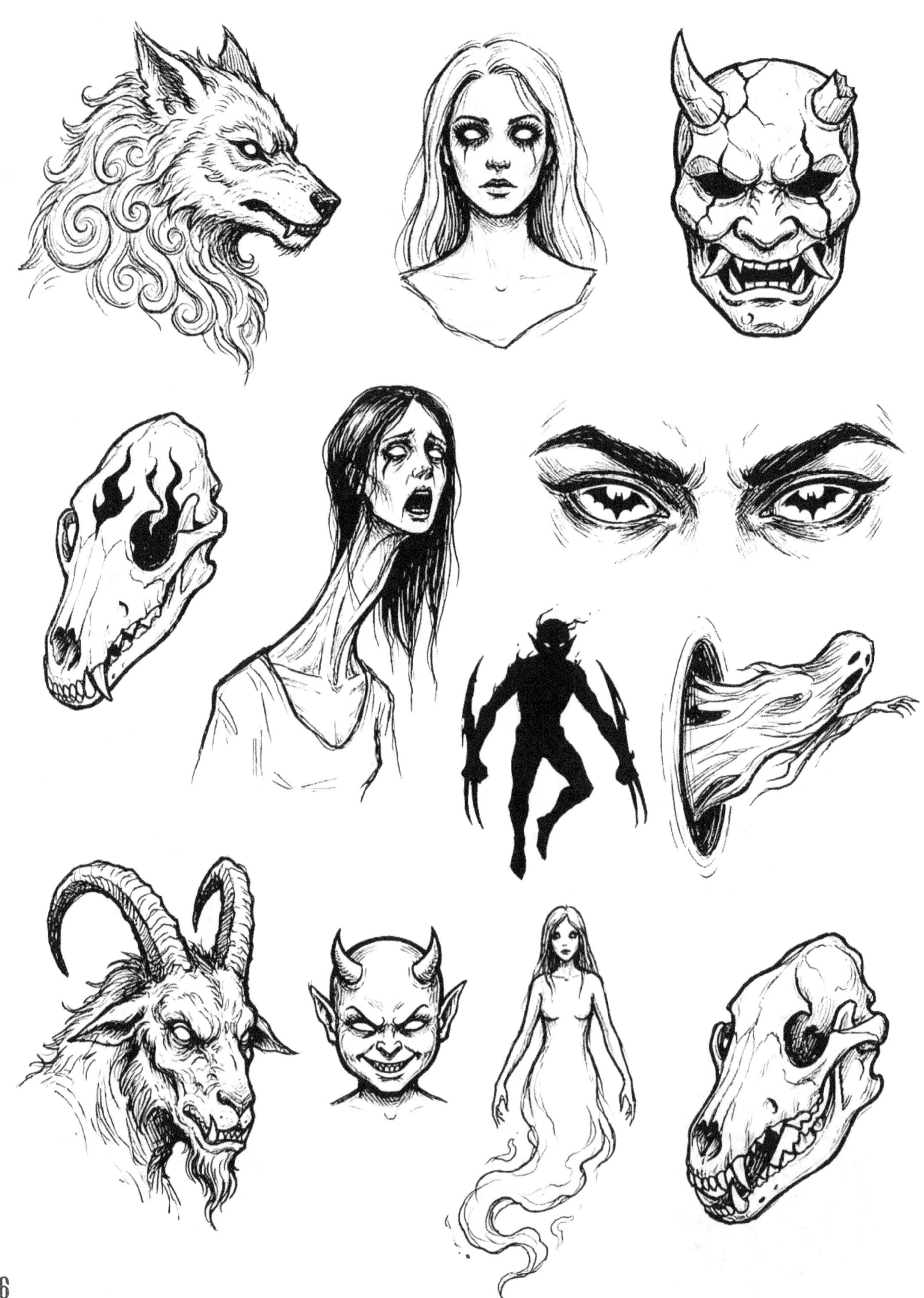

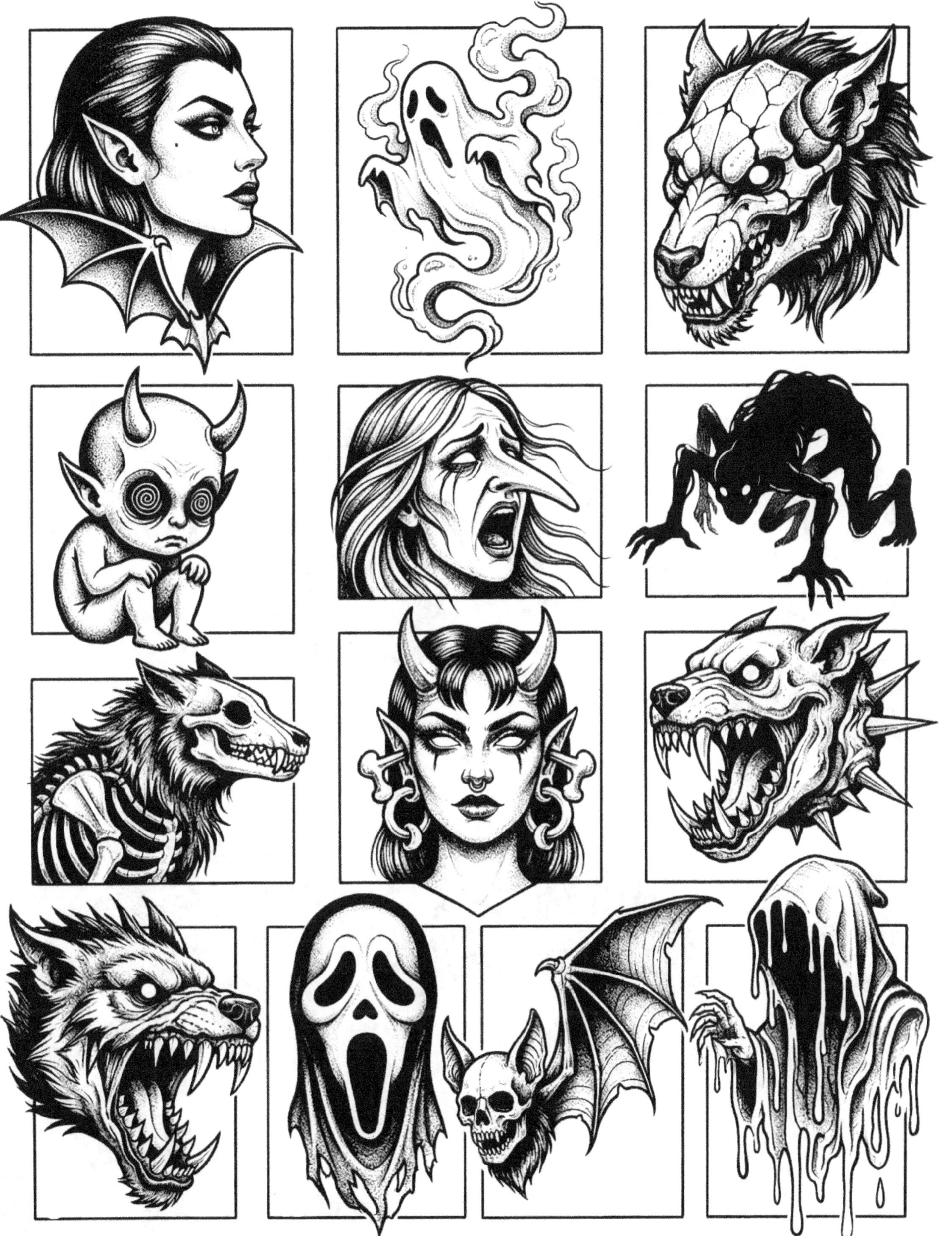

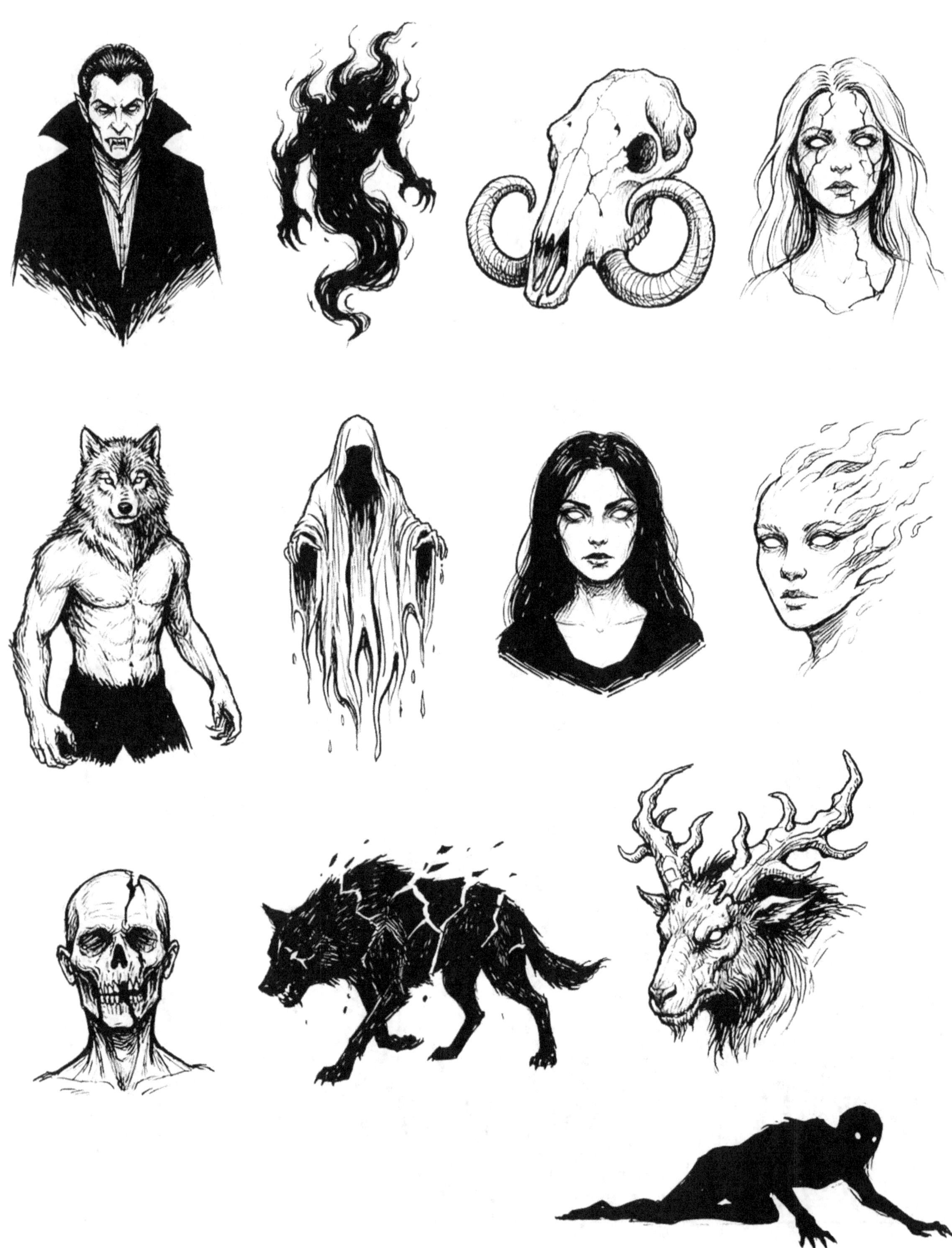

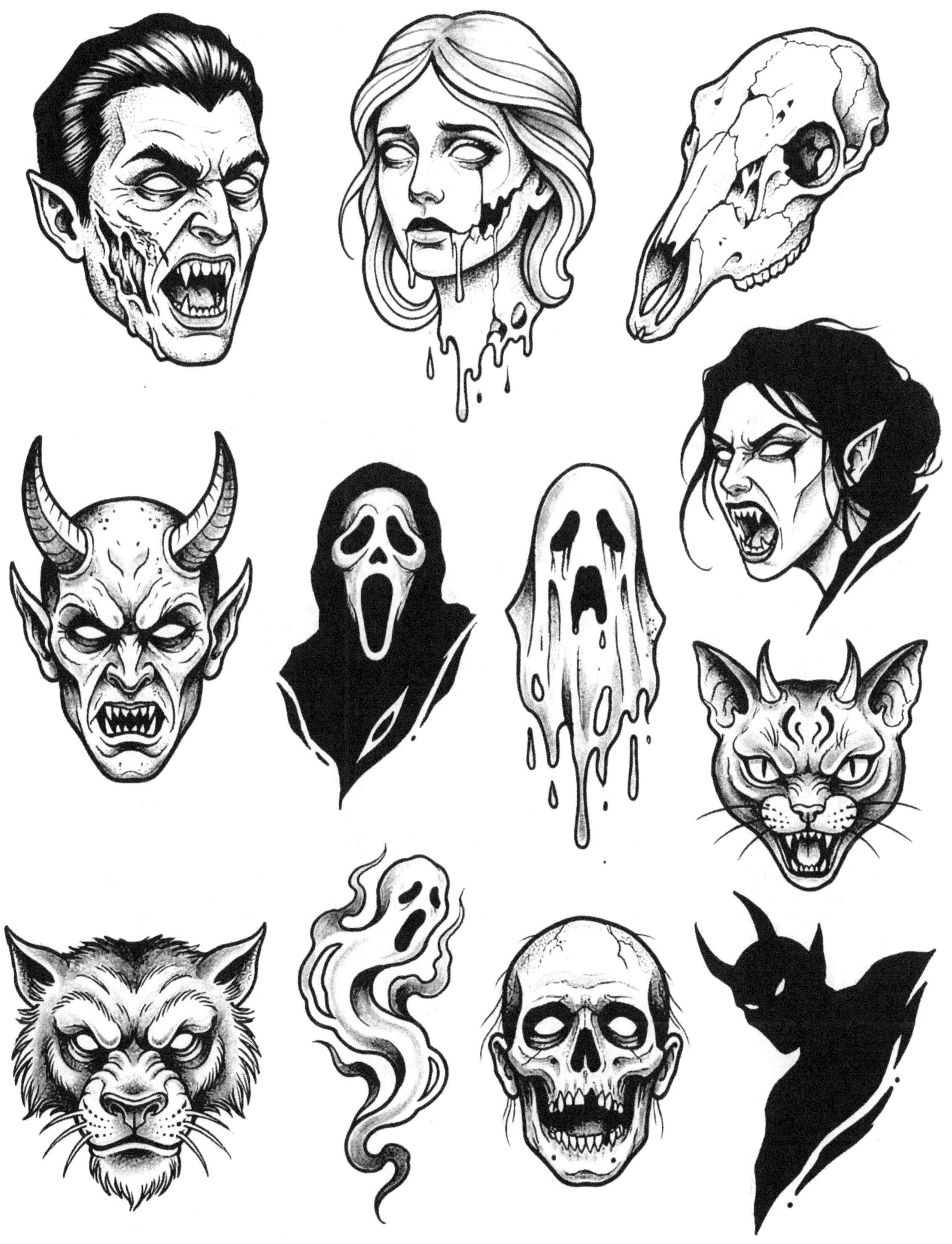

MACABRE SKULL VARIATIONS

Few symbols in tattoo art are as enduring and versatile as the skull. It bridges cultures, eras and artistic styles, carrying meanings that shift depending on its form. A skull can represent mortality, strength, rebellion, memory, transformation or acceptance. It can be grim, elegant, humorous, symbolic or deeply emotional. Its power lies in its simplicity — and in the endless ways it can be reimagined.

In the world of macabre aesthetics, skulls become more than anatomical structures. They turn into characters. Cracked surfaces, broken jaws, hollow expressions, exaggerated features, glowing elements or ornamental details all influence the story behind the design. A skull can look ancient, demonic, mechanical, ritualistic or abstract, making it one of the most adaptable focal points in tattoo composition.

This chapter explores skull imagery from multiple angles: twisted forms, hybrid silhouettes, fragmented structures, expressive eyesockets and stylized distortions. Each variation highlights a different emotional tone — from aggressive and intimidating to mysterious or surreal. These designs can serve as strong standalone tattoos, or act as central elements in larger works such as sleeves, back pieces or mixed symbolic compositions.

Use this chapter to study texture, shadow placement, structural exaggeration and how subtle shifts in proportion can dramatically change mood. Skull-based designs are ideal for practicing contrast, experimenting with line weight and building depth through shading. They give you the freedom to create something instantly recognizable yet completely unique.

This is where anatomy meets symbolism,

where decay becomes design,

and where every fracture tells its own story.

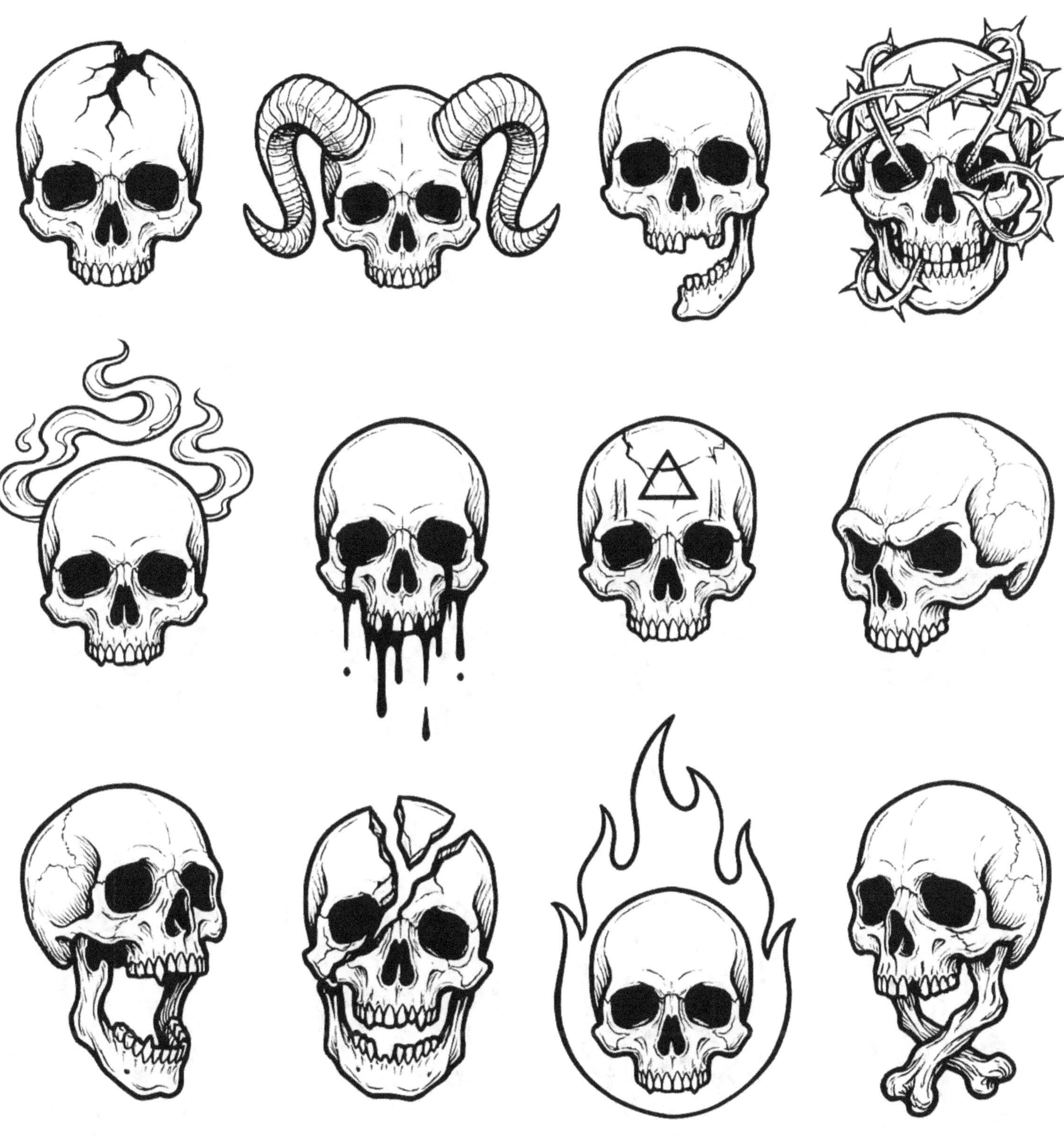

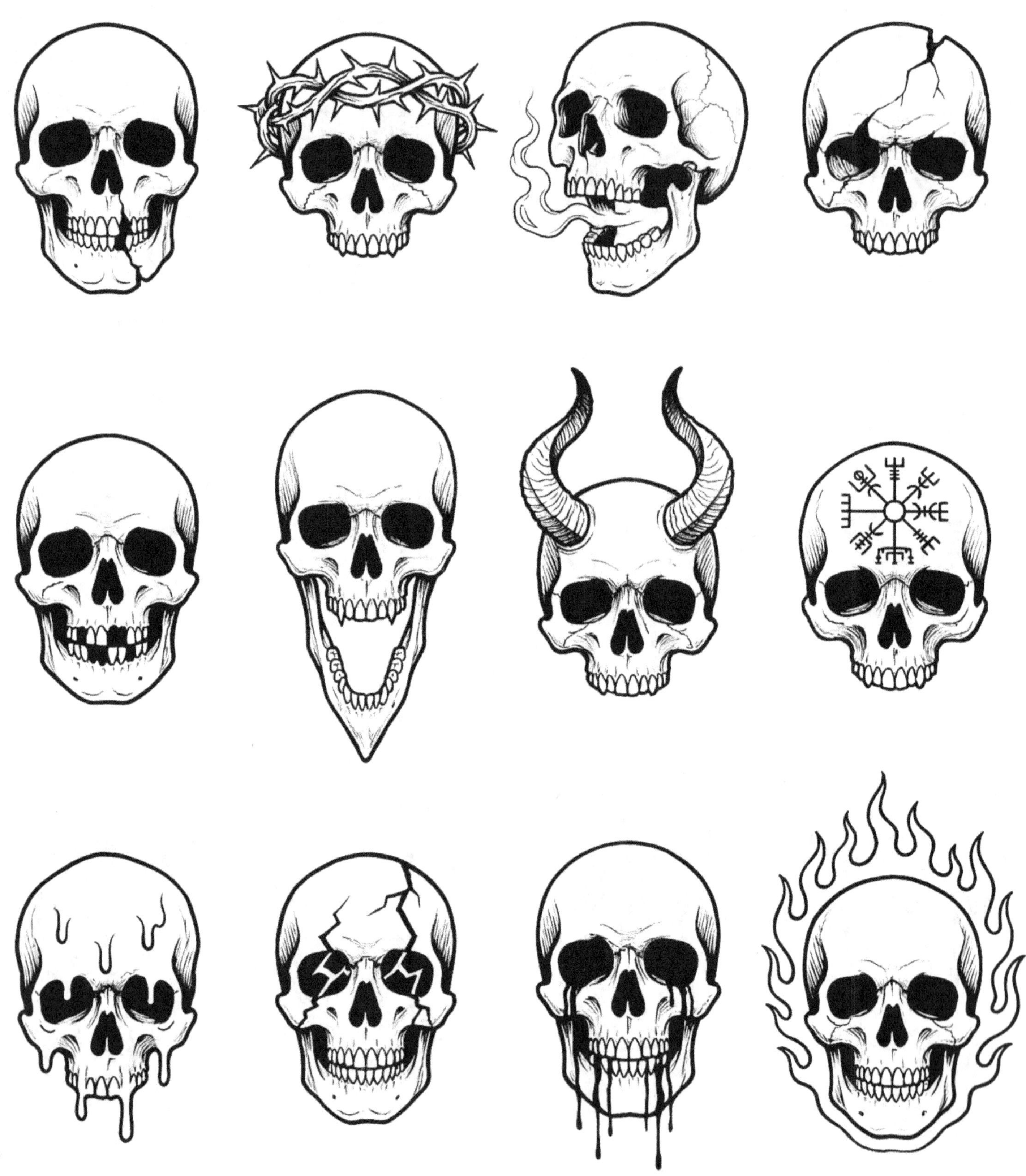

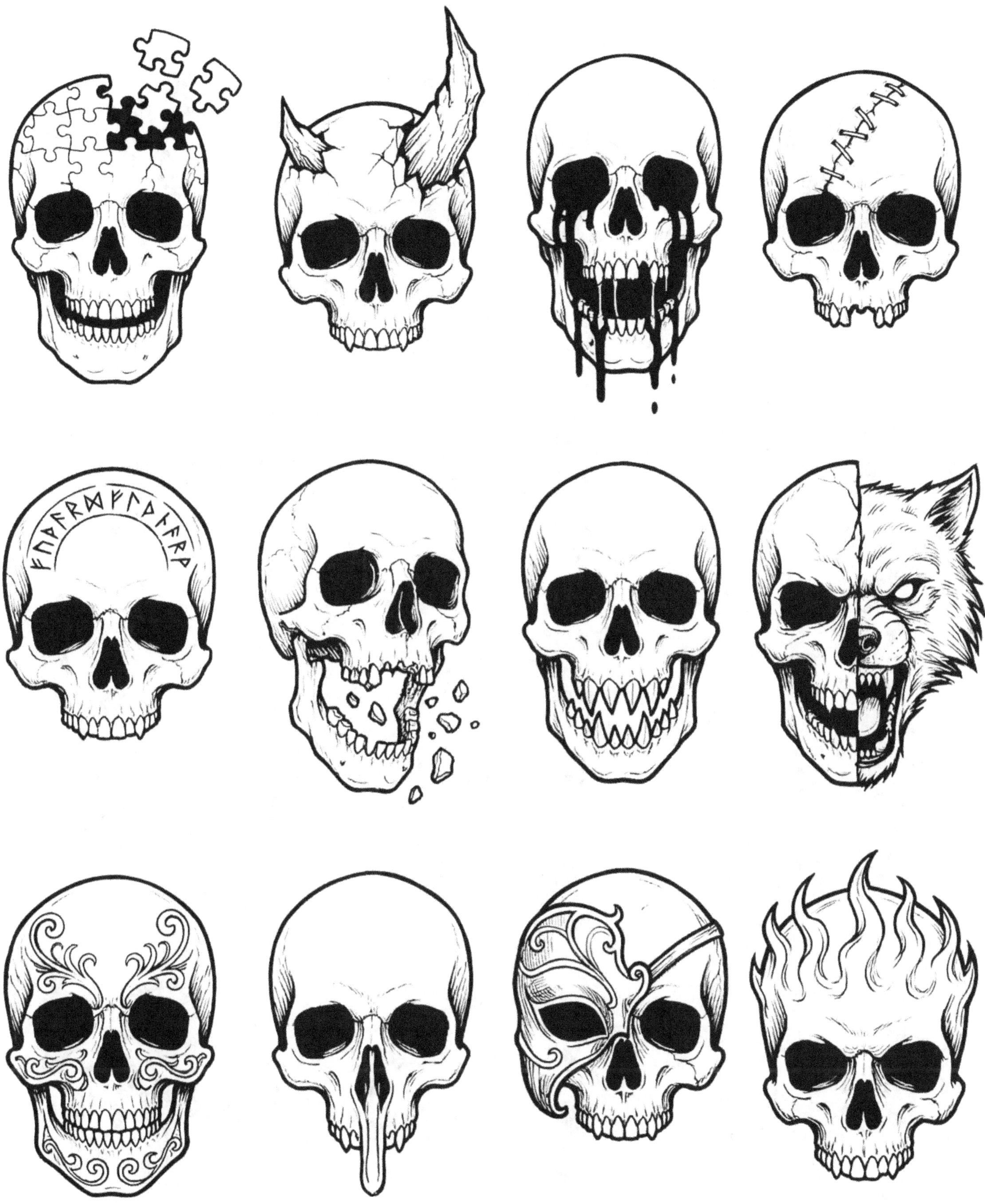

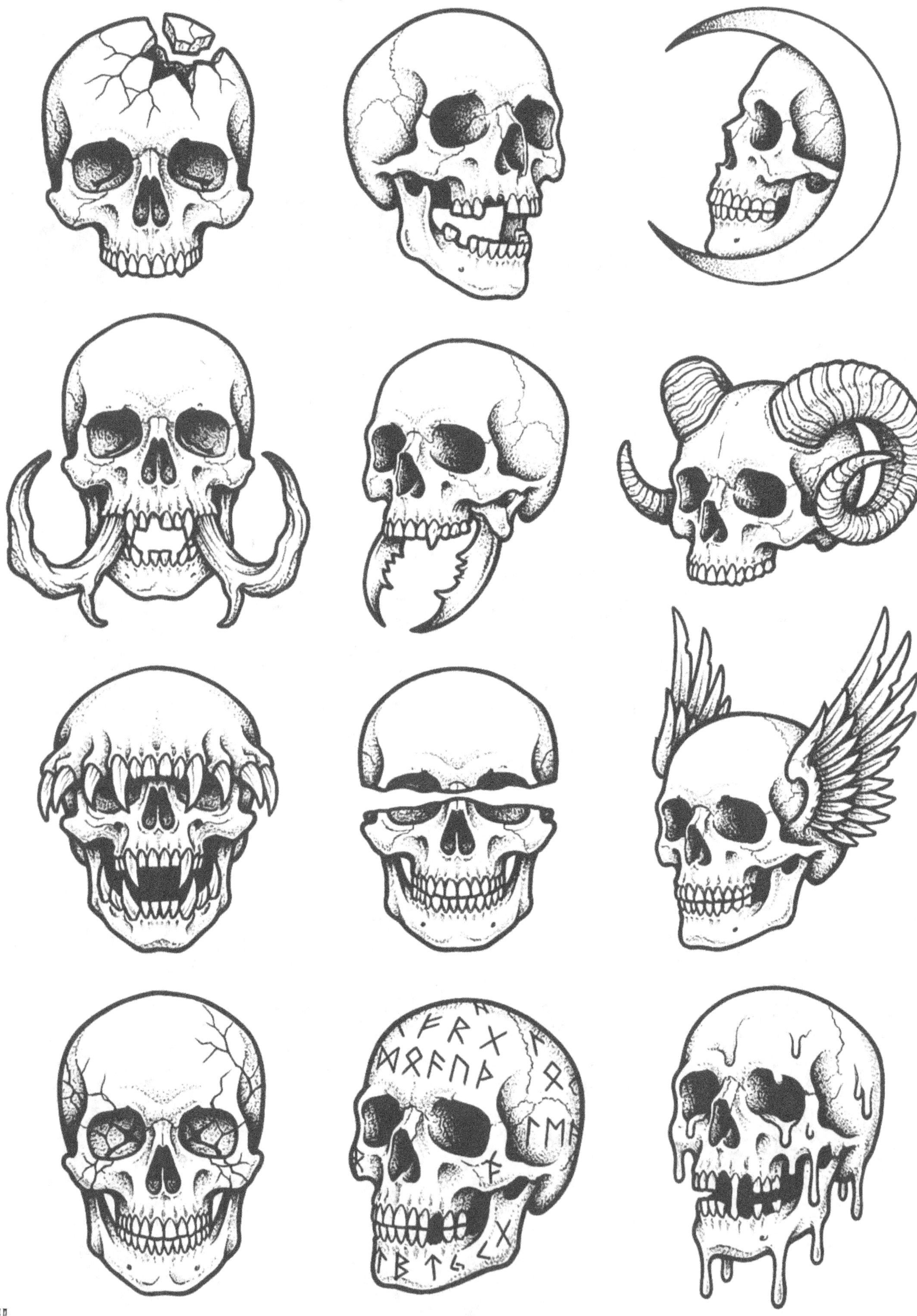

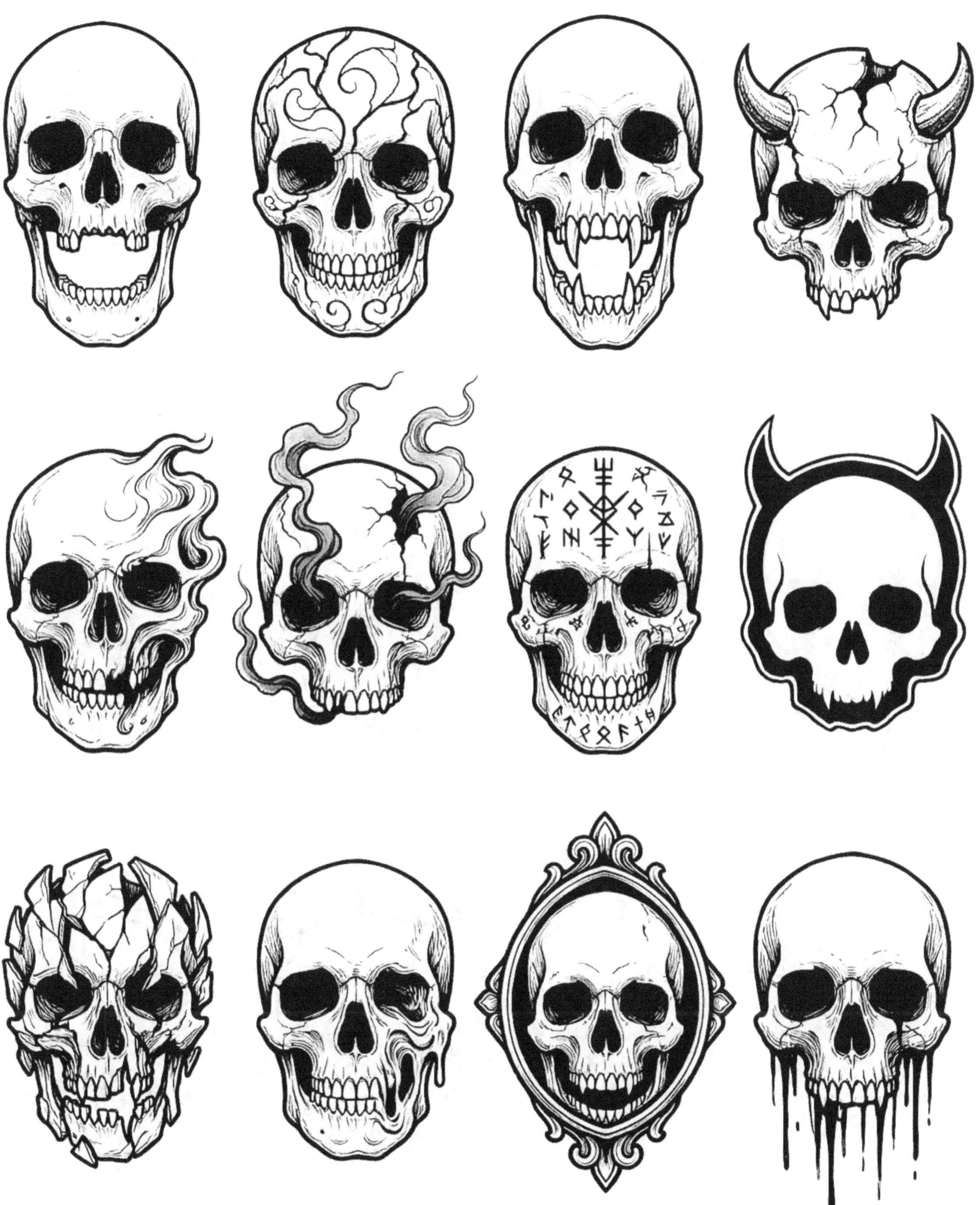

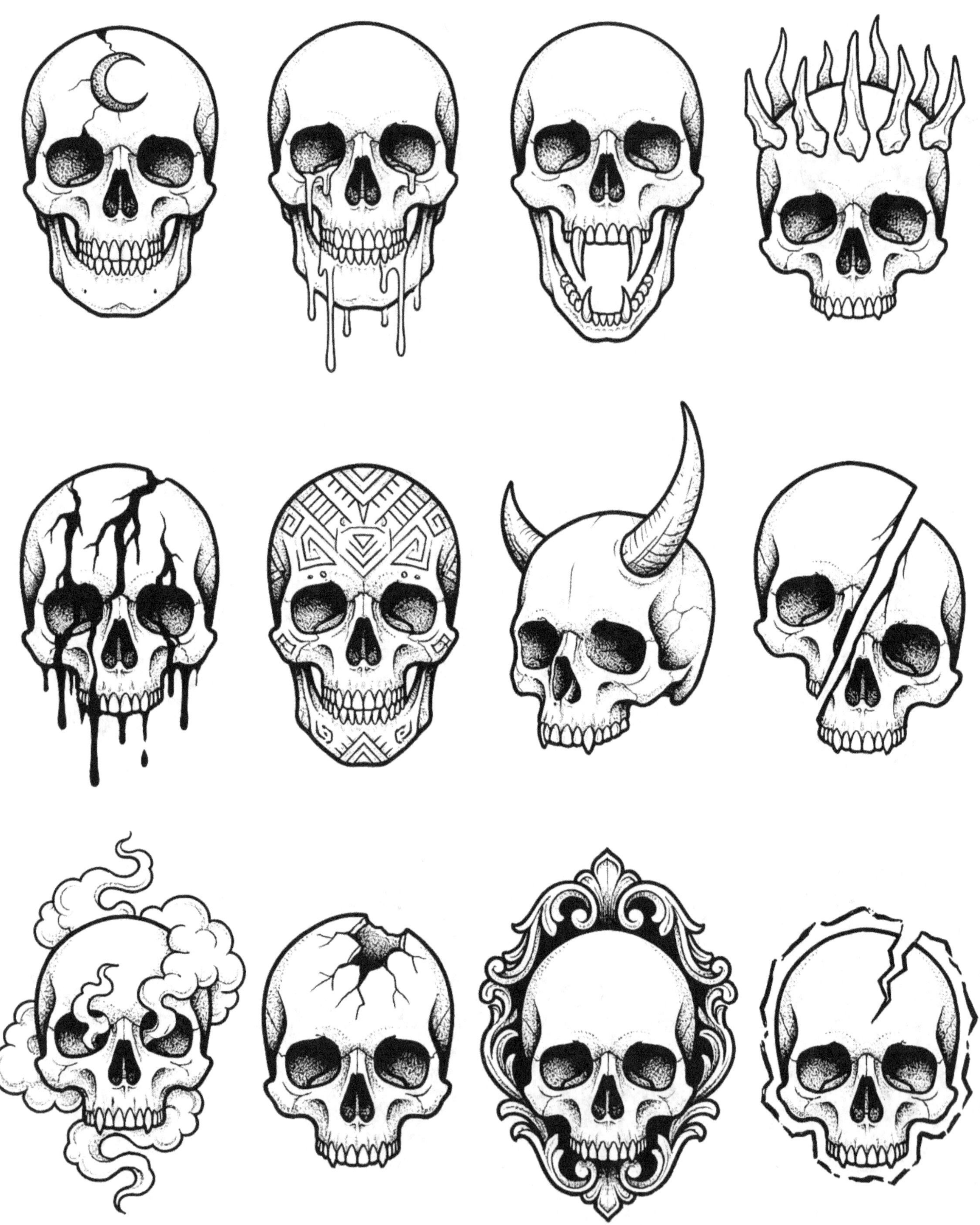

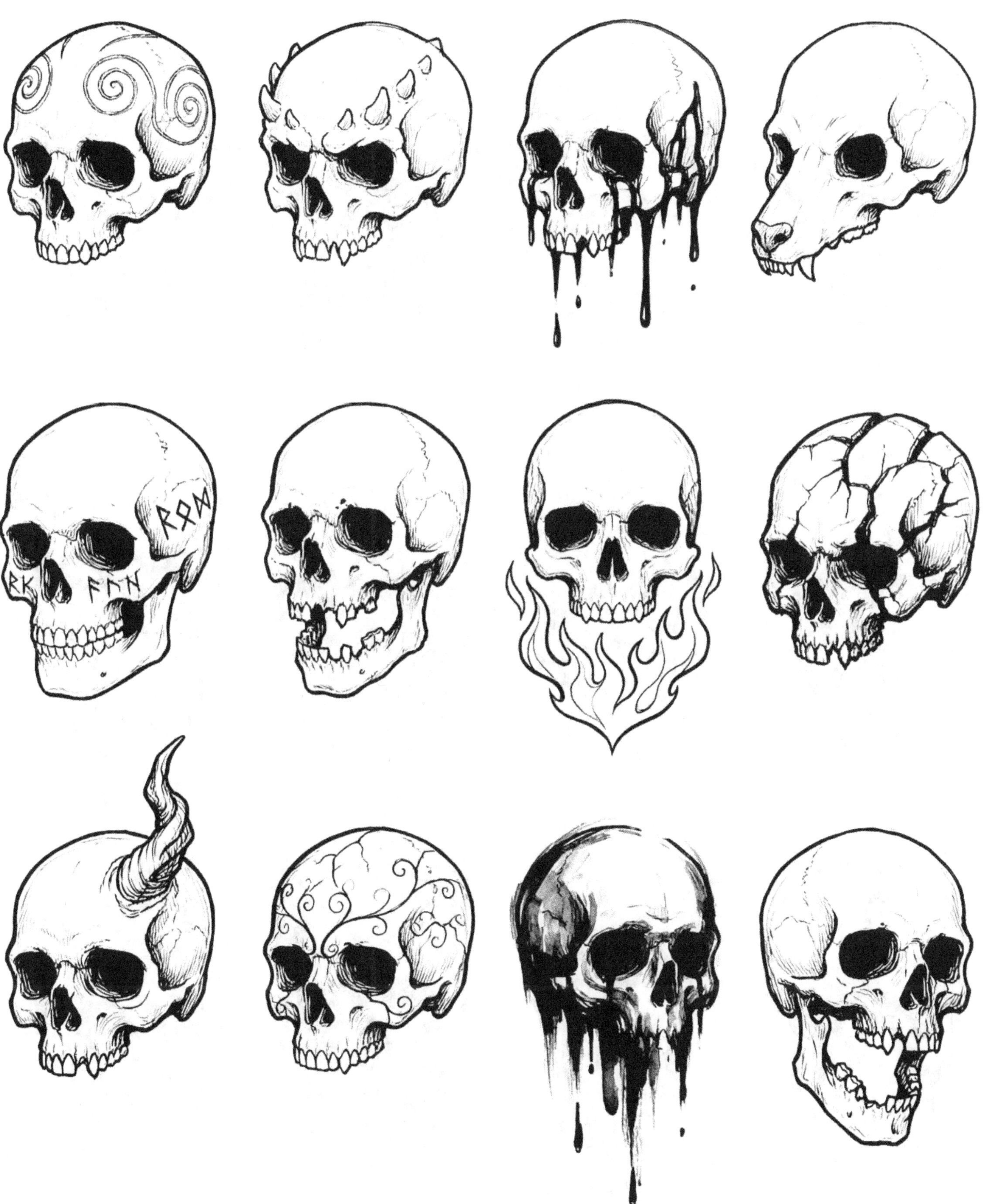

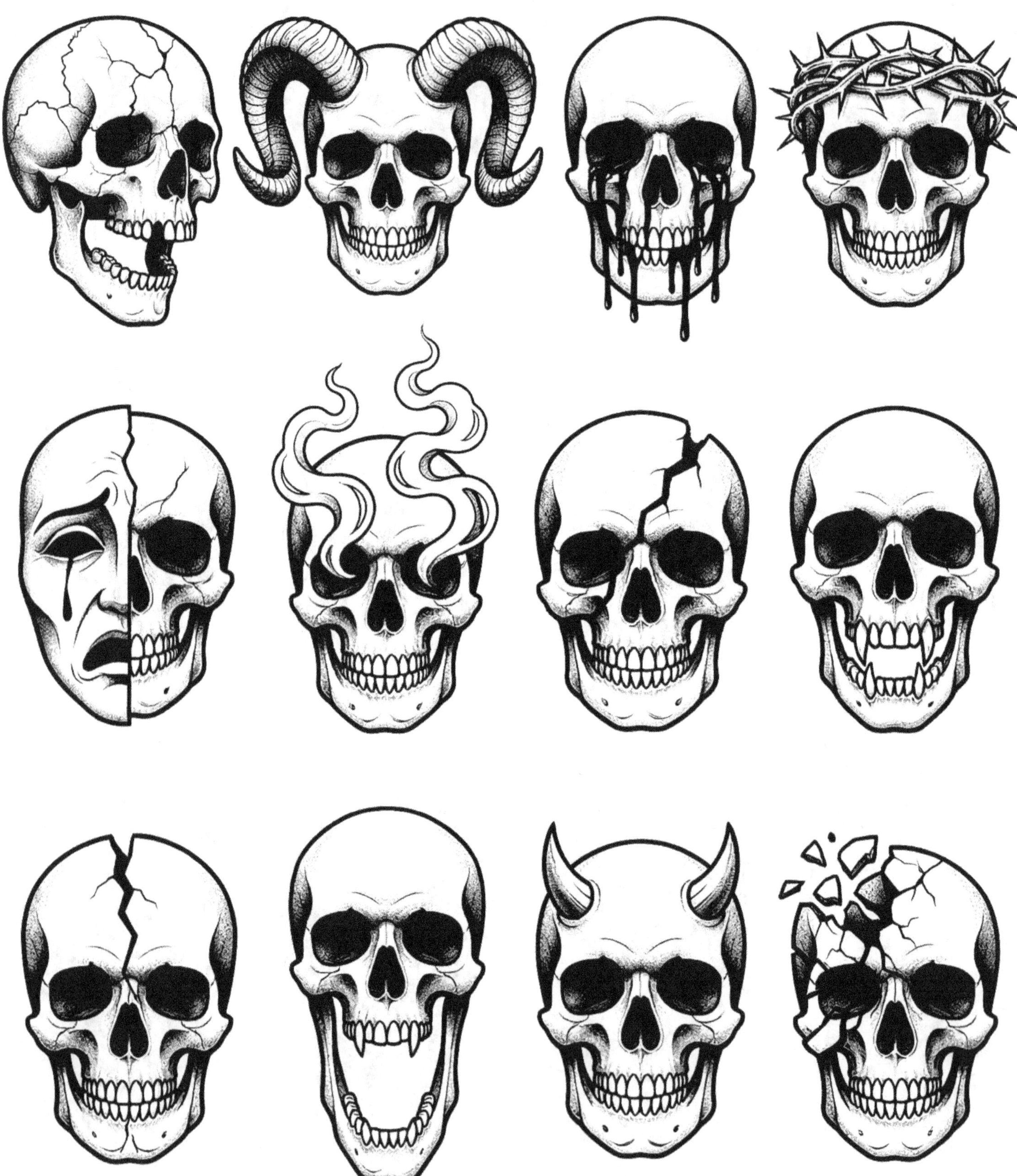

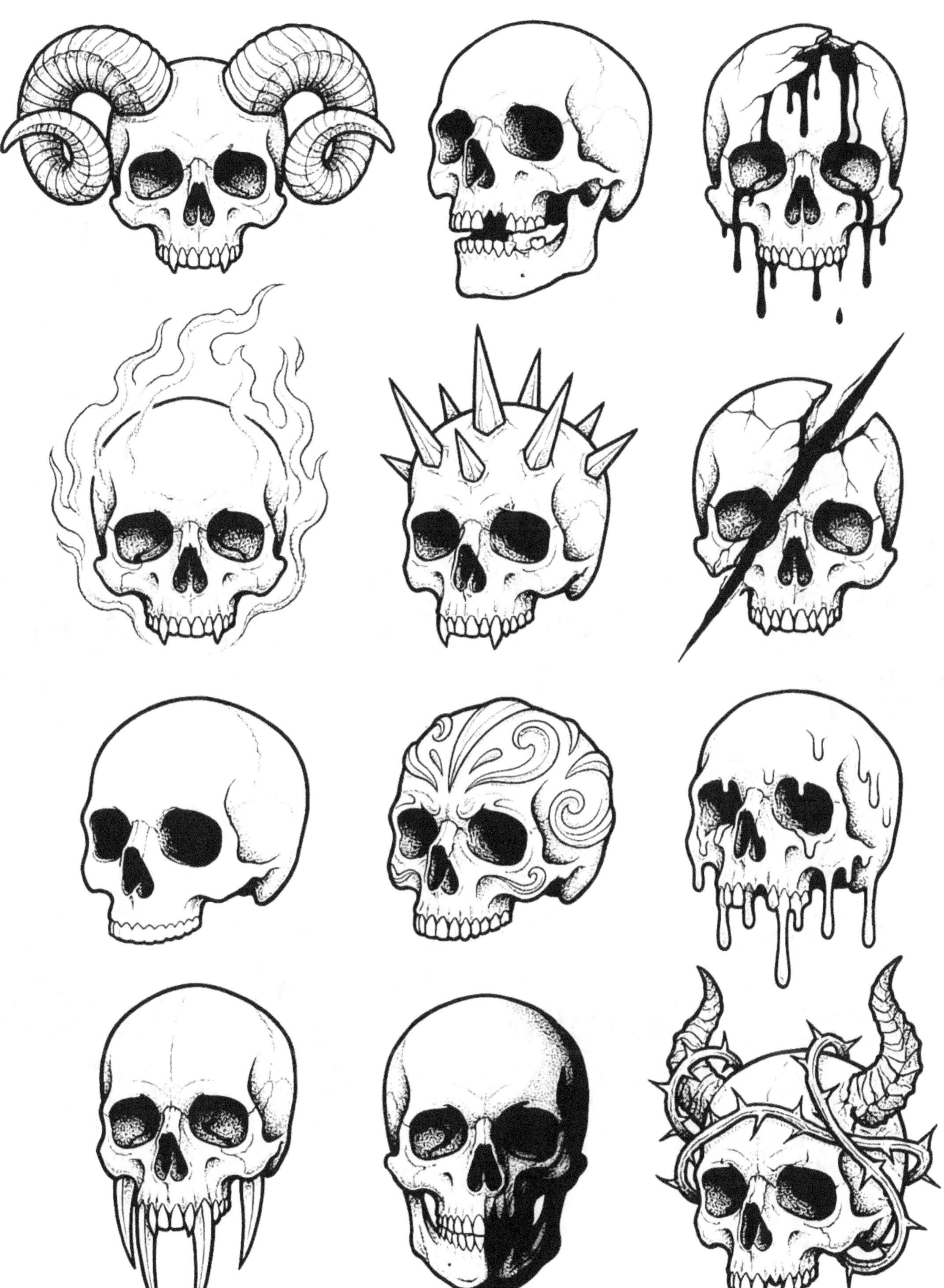

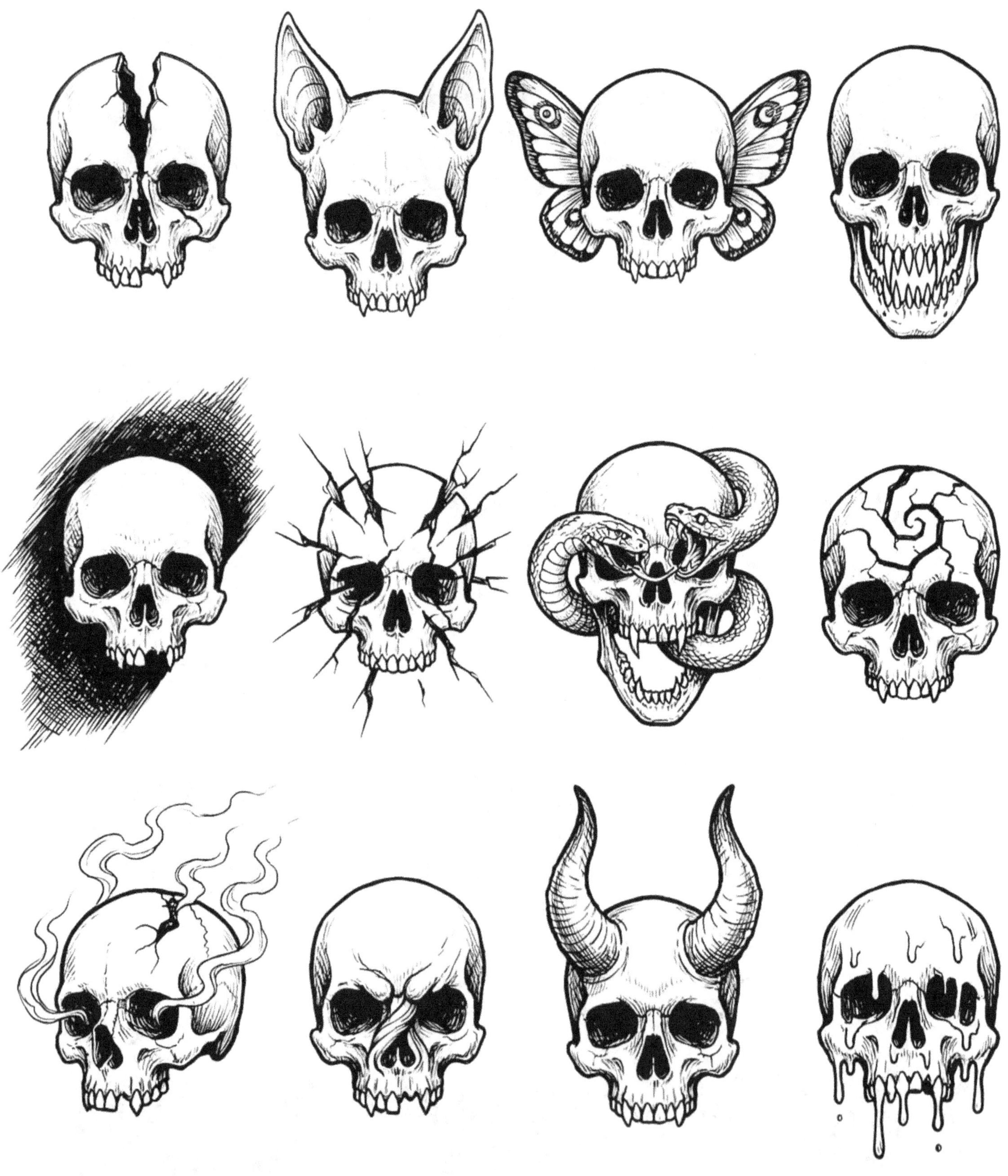

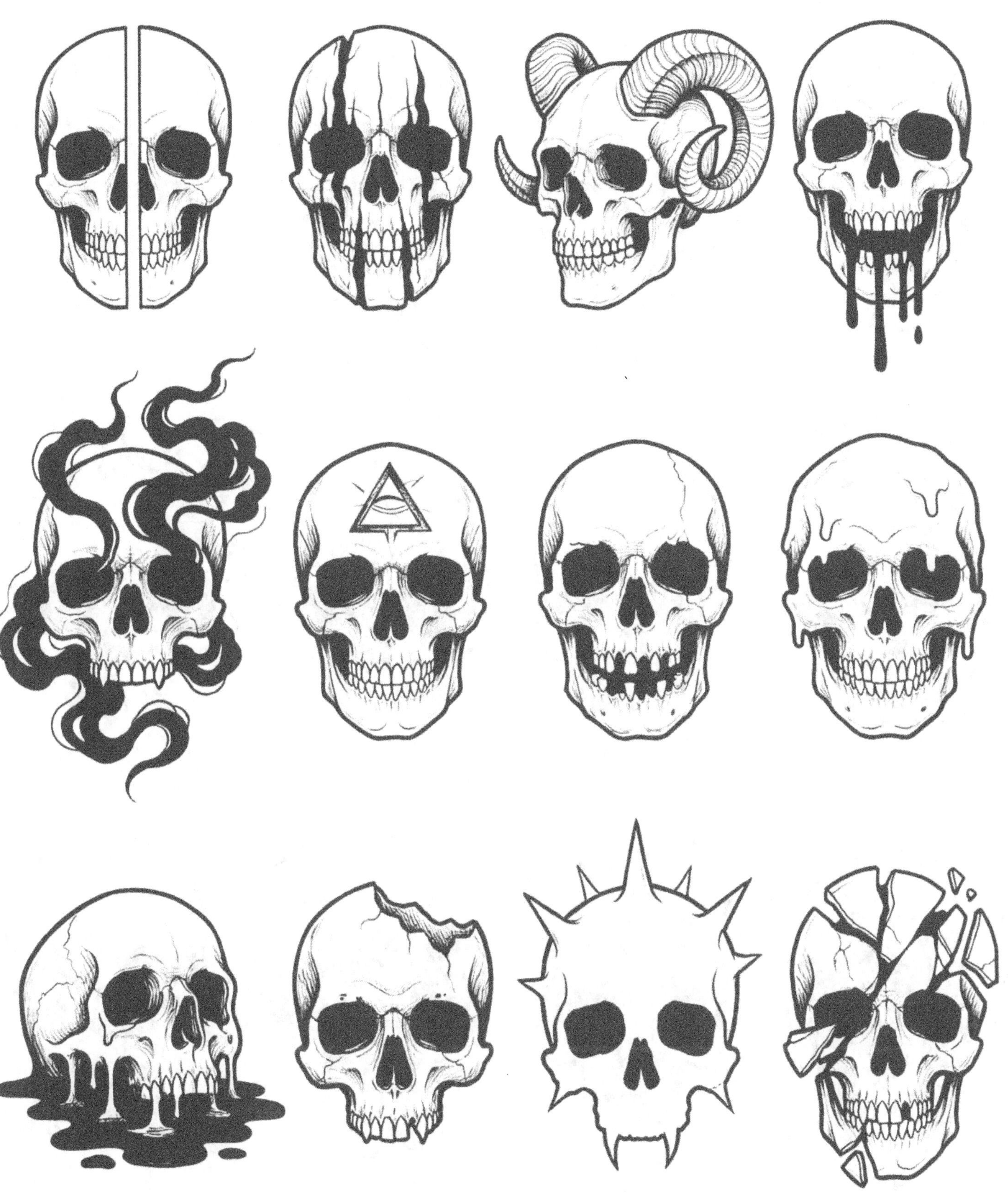

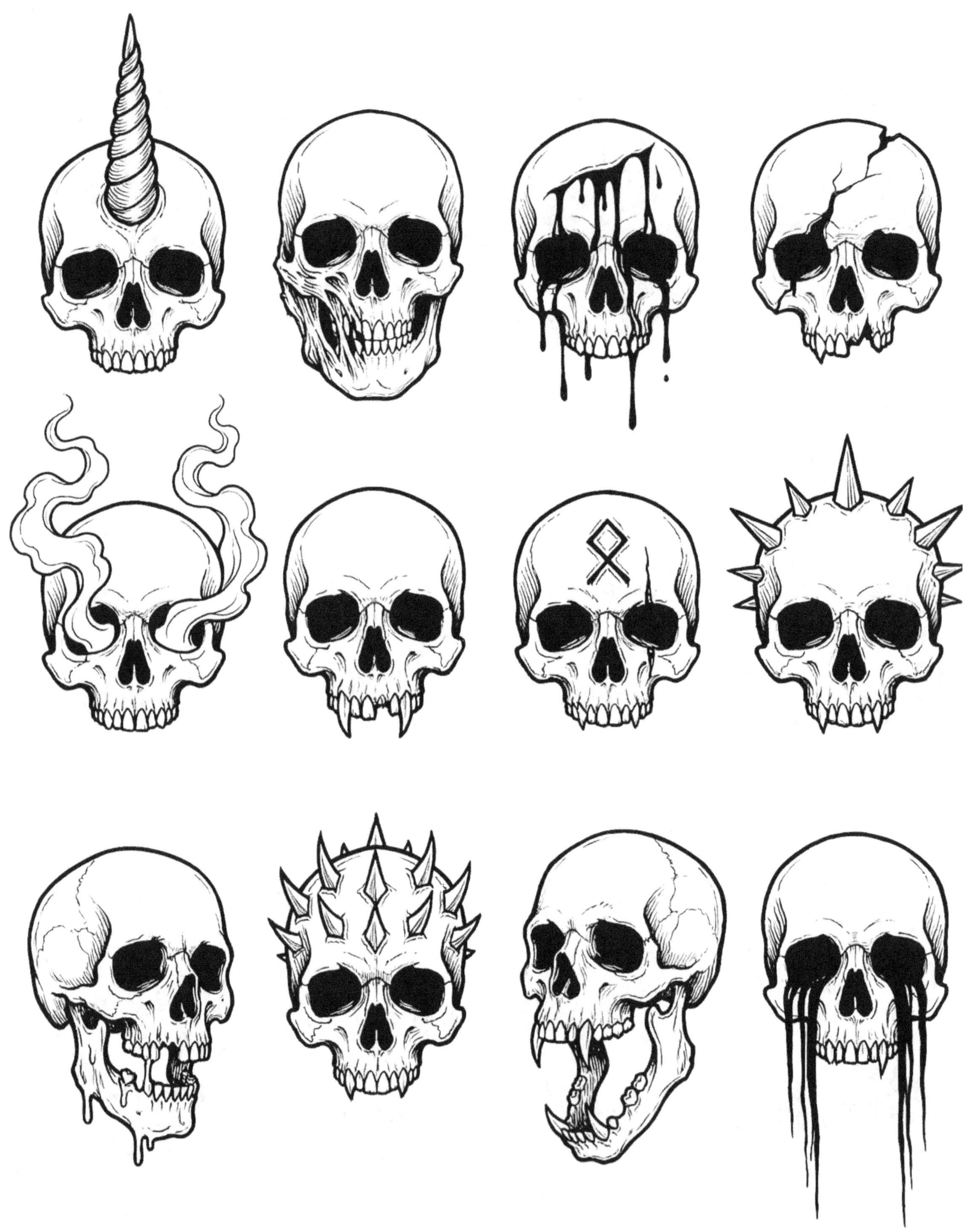

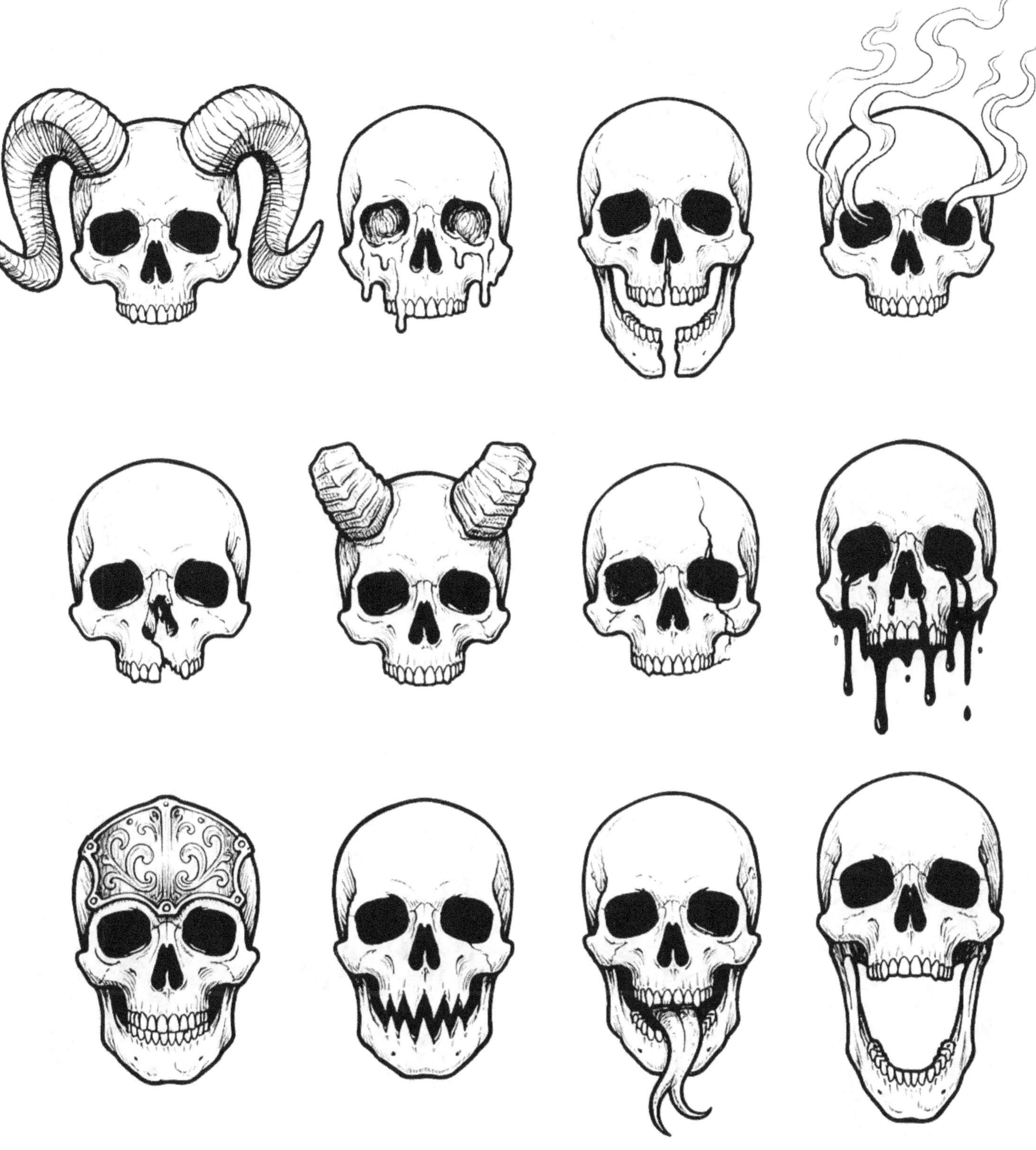

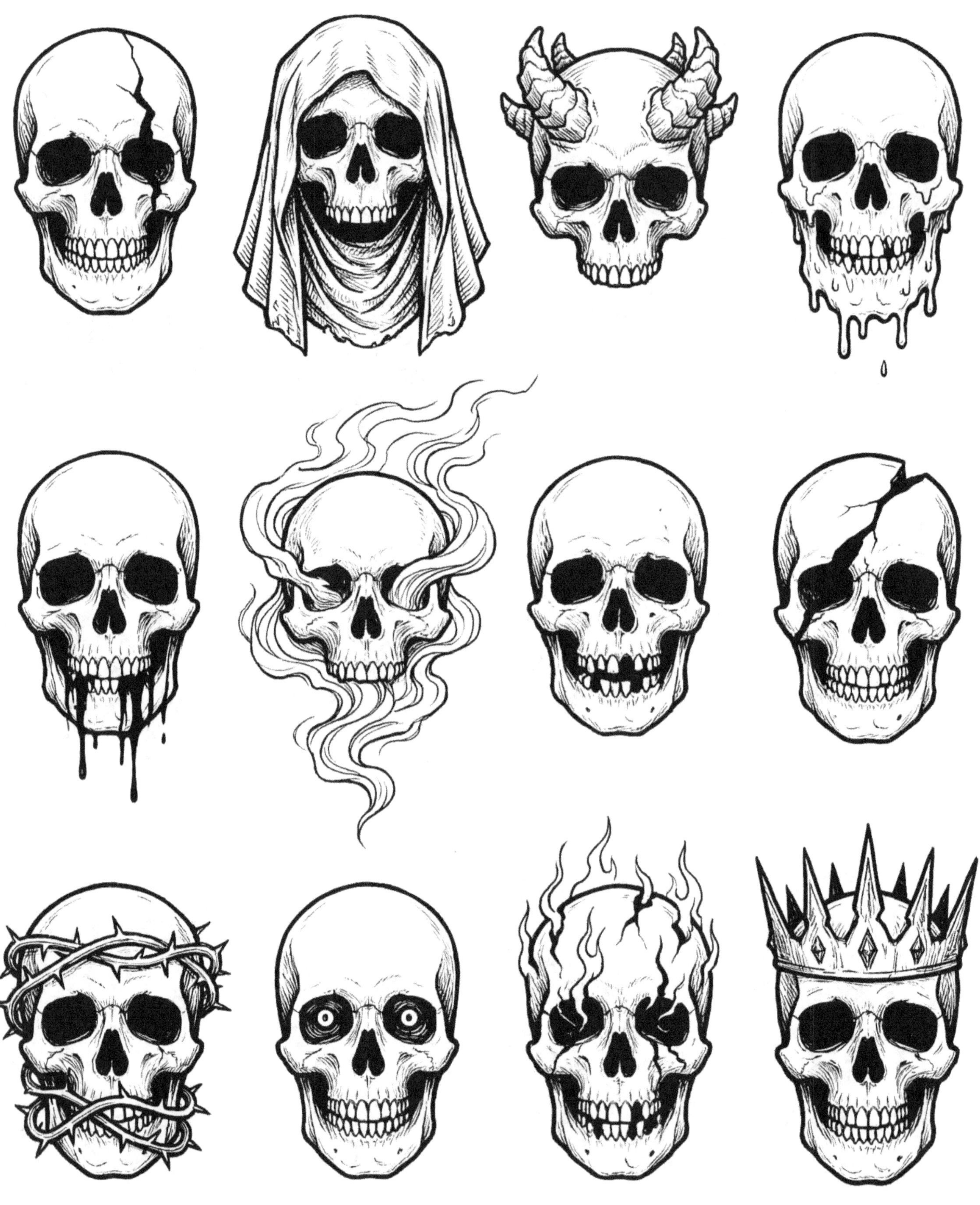

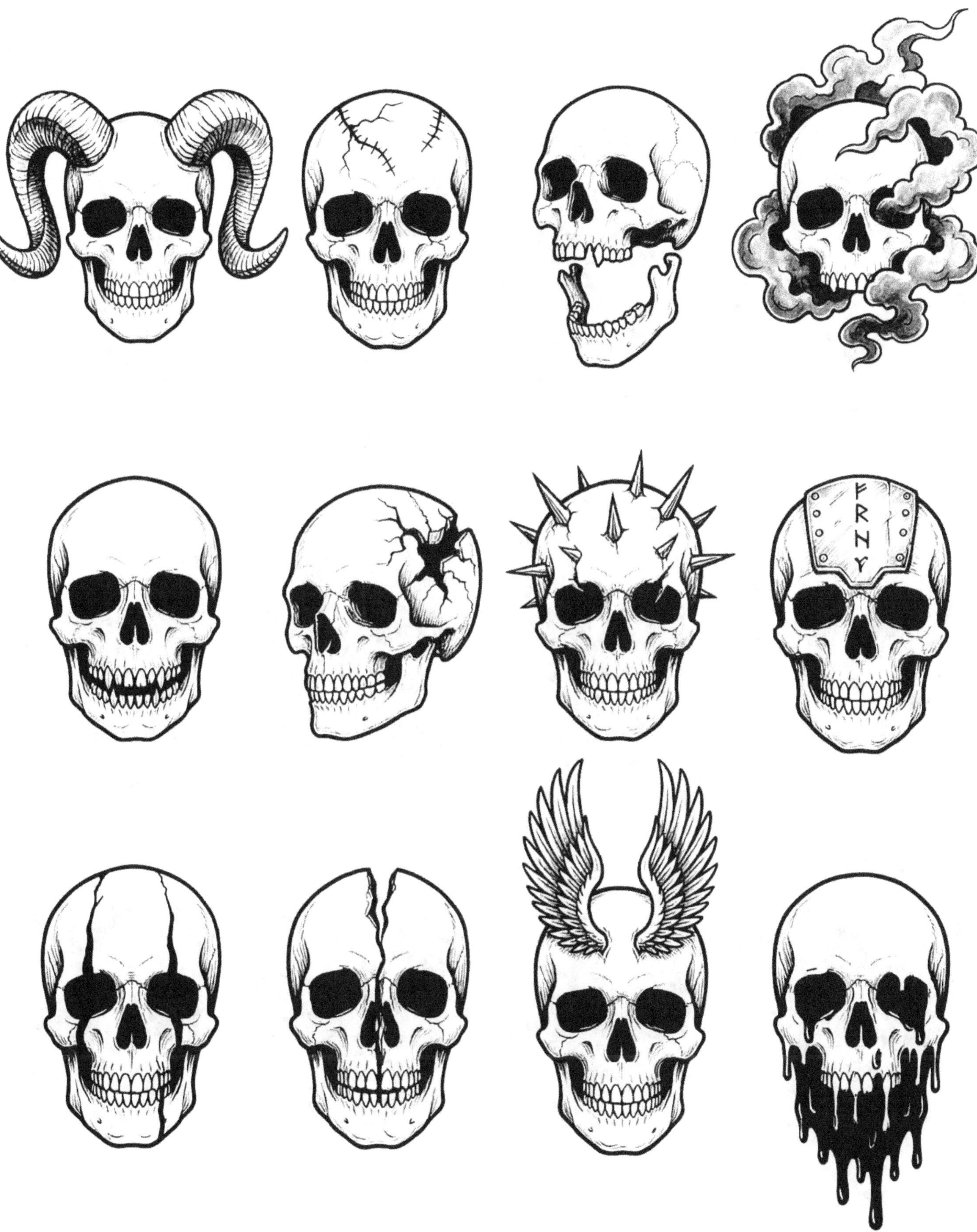

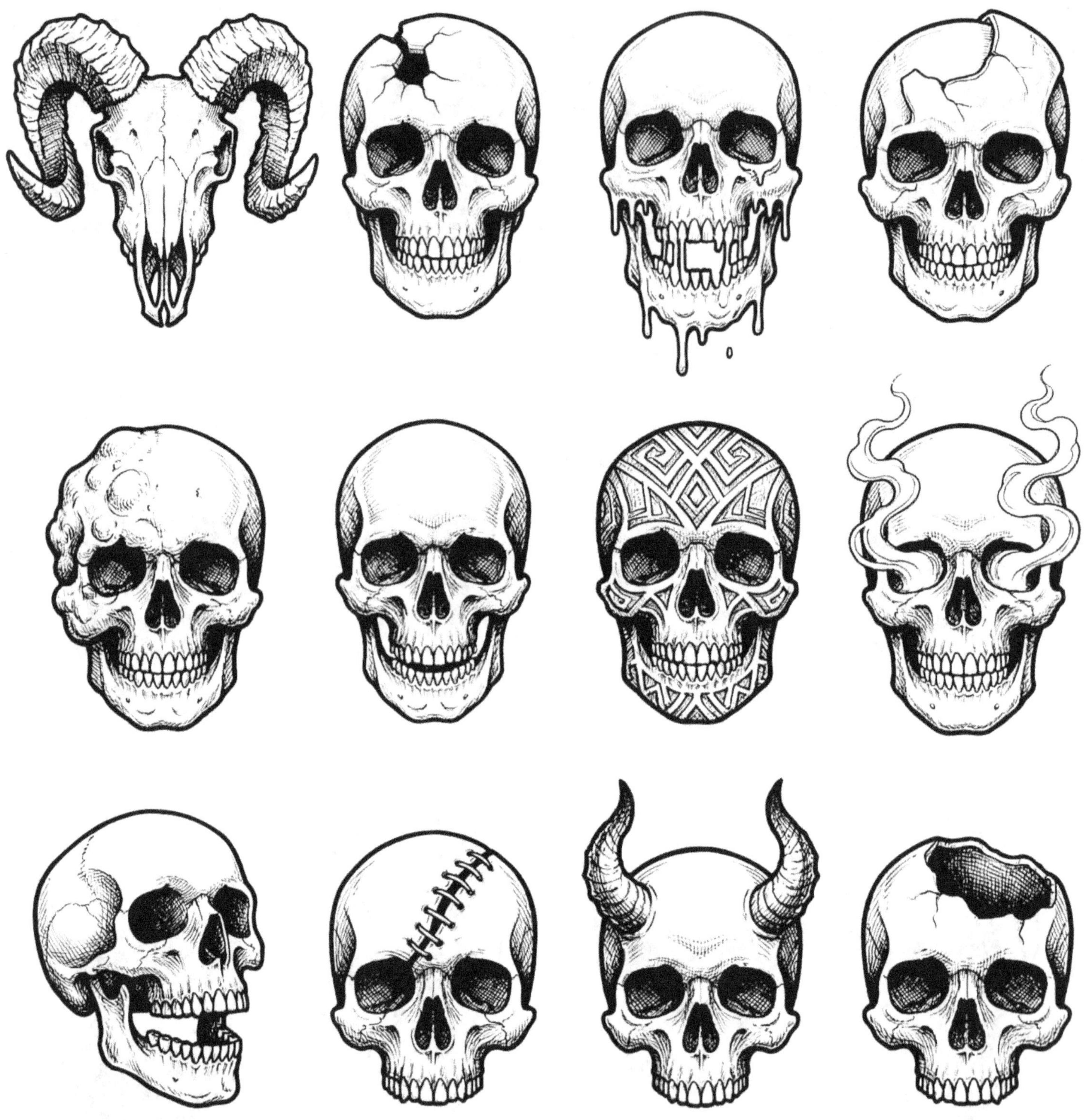

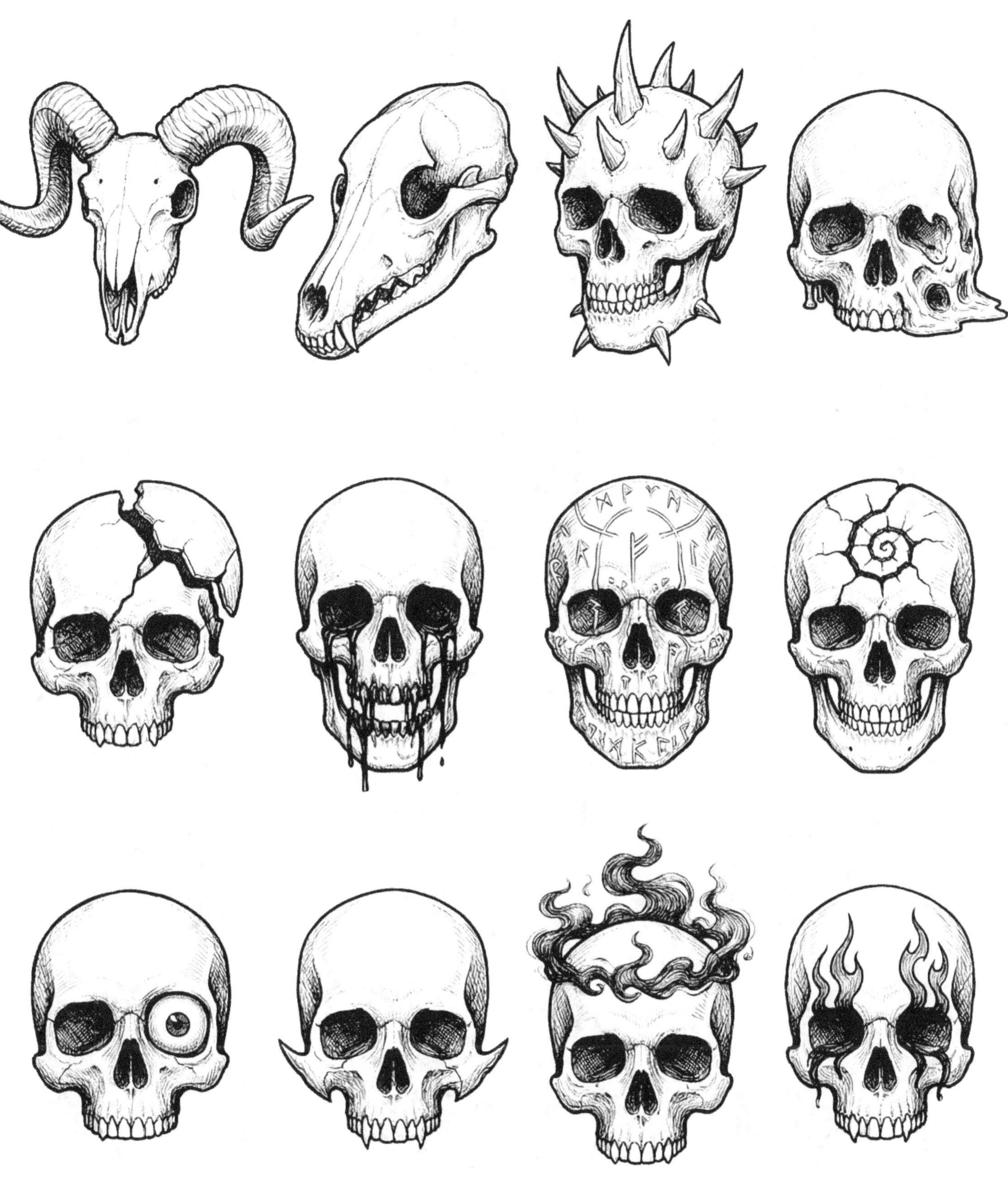

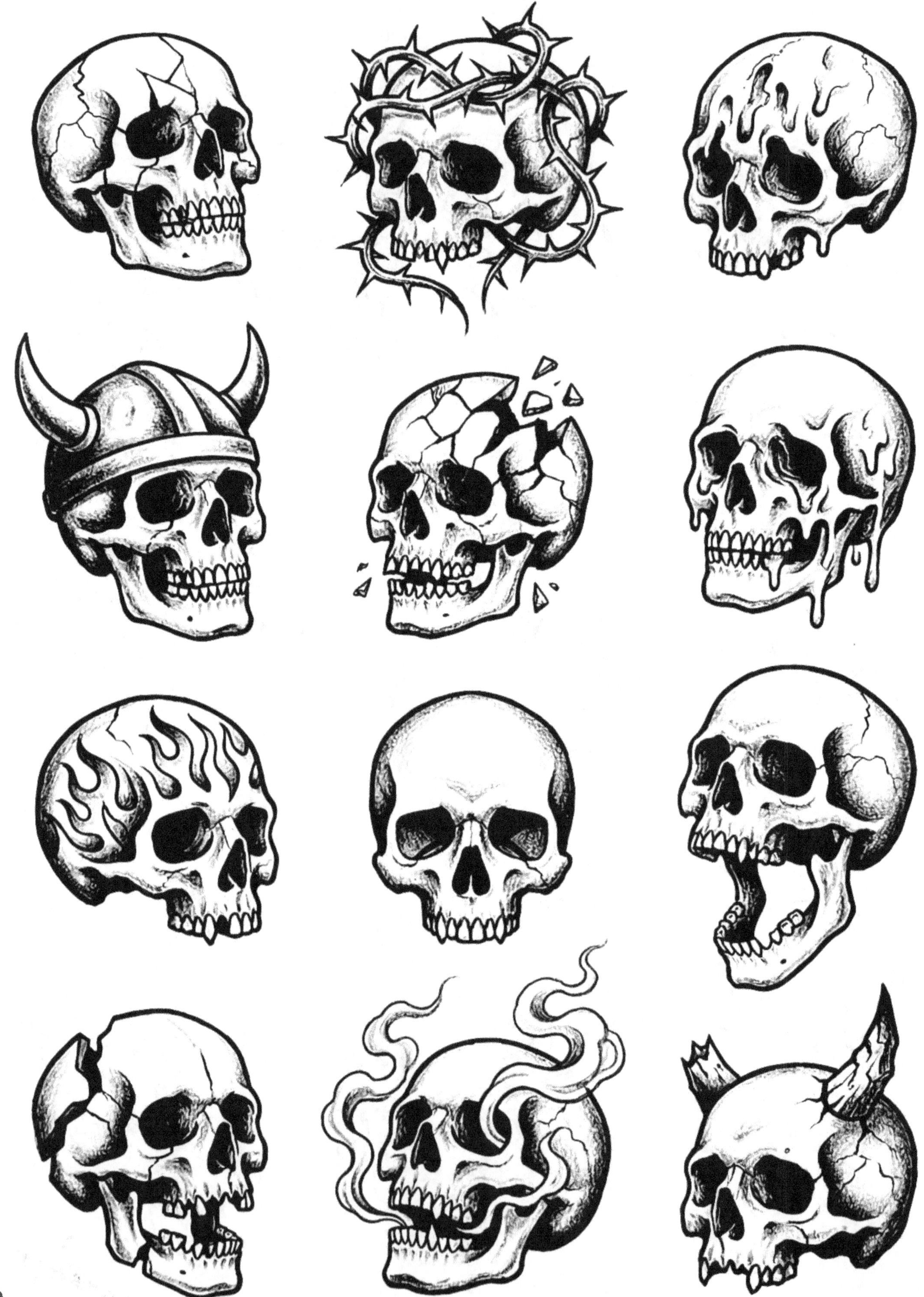

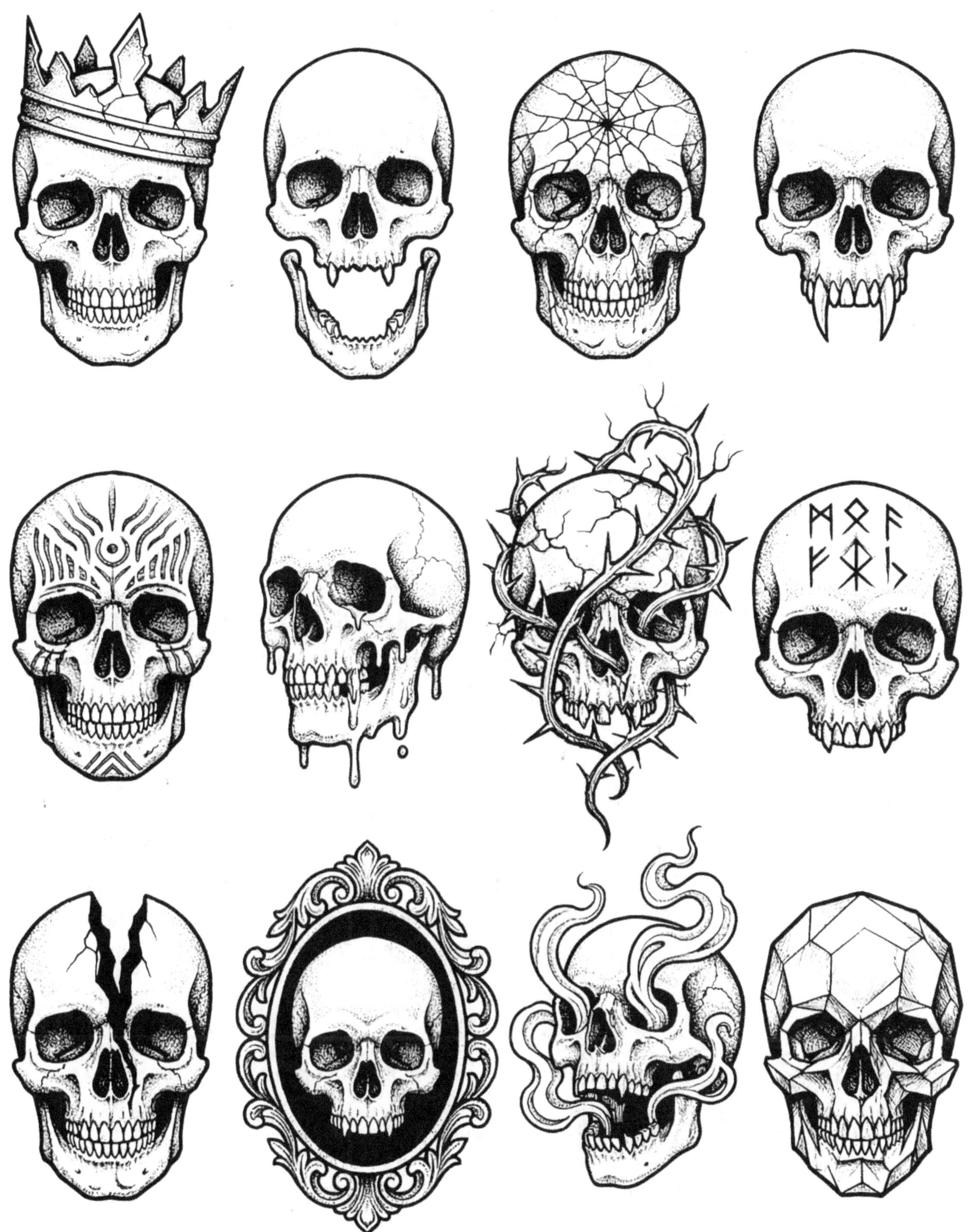

RAVEN & CROW DESIGNS

Ravens and crows have always held a special place in dark art and symbolism. Intelligent, observant and connected with myth across countless cultures, they represent mystery, prophecy, transformation and the thin line between life and death. Their presence carries weight — sometimes ominous, sometimes protective, always meaningful.

In tattoo art, these birds offer a perfect balance between realism and symbolism. Their silhouettes are strong and instantly recognizable, while their textures — layered feathers, sharp beaks, reflective eyes — create opportunities for depth, contrast and expressive detail. A single wing shape can generate movement; a perched crow can set an entire atmosphere; a raven in flight can fill a composition with energy and direction.

This chapter explores ravens and crows through a wide range of stylistic angles: bold silhouettes, elegant feathers, dramatic poses, symbolic arrangements and compositions that pair the birds with elements like skulls, moons, frames or branches. Some designs lean toward realism, others toward graphic minimalism or gothic ornament, but all of them share the same core: presence and personality.

Use these designs to study motion, feather patterns, negative space and how a bird's posture affects the mood of a tattoo. Ravens and crows work beautifully as standalone pieces on arms, backs or ribs, but they also integrate naturally into larger dark-themed works. Their shape allows for clean flow along the body, and their symbolism opens endless narrative possibilities.

This is the place where shadow takes flight,

where intelligence meets mystery,

and where every feather carries a story.

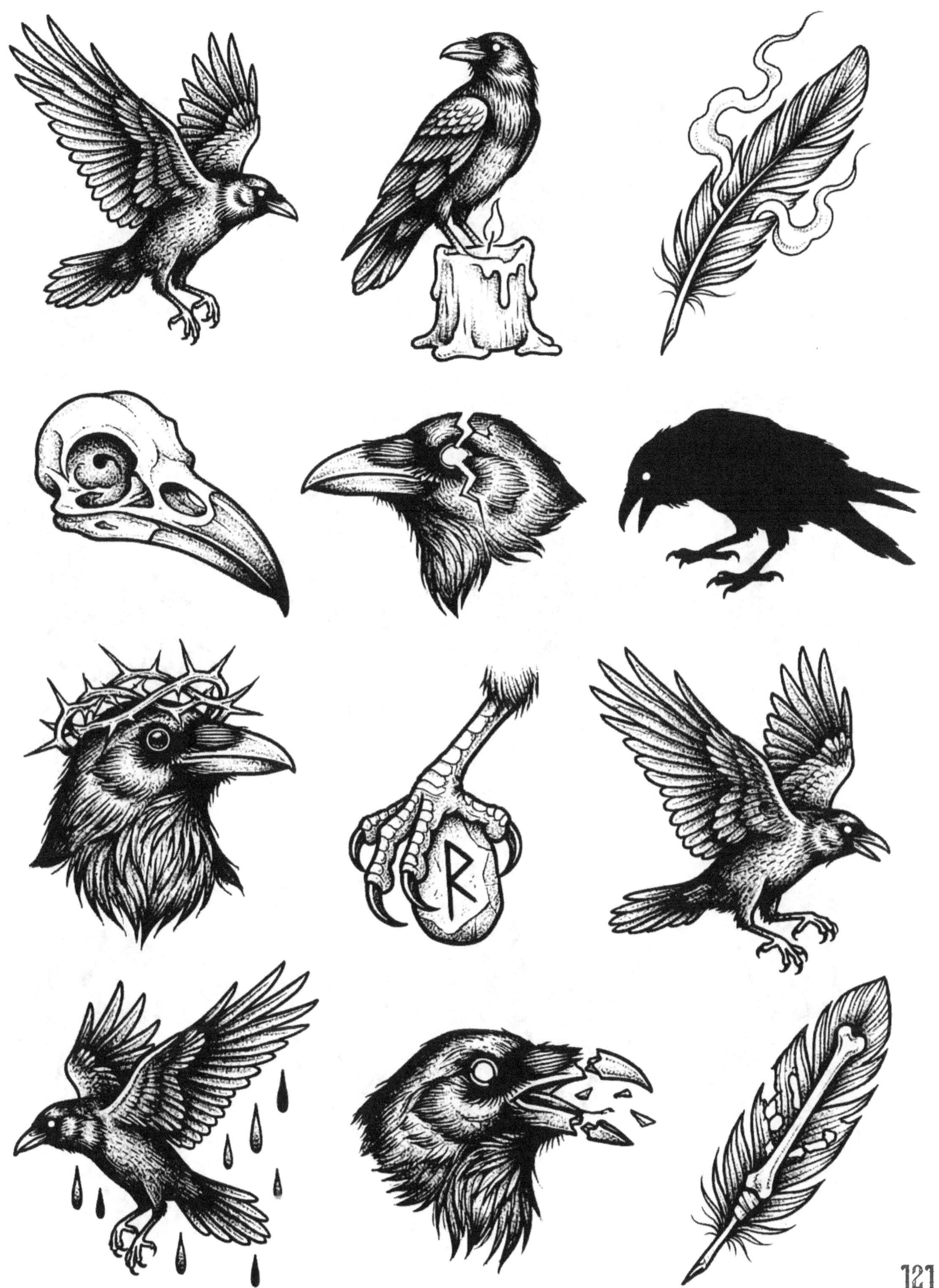

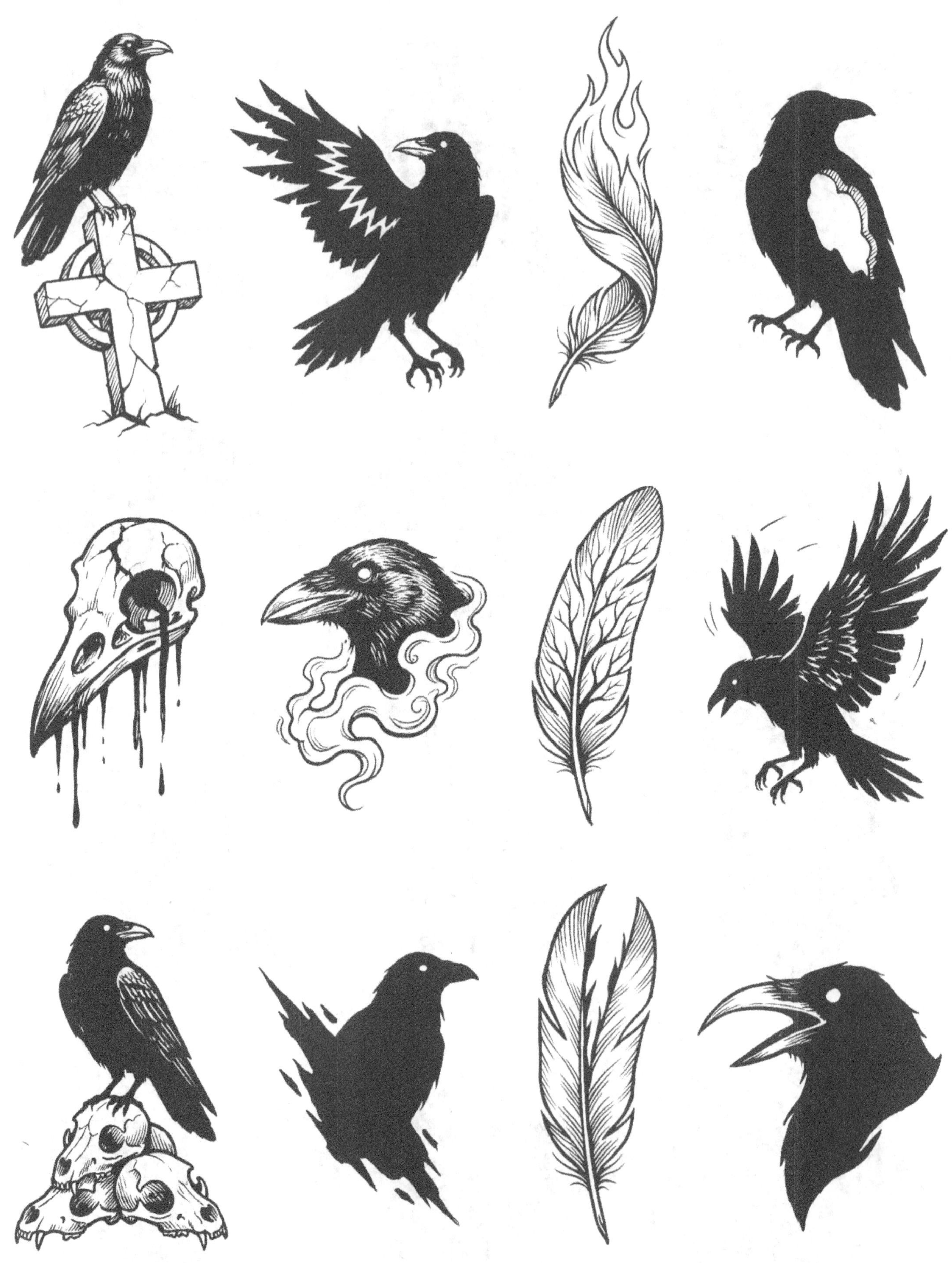

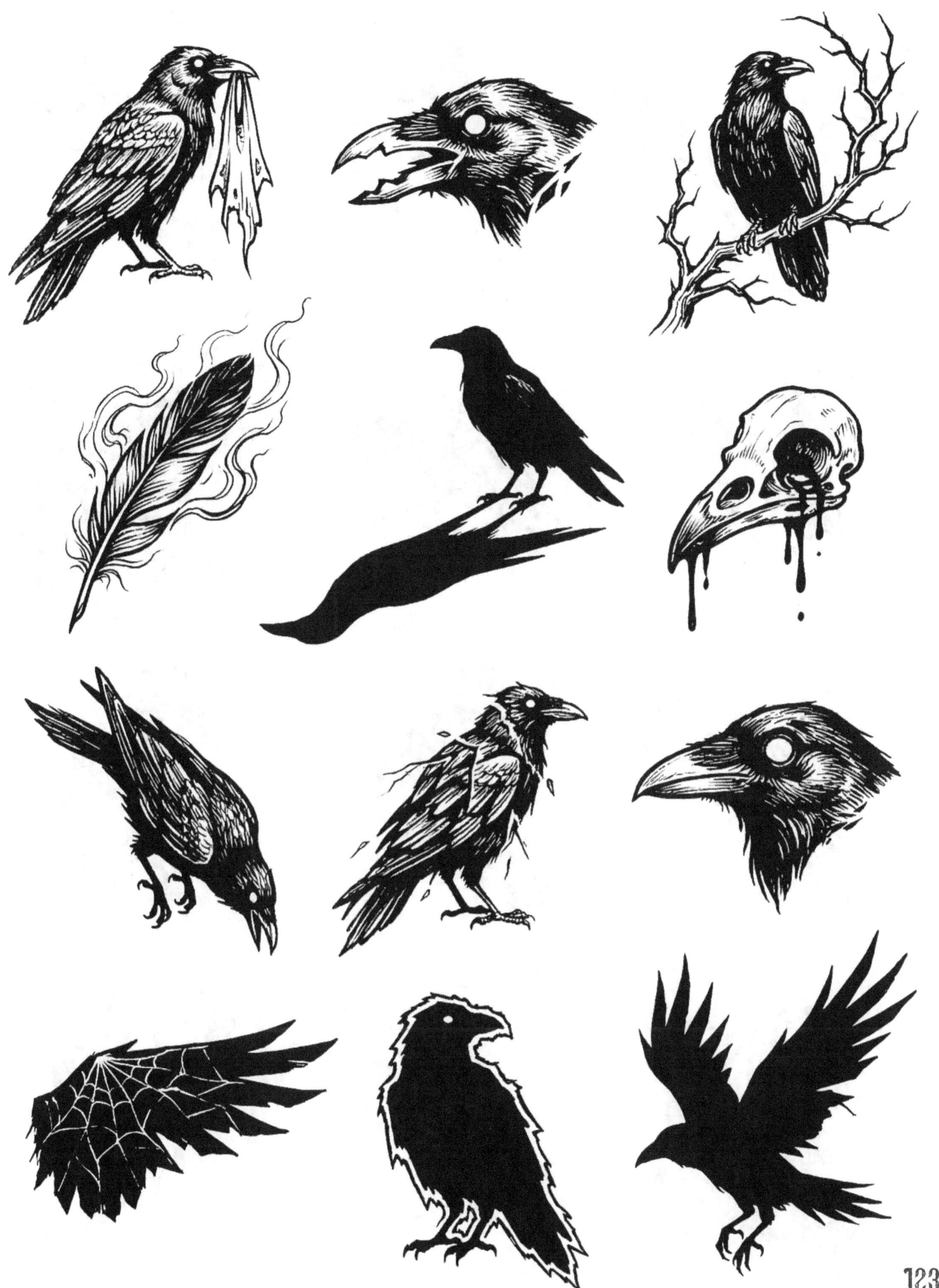

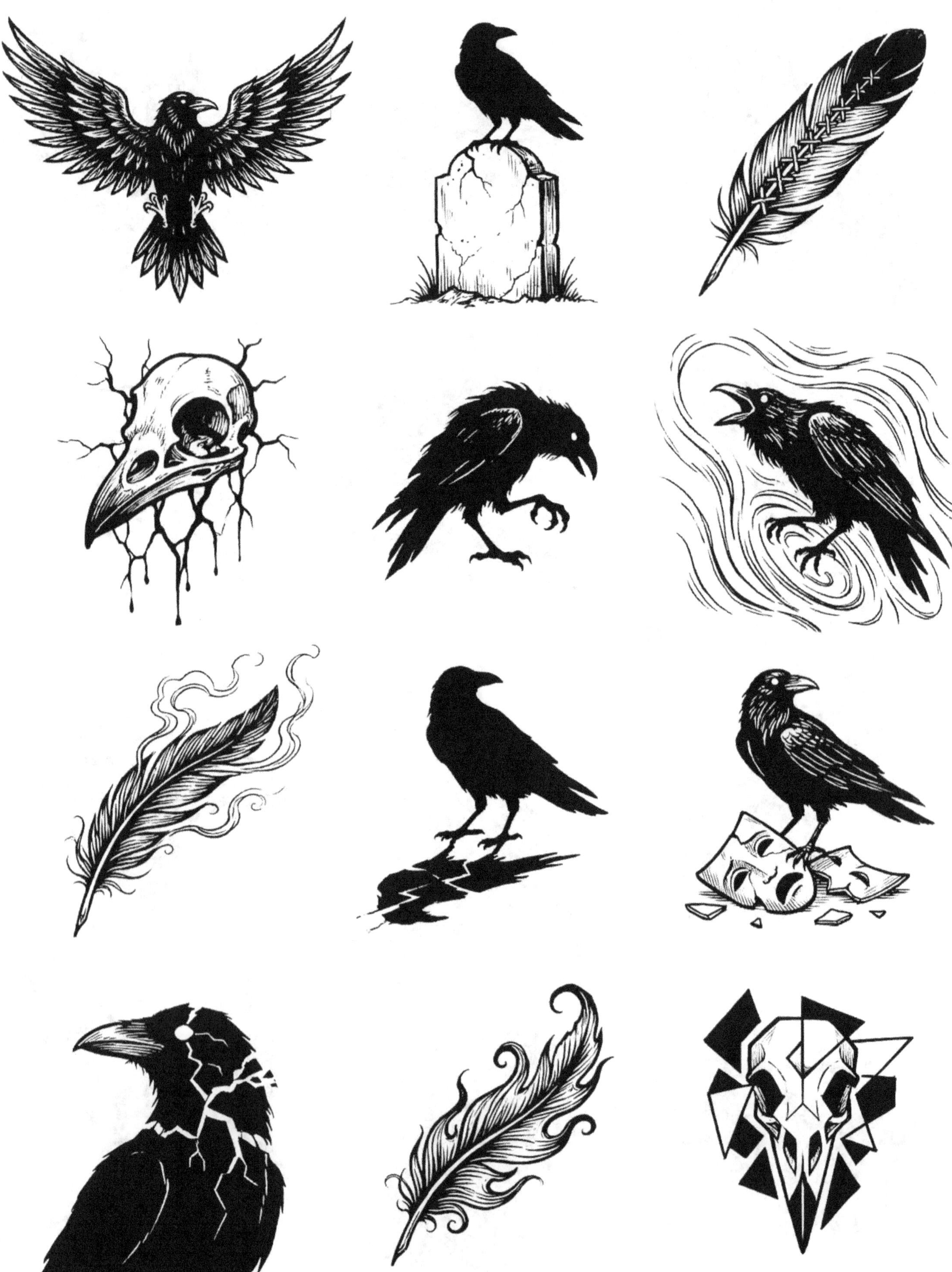

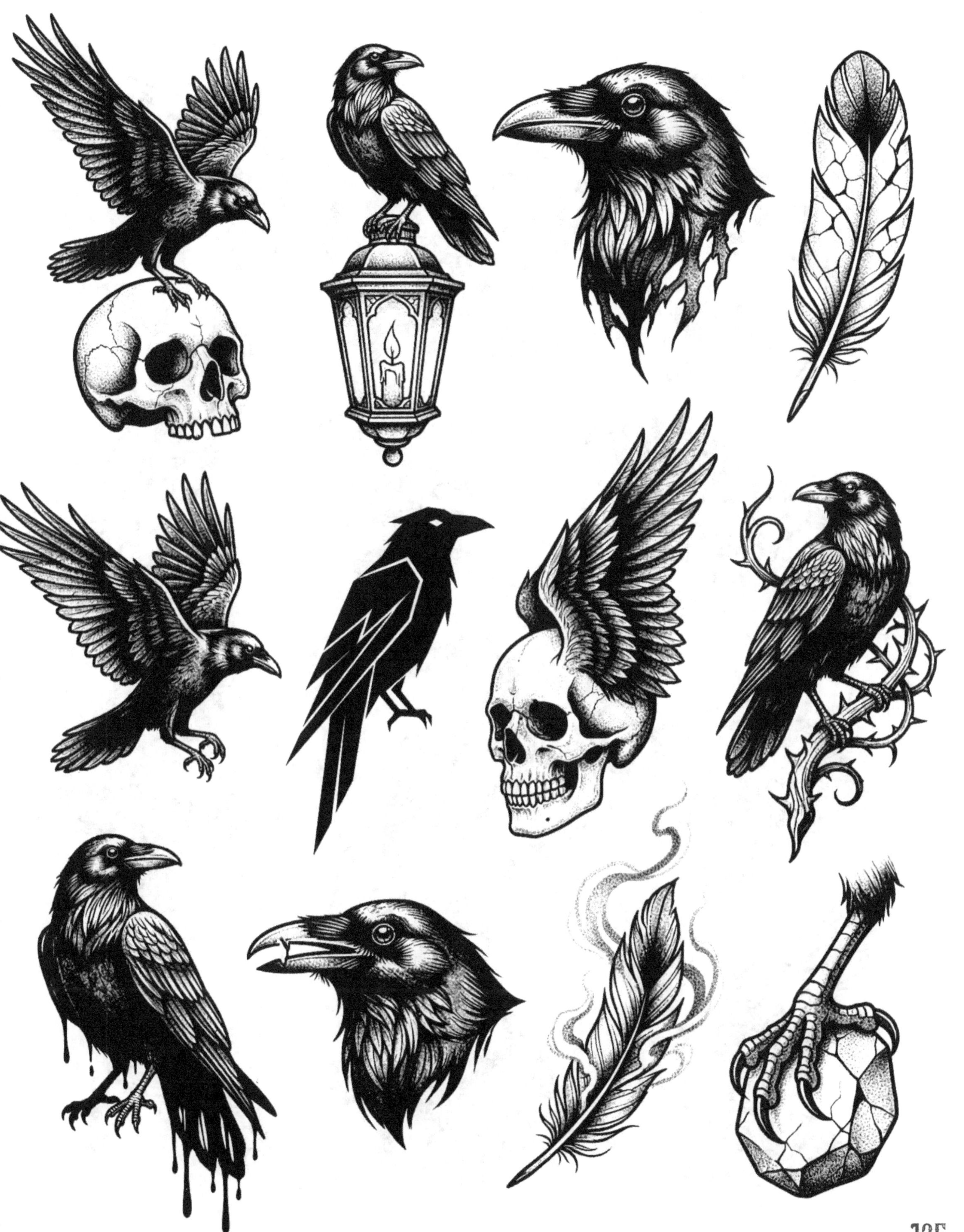

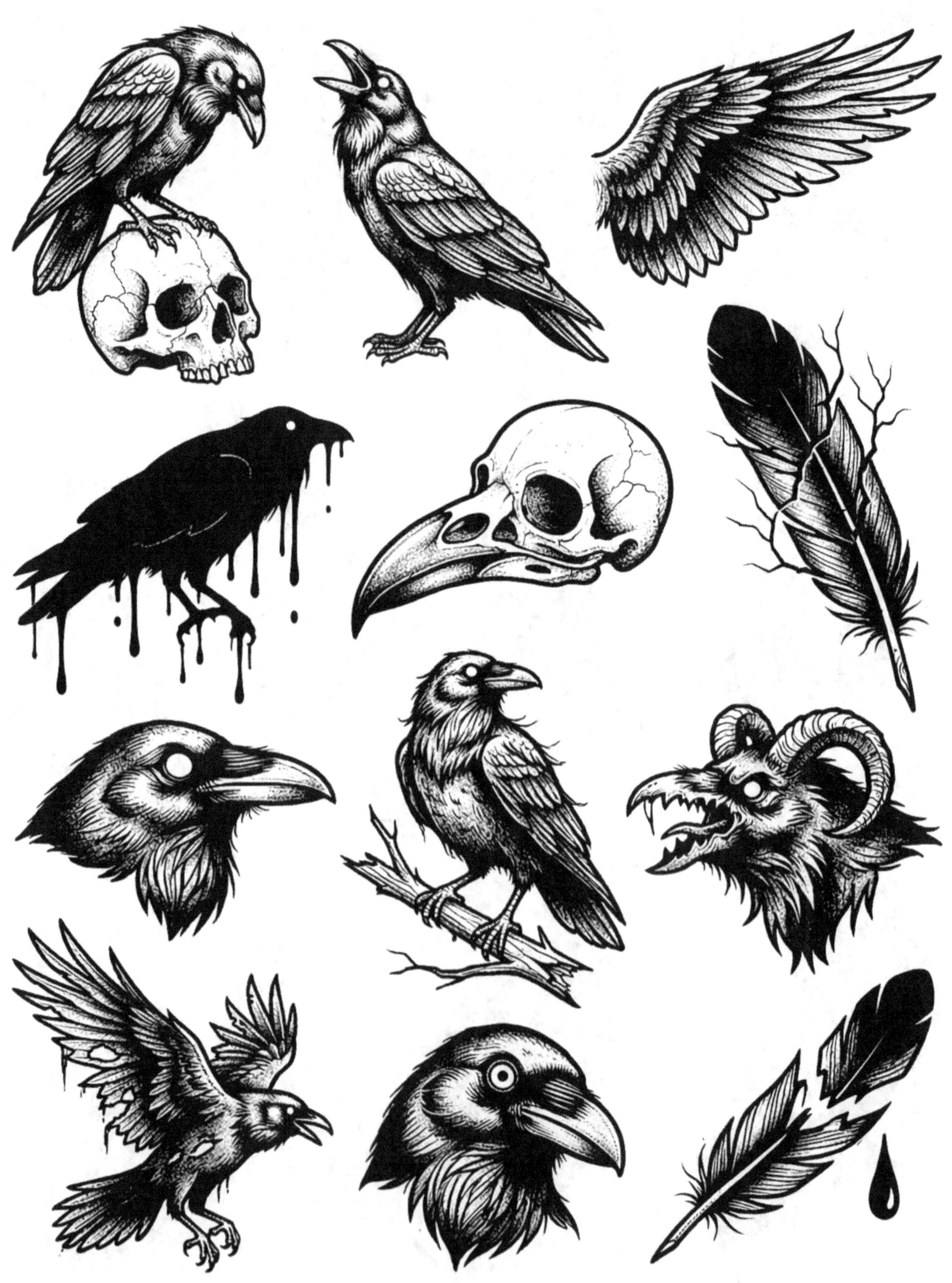

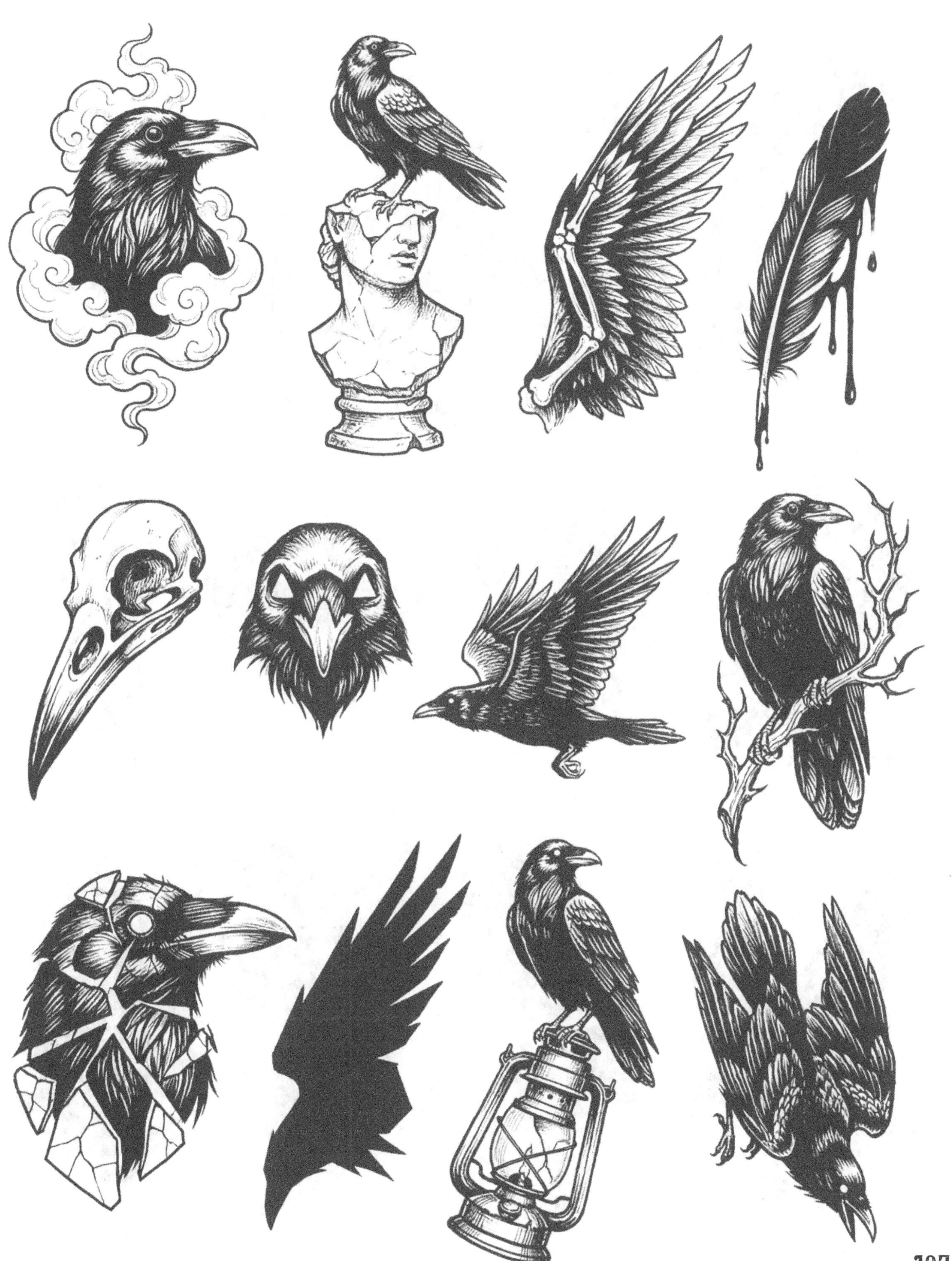

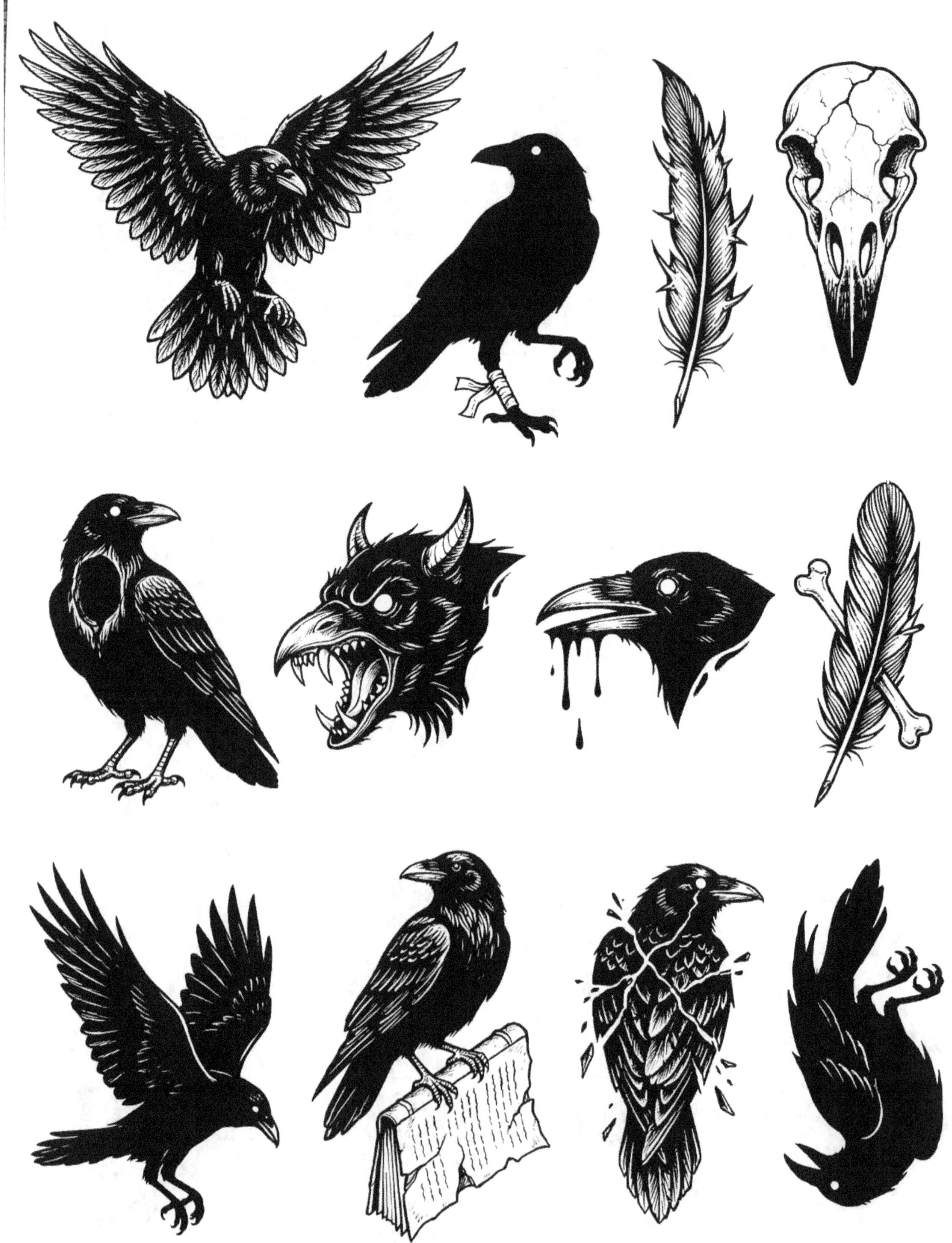

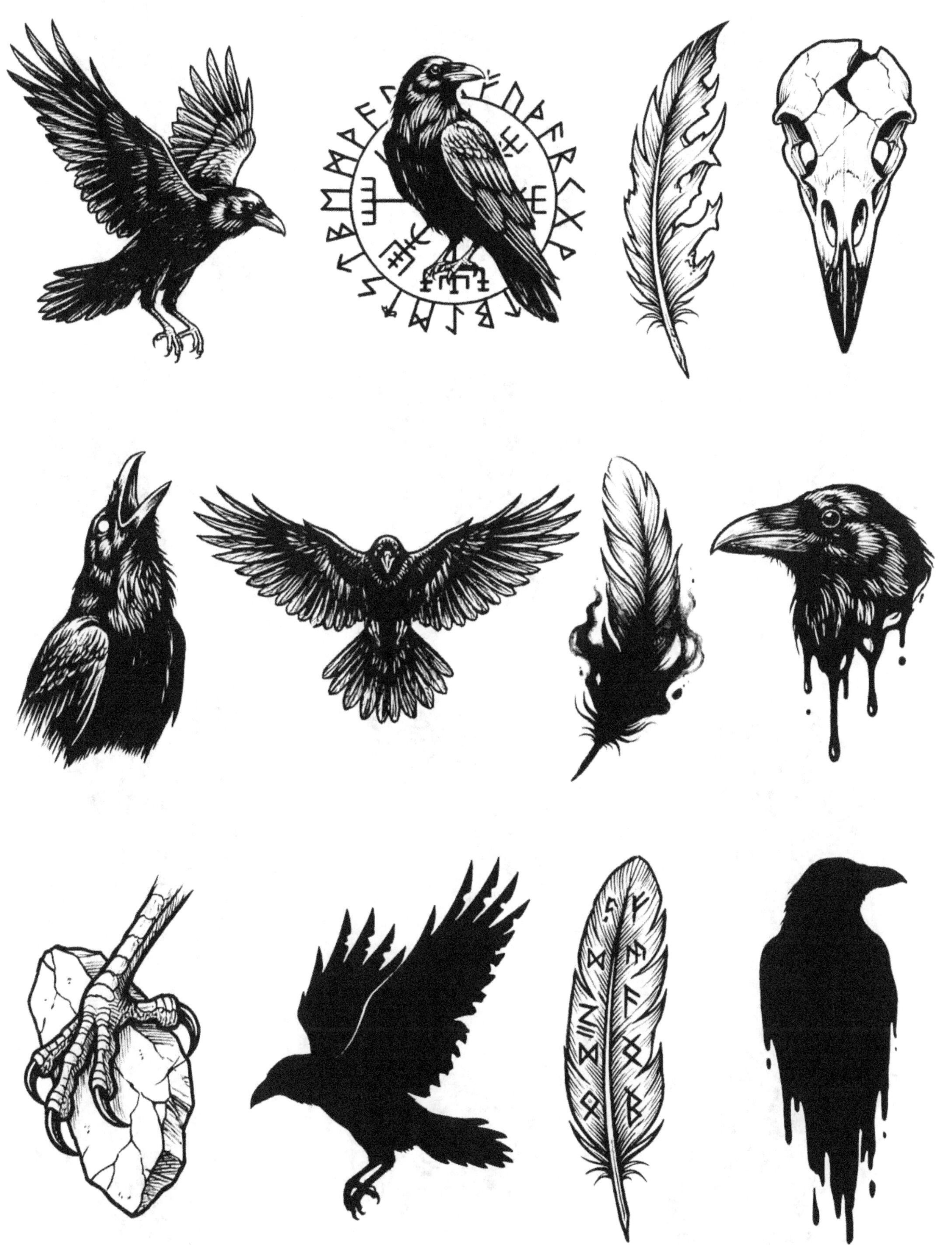

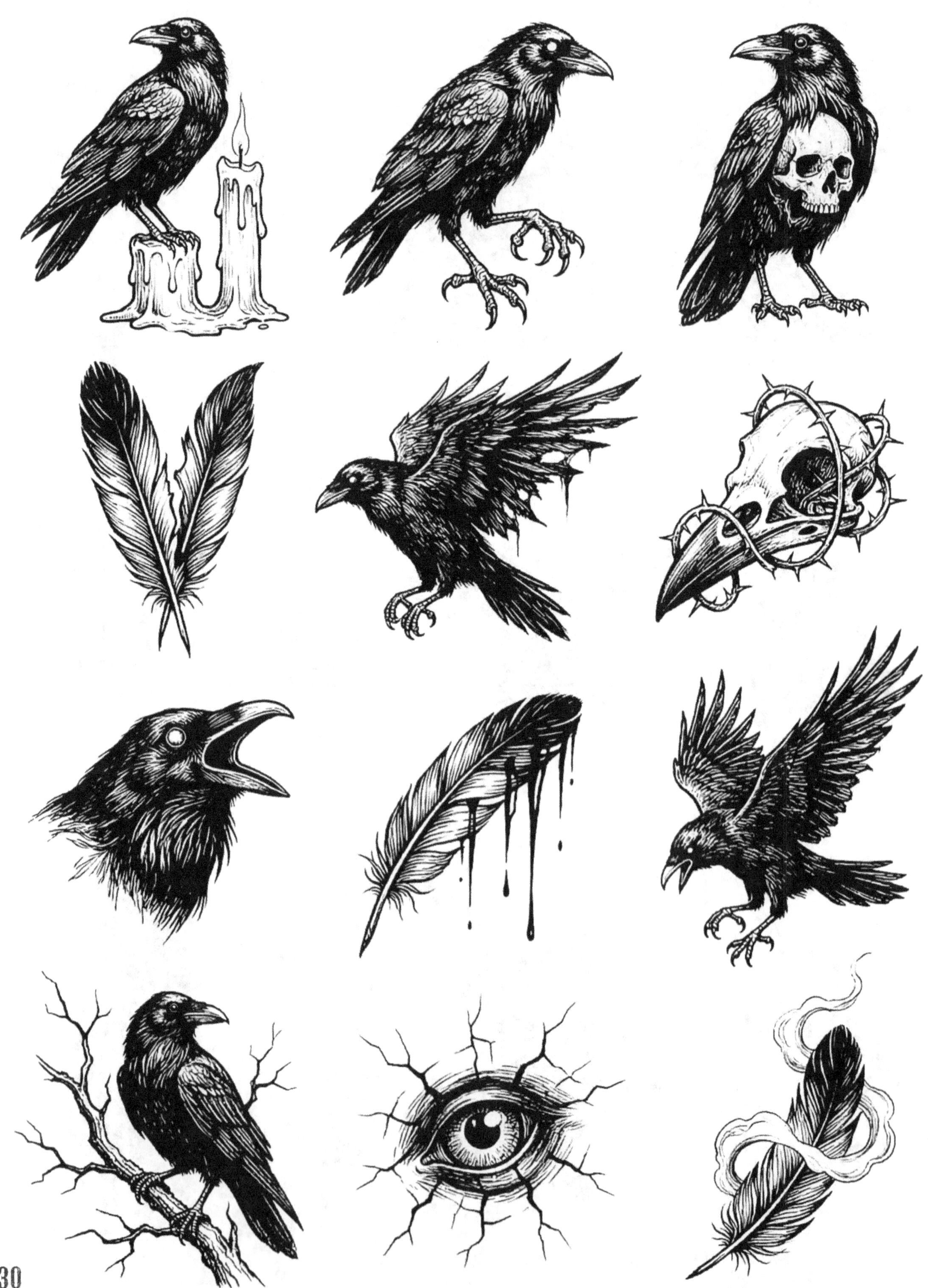

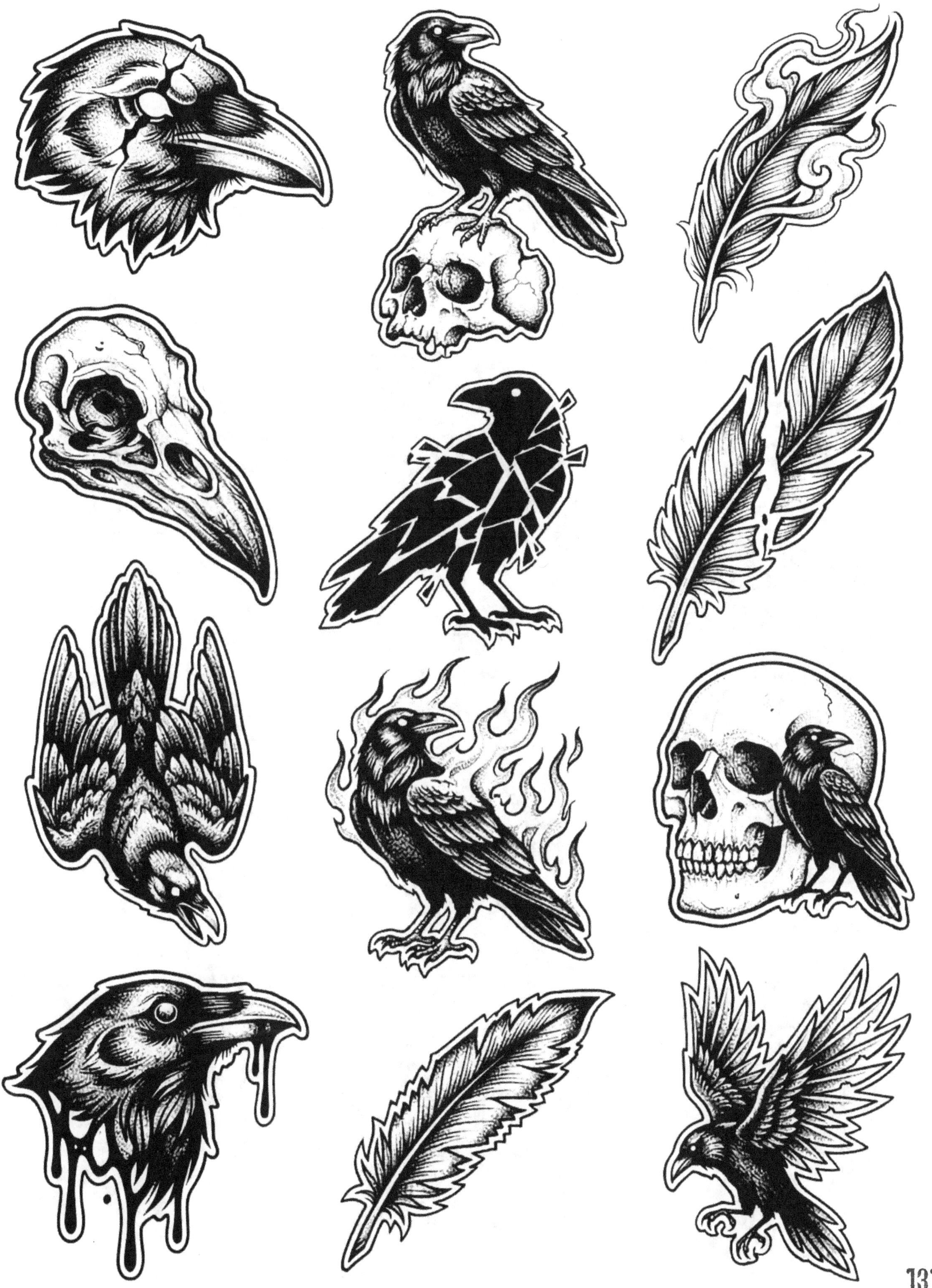

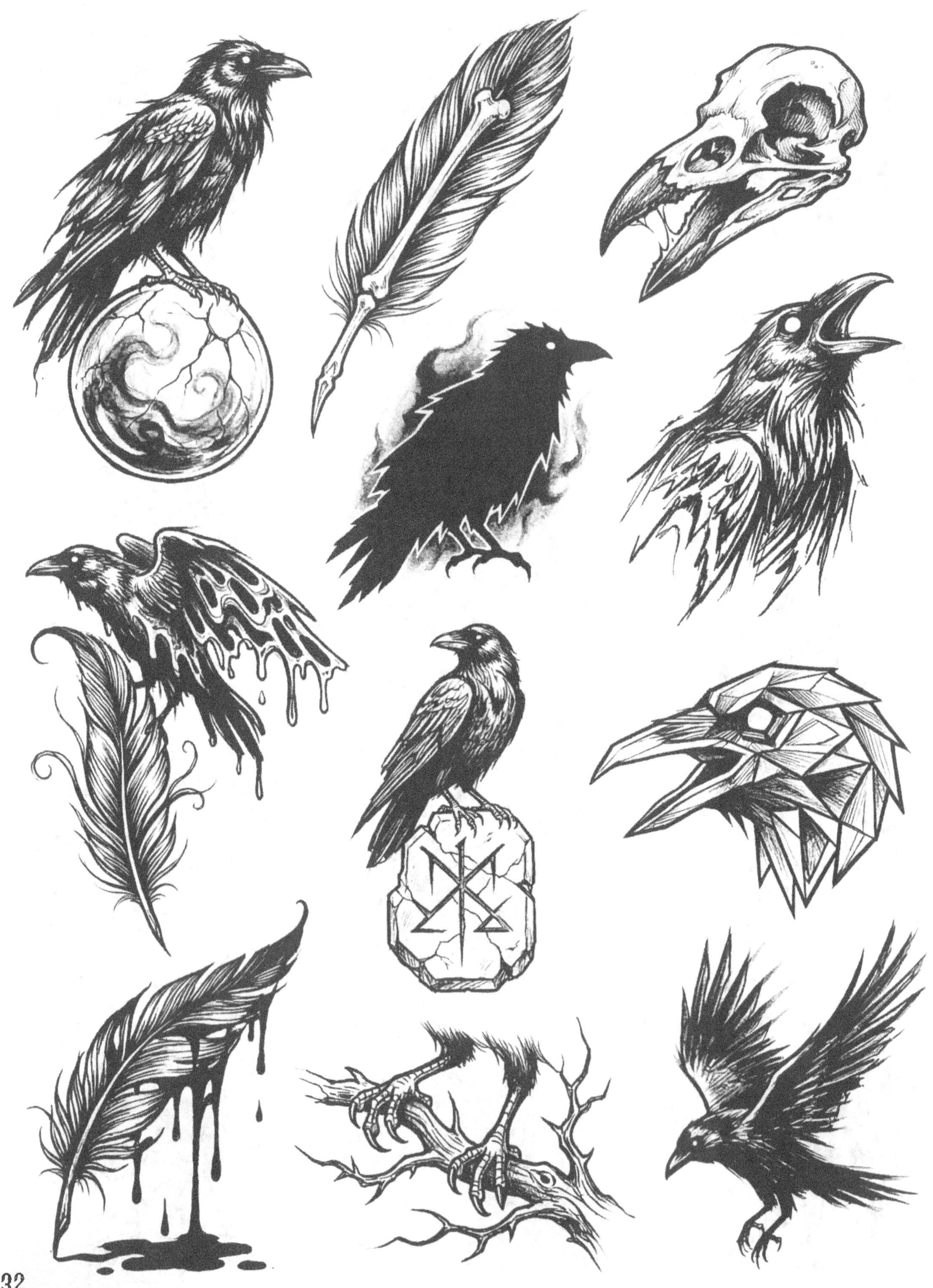

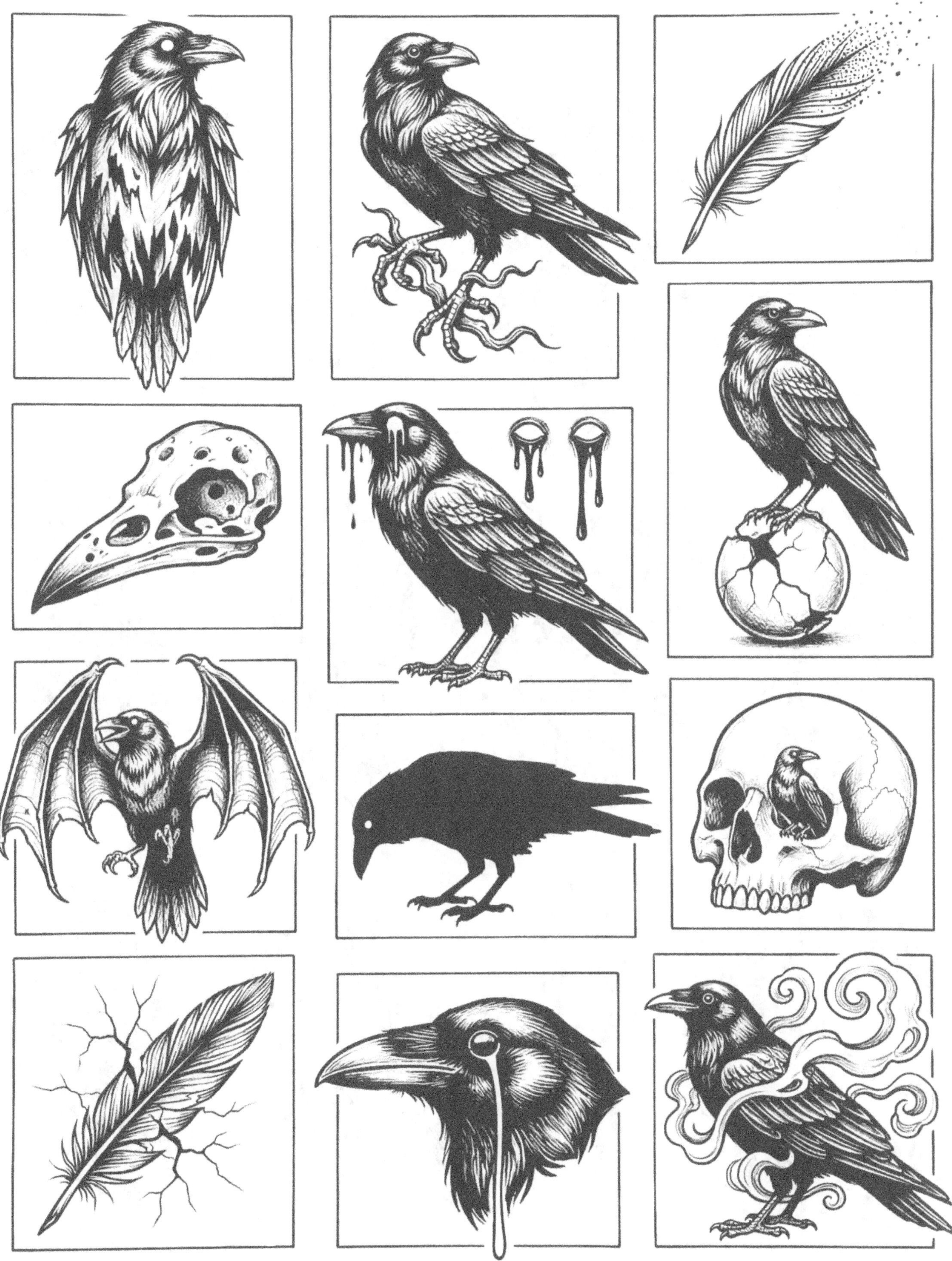

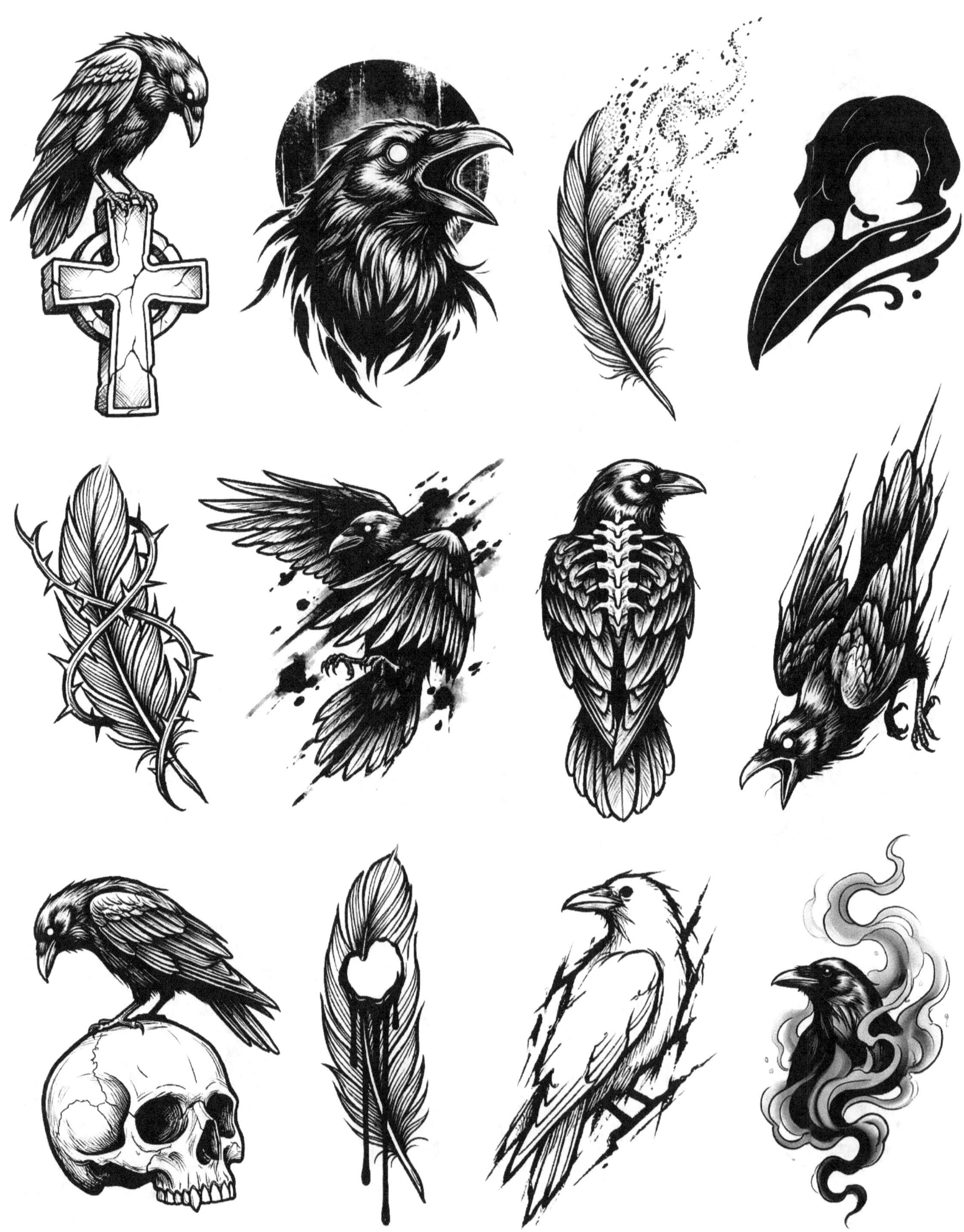

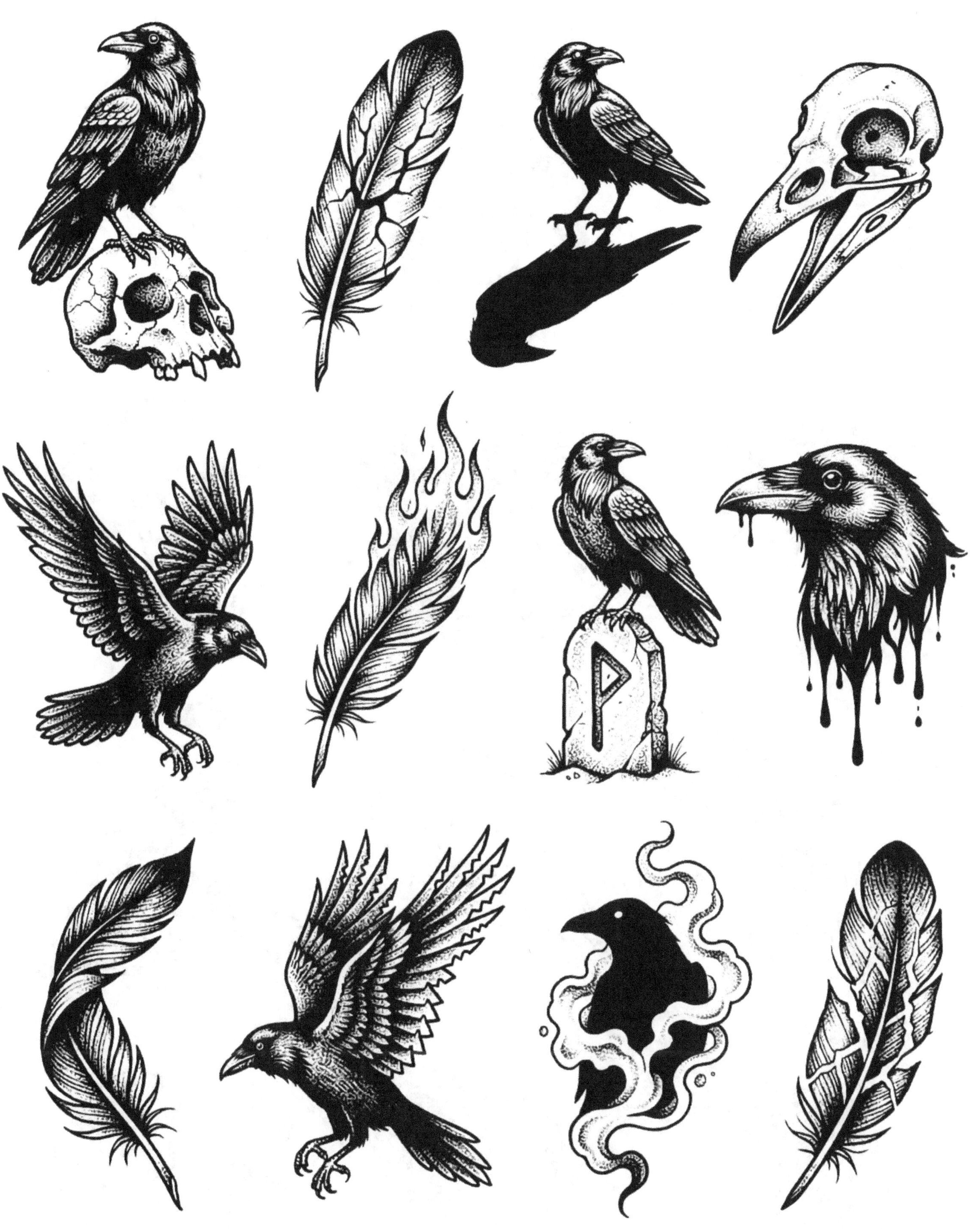

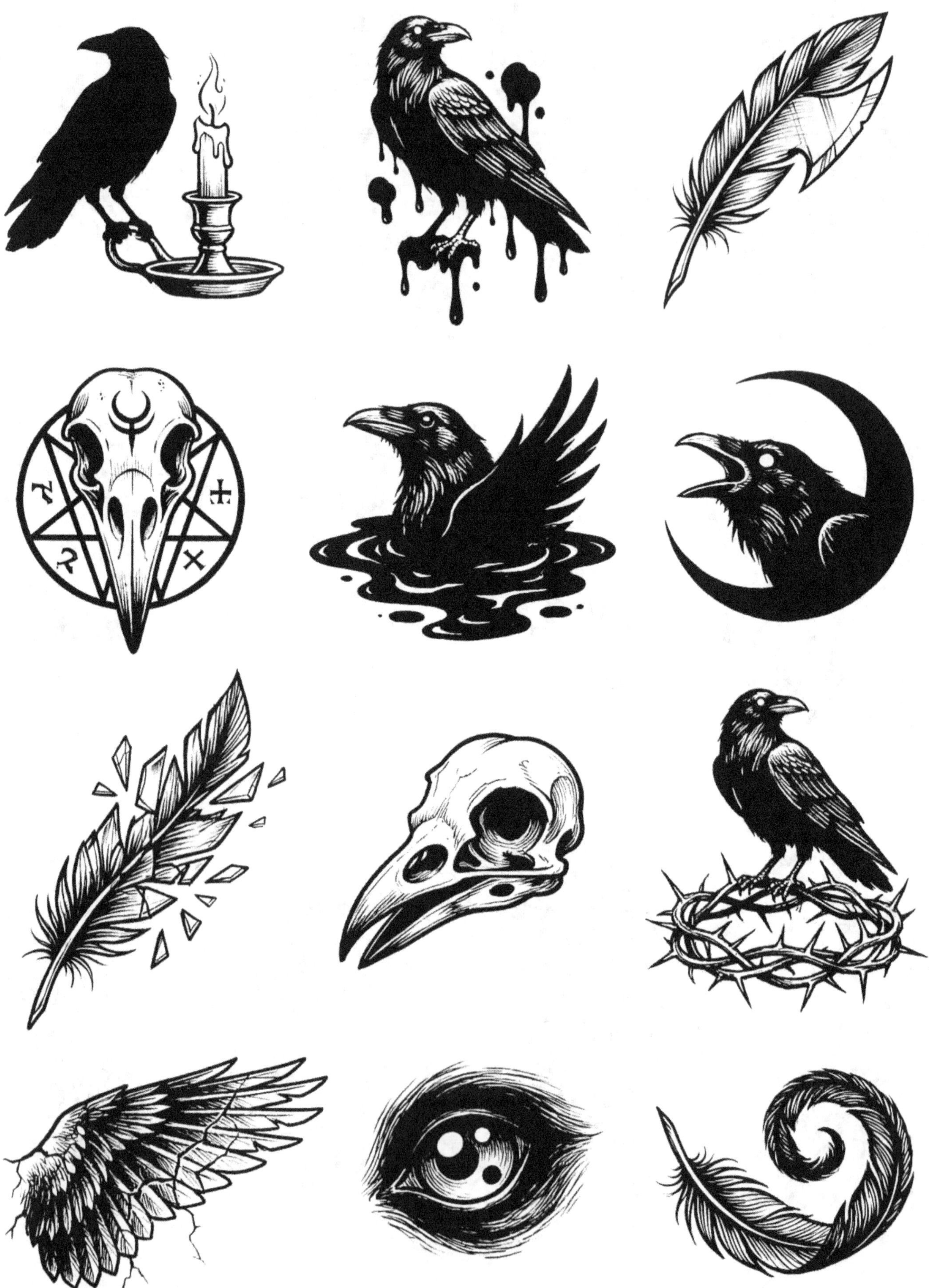

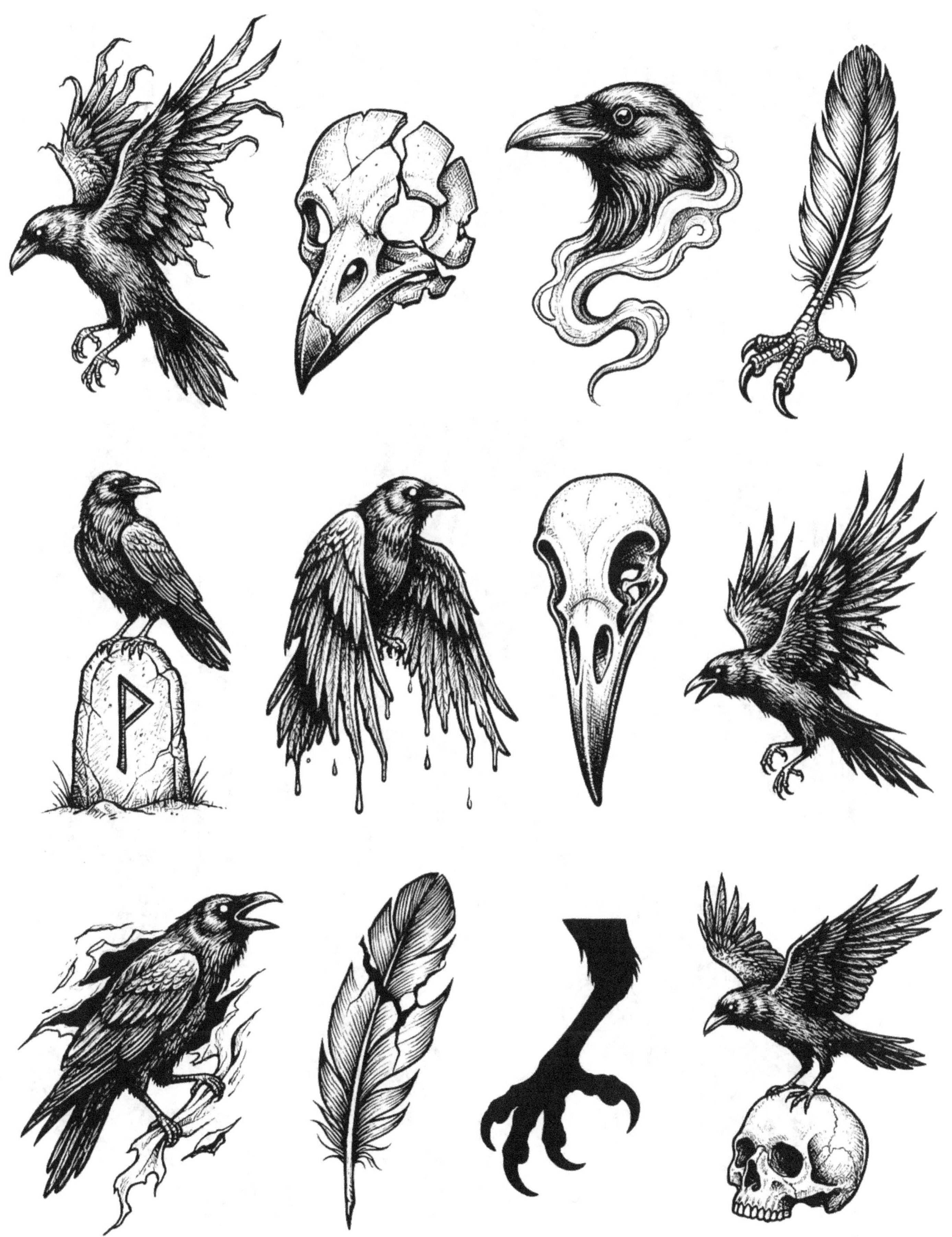

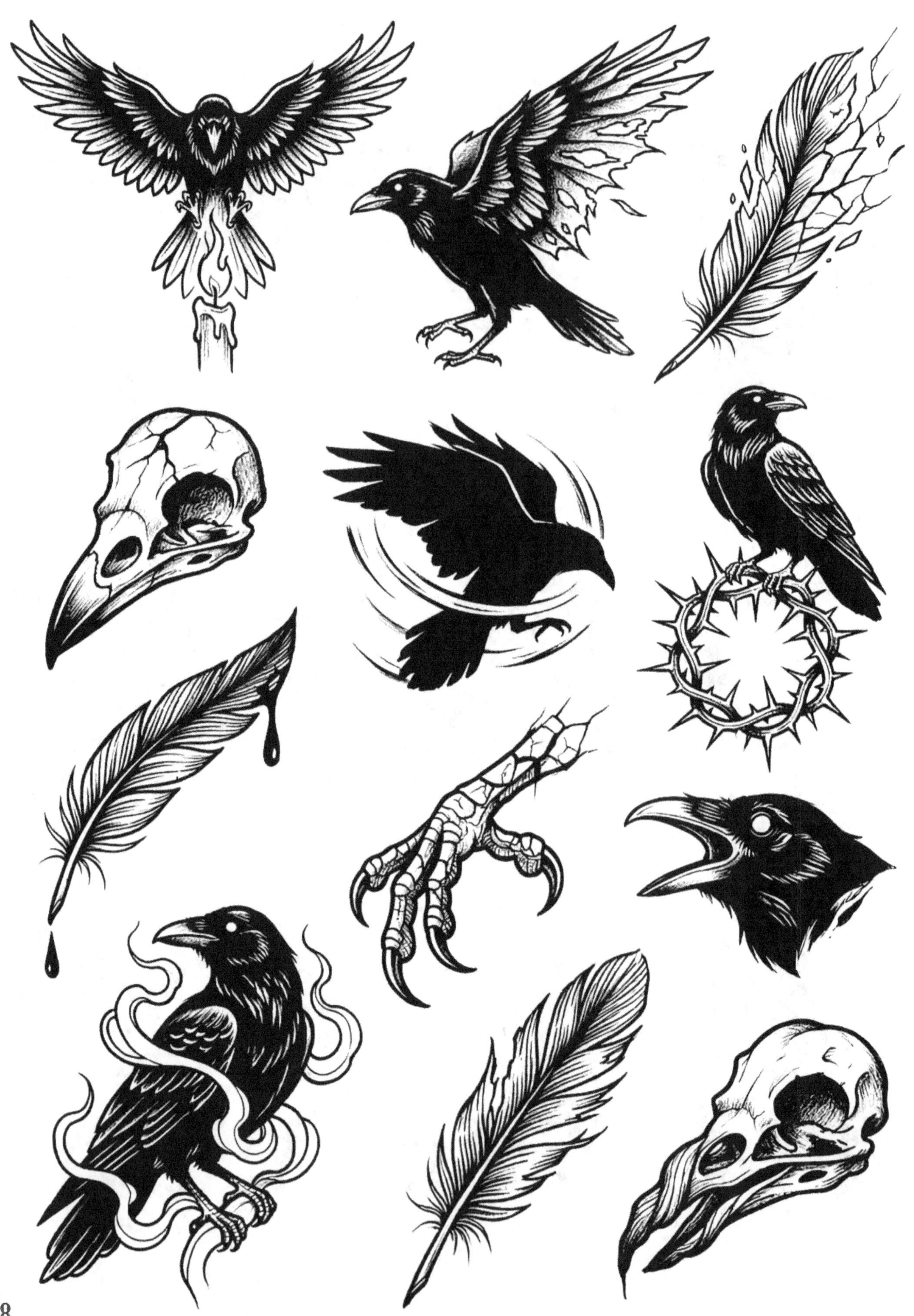

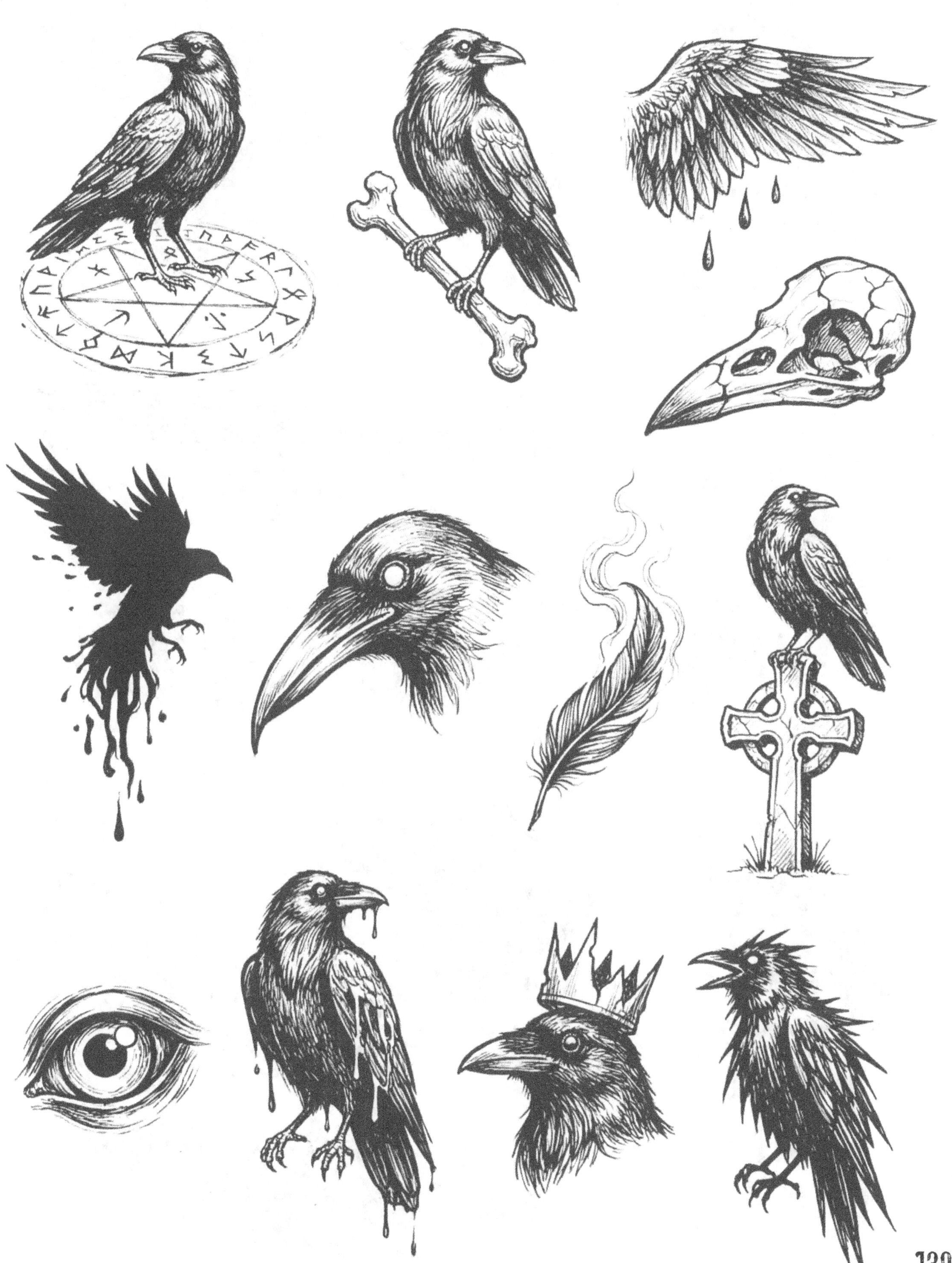

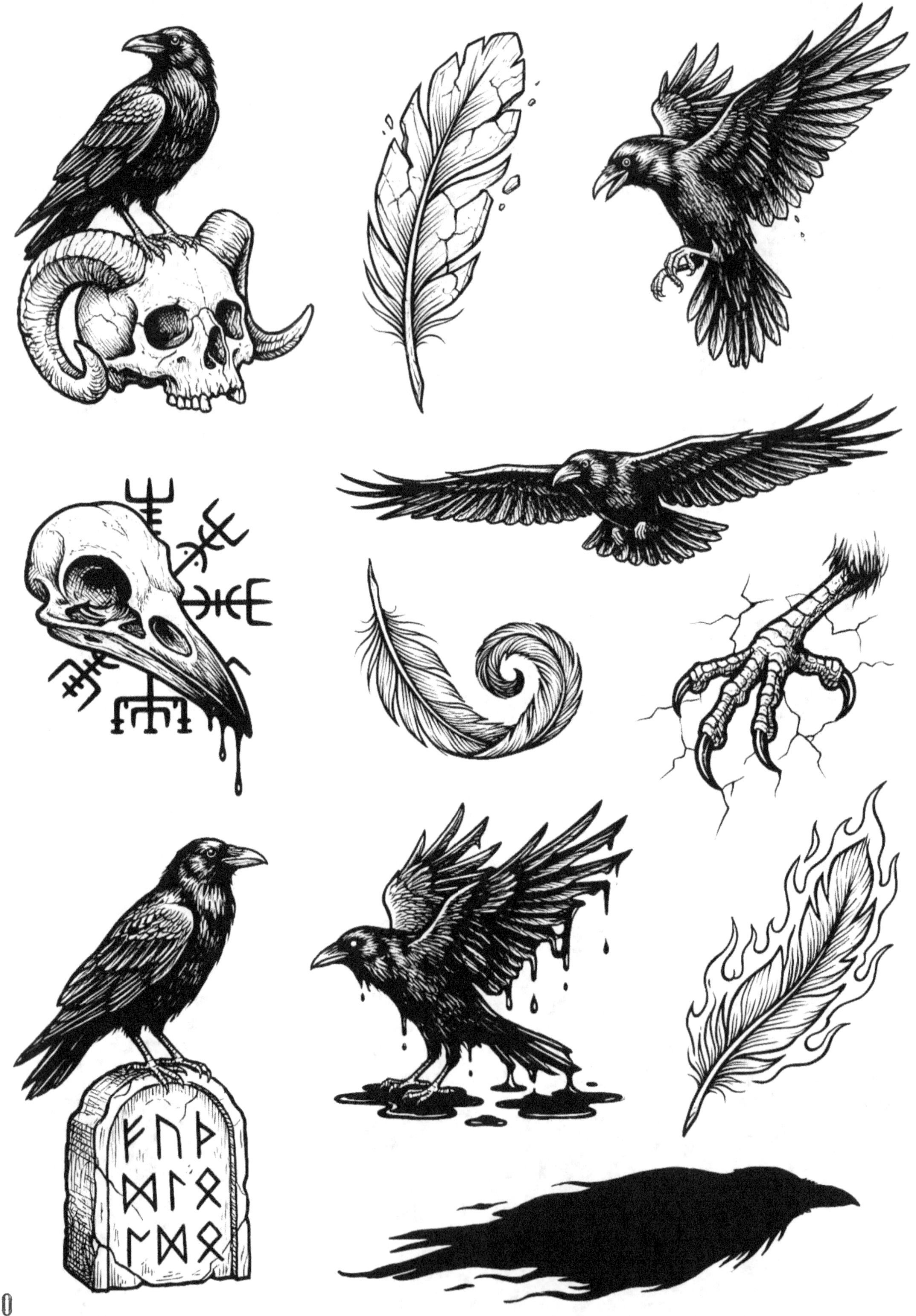

TRADITIONAL AMERICAN

Traditional American tattooing is one of the most iconic and influential styles in the history of the craft. Bold lines, solid shapes, clear storytelling and a palette built around strong contrasts — wszystko to sprawia, że old-schoolowe motywy są natychmiast rozpoznawalne. This style was born from a time when tattoos needed to survive sun, salt, sweat and years of aging, and its visual language reflects that toughness and clarity.

Classic symbols such as hearts, roses, daggers, eagles, anchors, banners and pin-up portraits carry cultural weight that has lasted for generations. They are direct, honest and expressive. Every shape has a purpose, every line supports the form, and every design has a story behind it — whether it's love, loyalty, courage, travel, rebellion or personal identity.

In tattoo art today, Traditional American remains timeless because of its versatility. These motifs can be used exactly as they are — bold and proud — or reinterpreted within modern compositions. The clean silhouettes make them ideal for patches, fillers, medium-sized standalone tattoos or larger themed pieces. Their strong visual foundation allows artists to experiment while still keeping the spirit of the style intact.

This chapter brings together a range of old-school designs meant to inspire both classic execution and modern adaptation. Study the weight of the lines, the rhythm of the shapes and the way the motifs balance simplicity with impact. Traditional American is not about complexity — it's about clarity, attitude and confidence.

This is the heart of tattoo heritage,

a style that echoes through decades,

and a reminder that simplicity, when done right,

never loses its power.

FORTITUDE

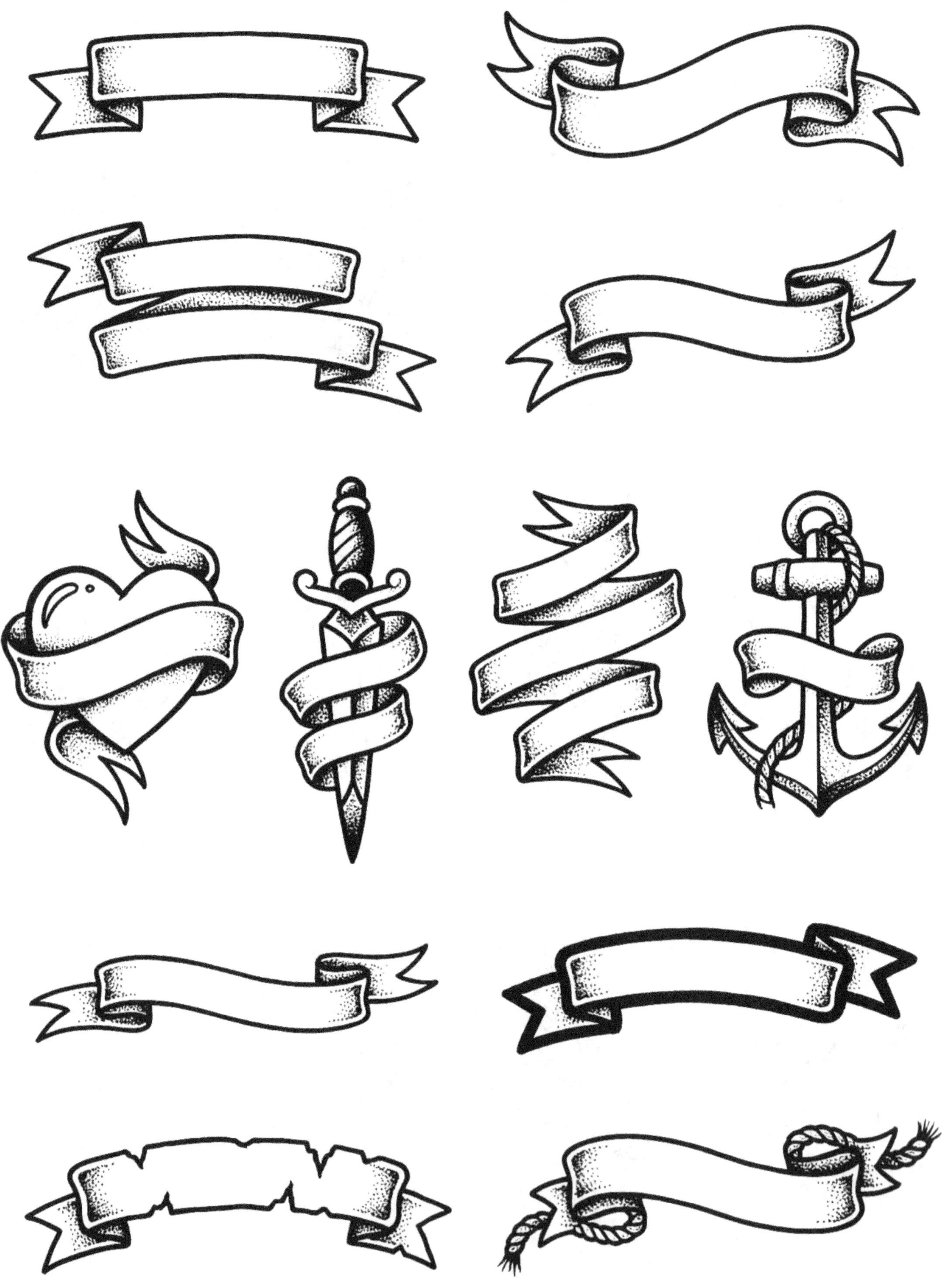

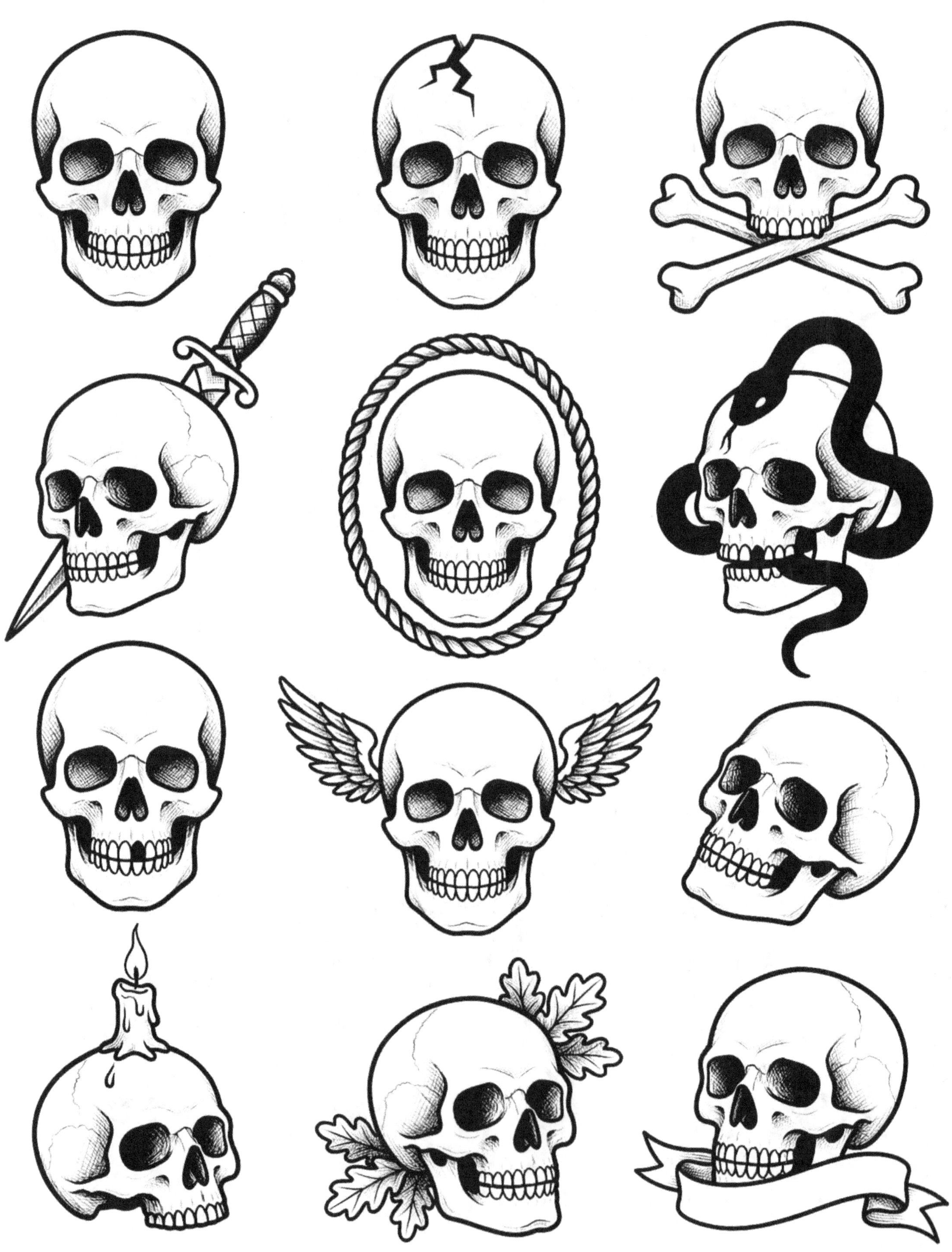

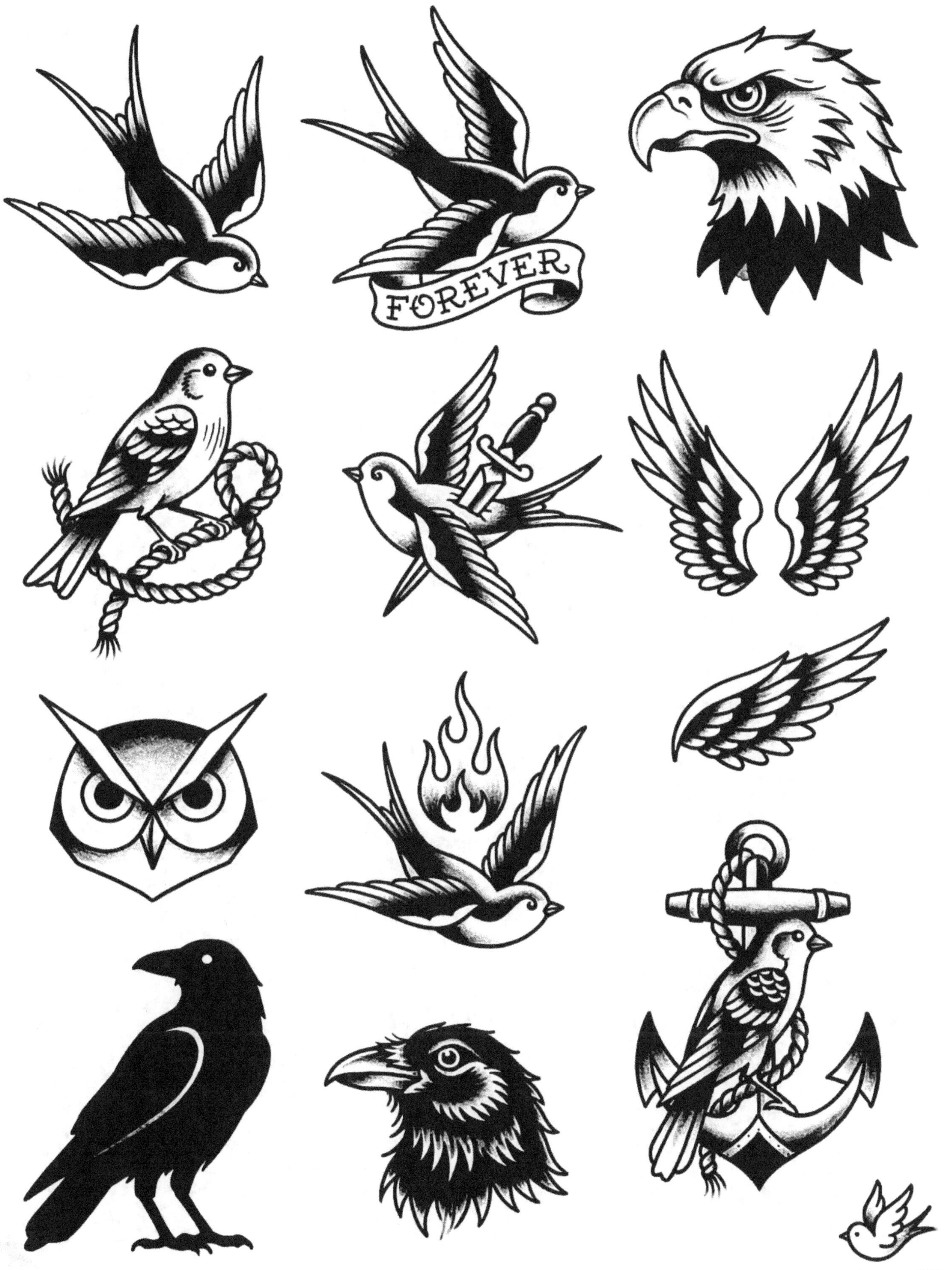
FOREVER

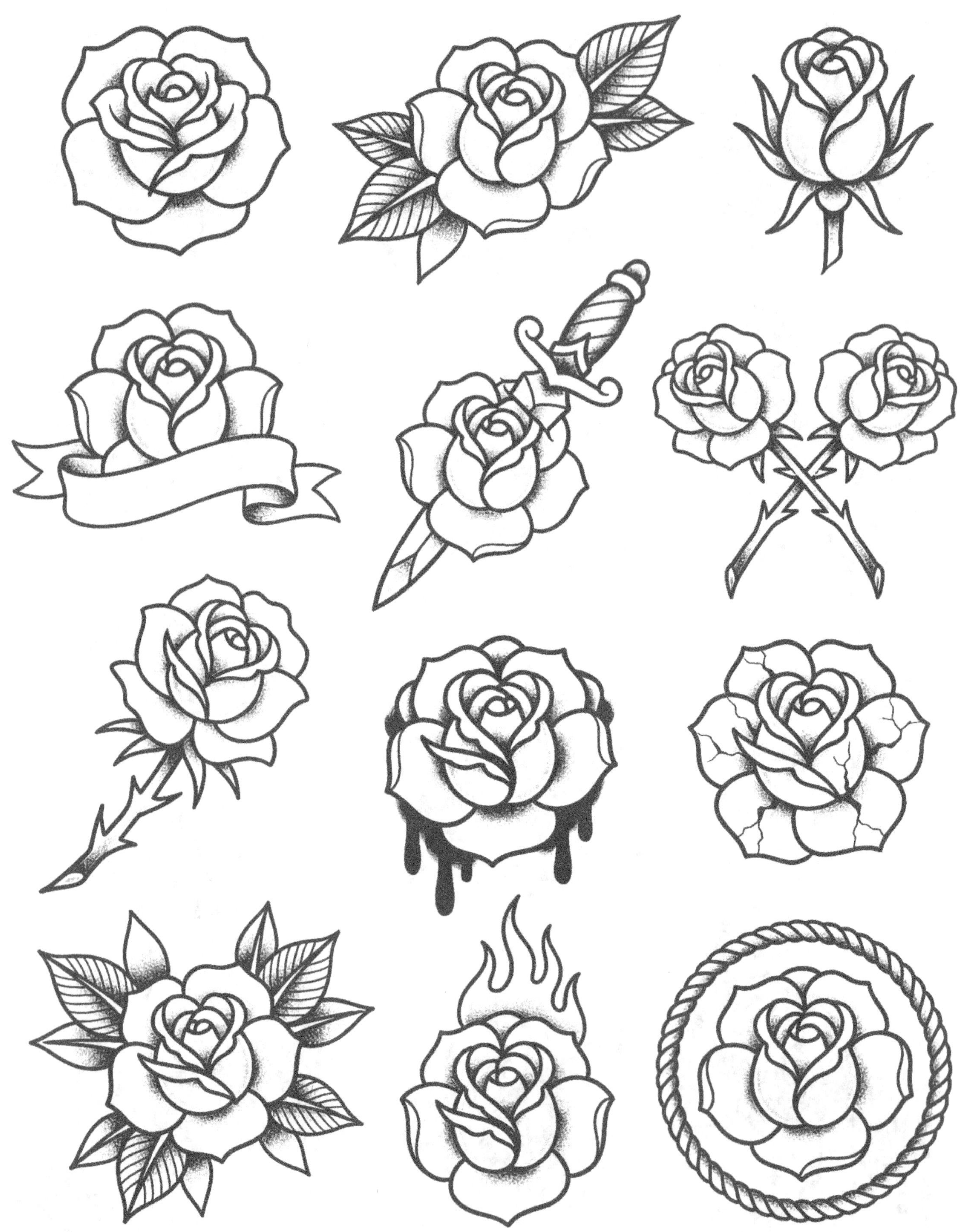

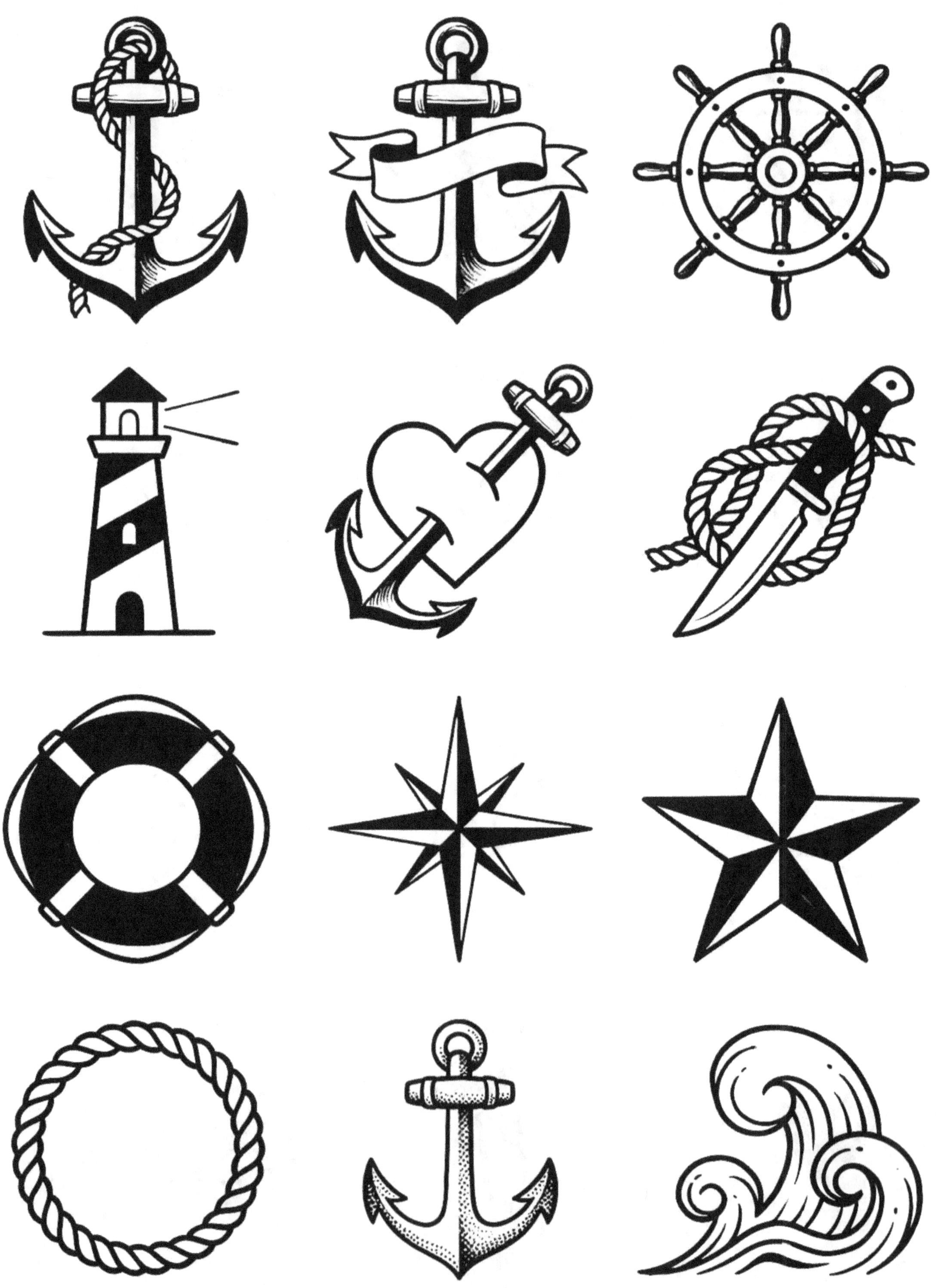

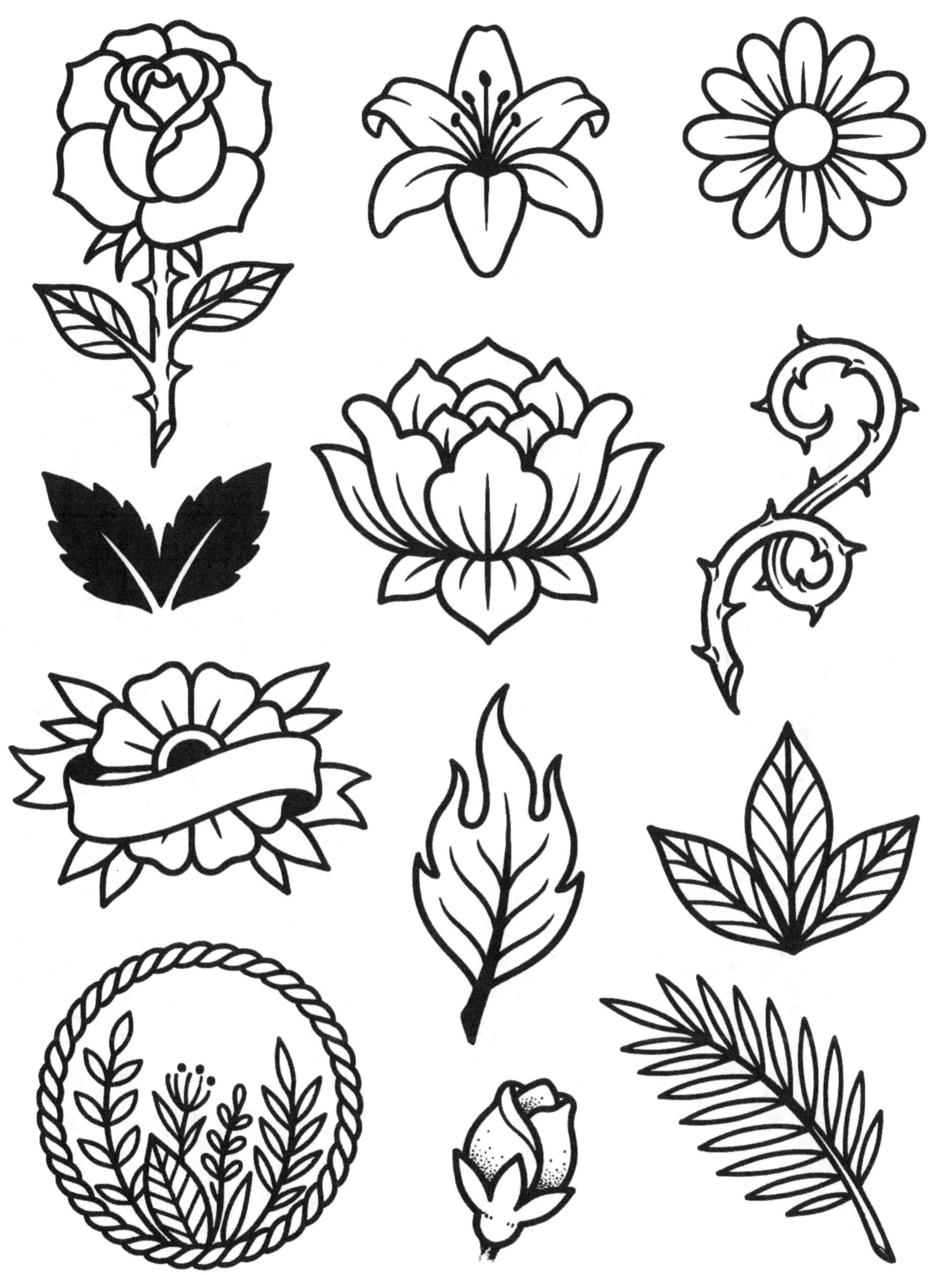

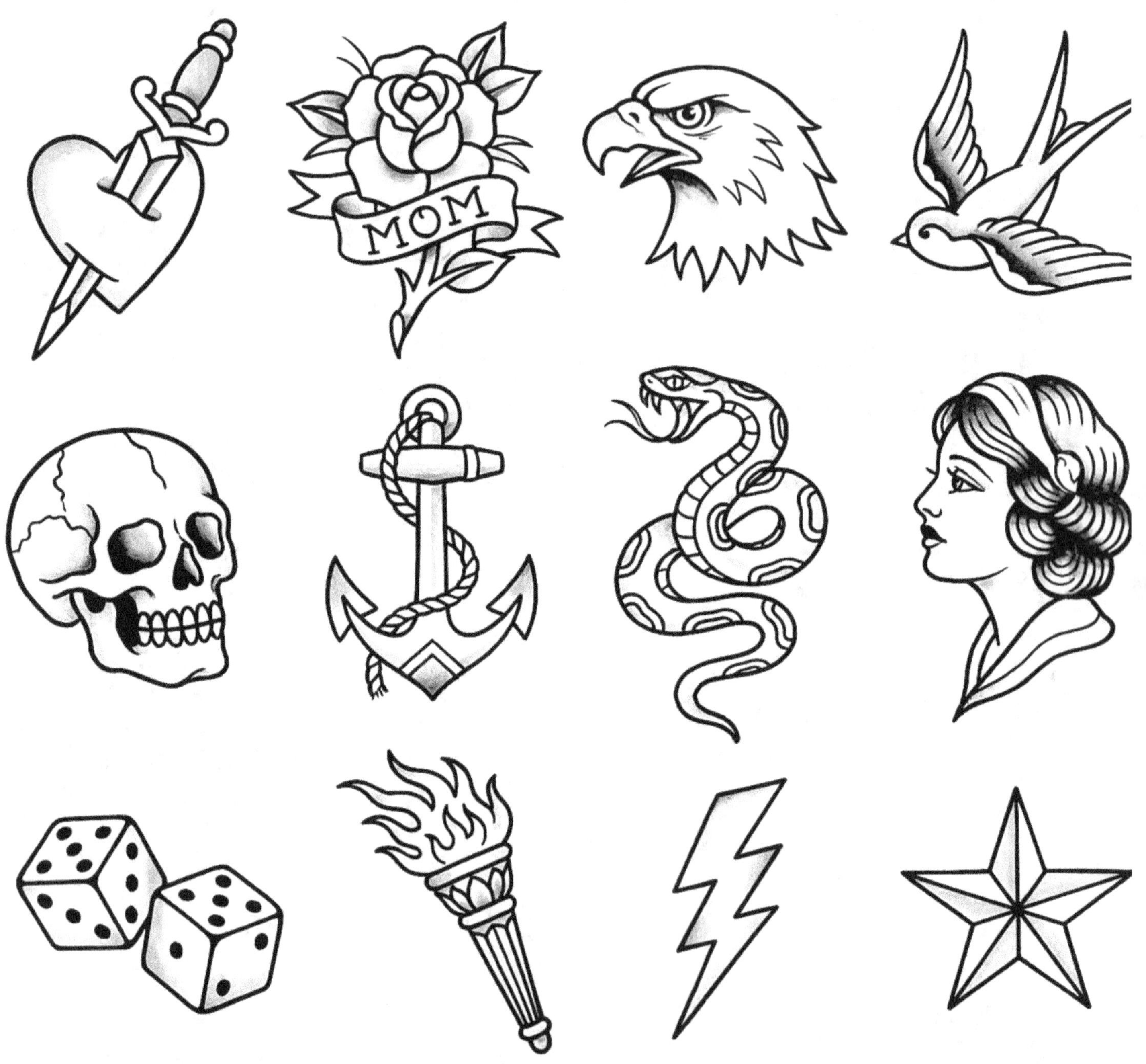

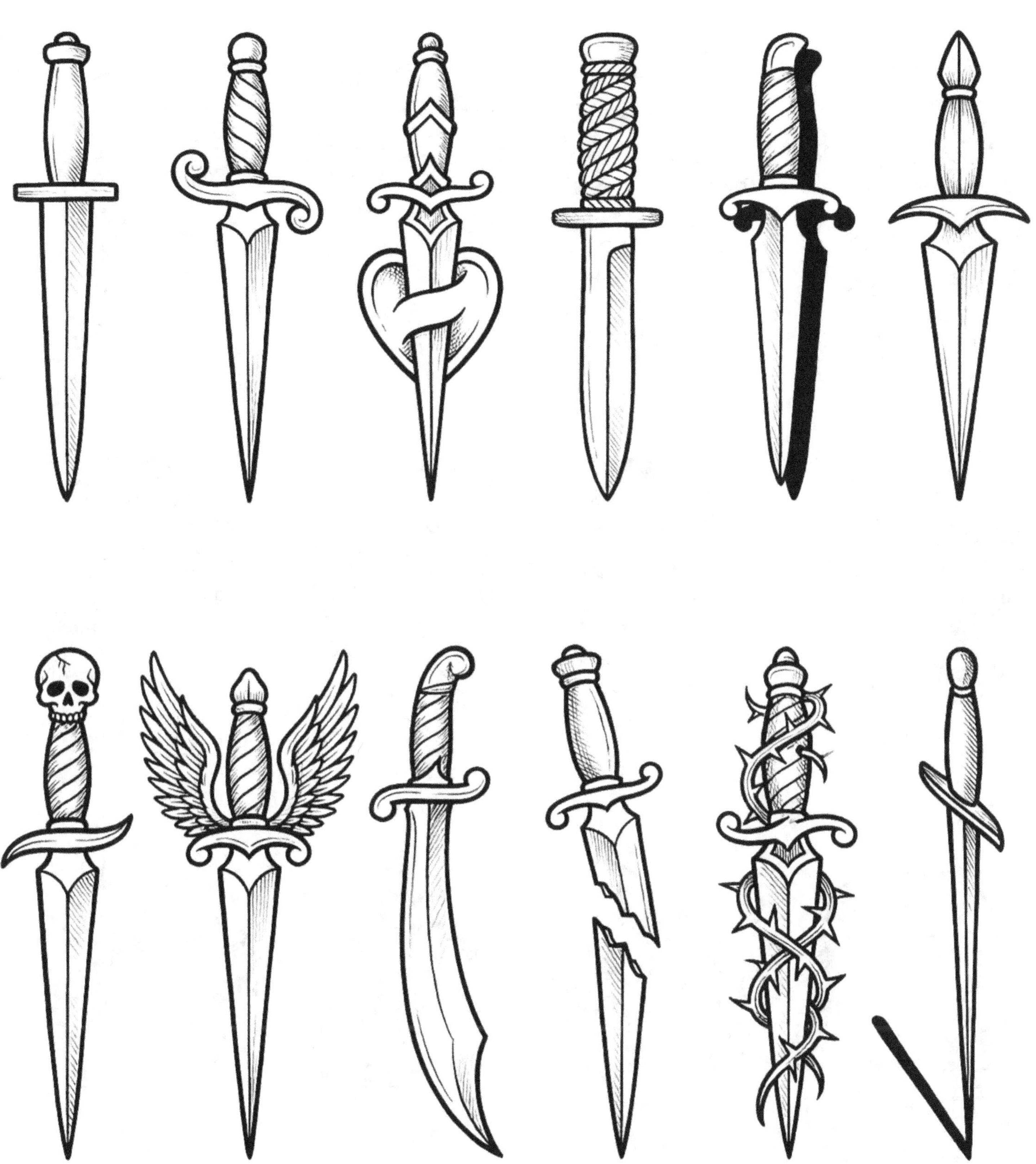

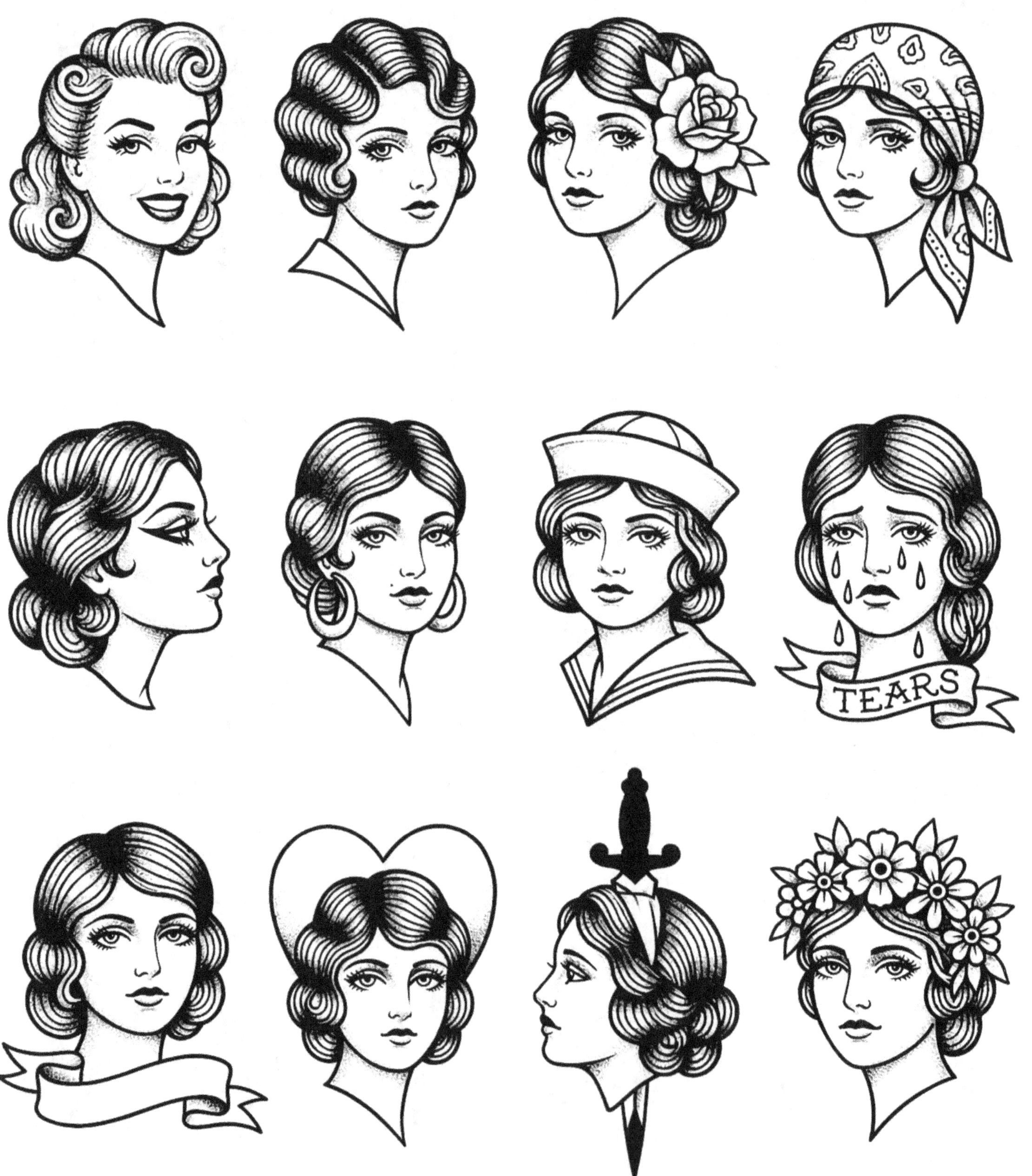

TEARS

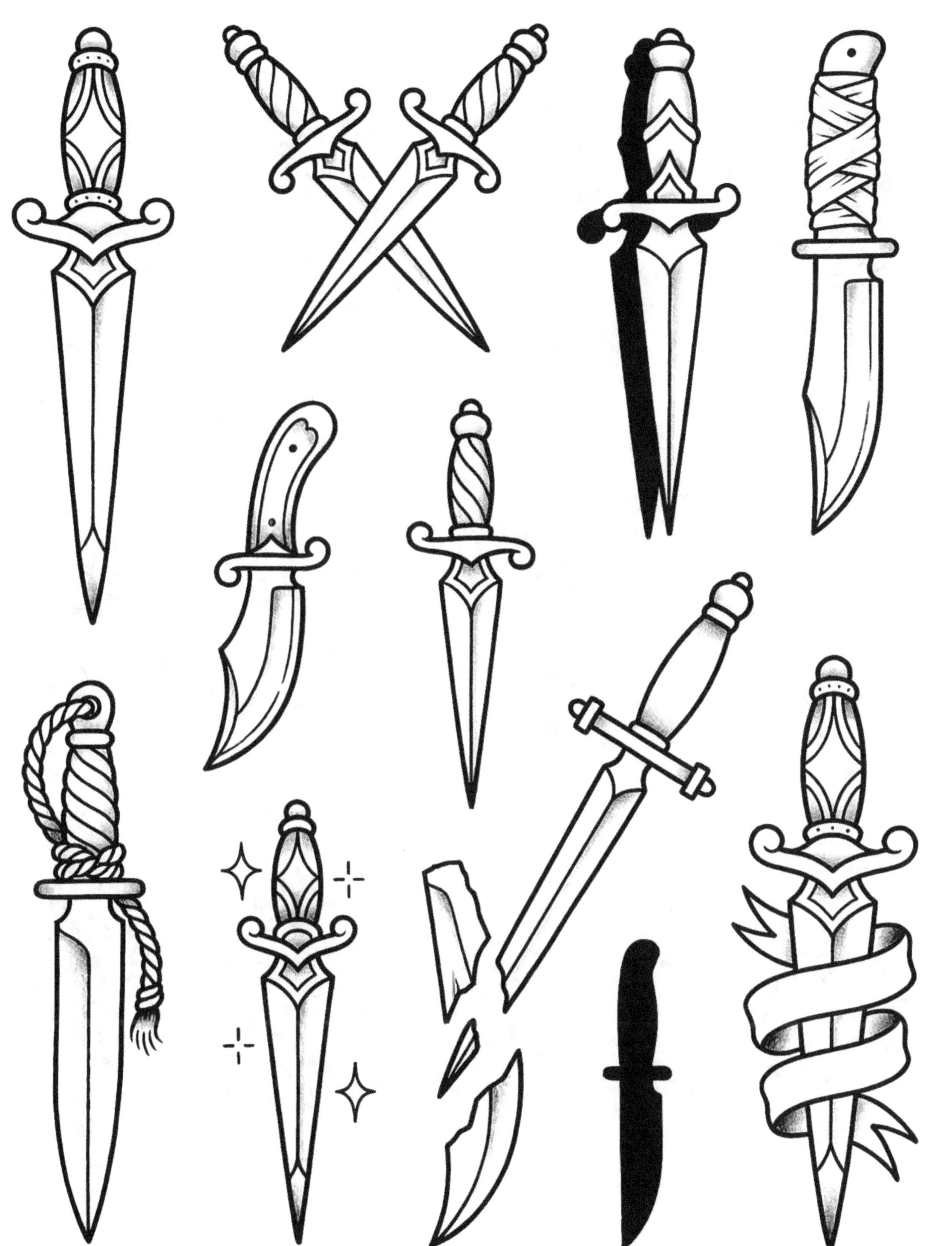

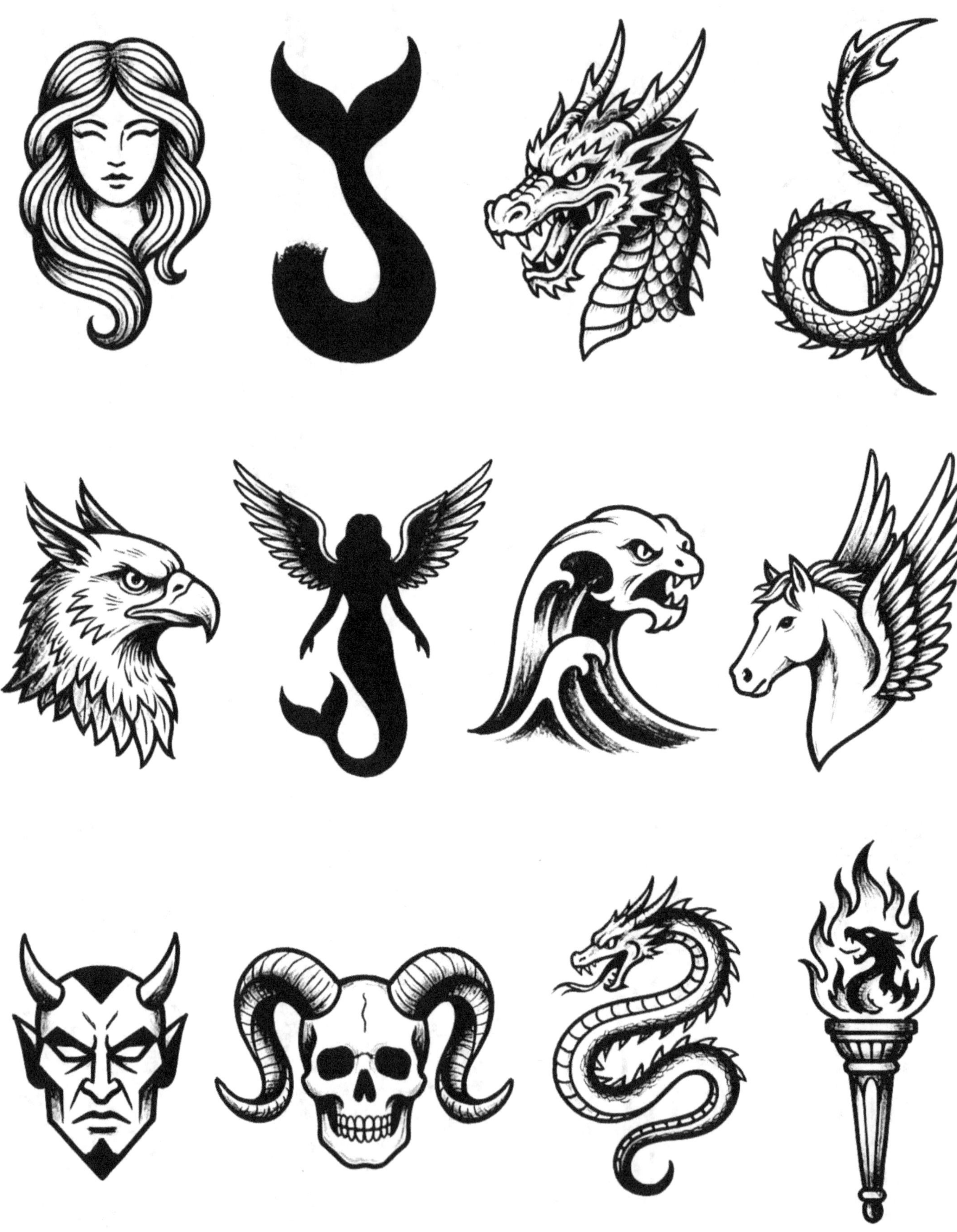

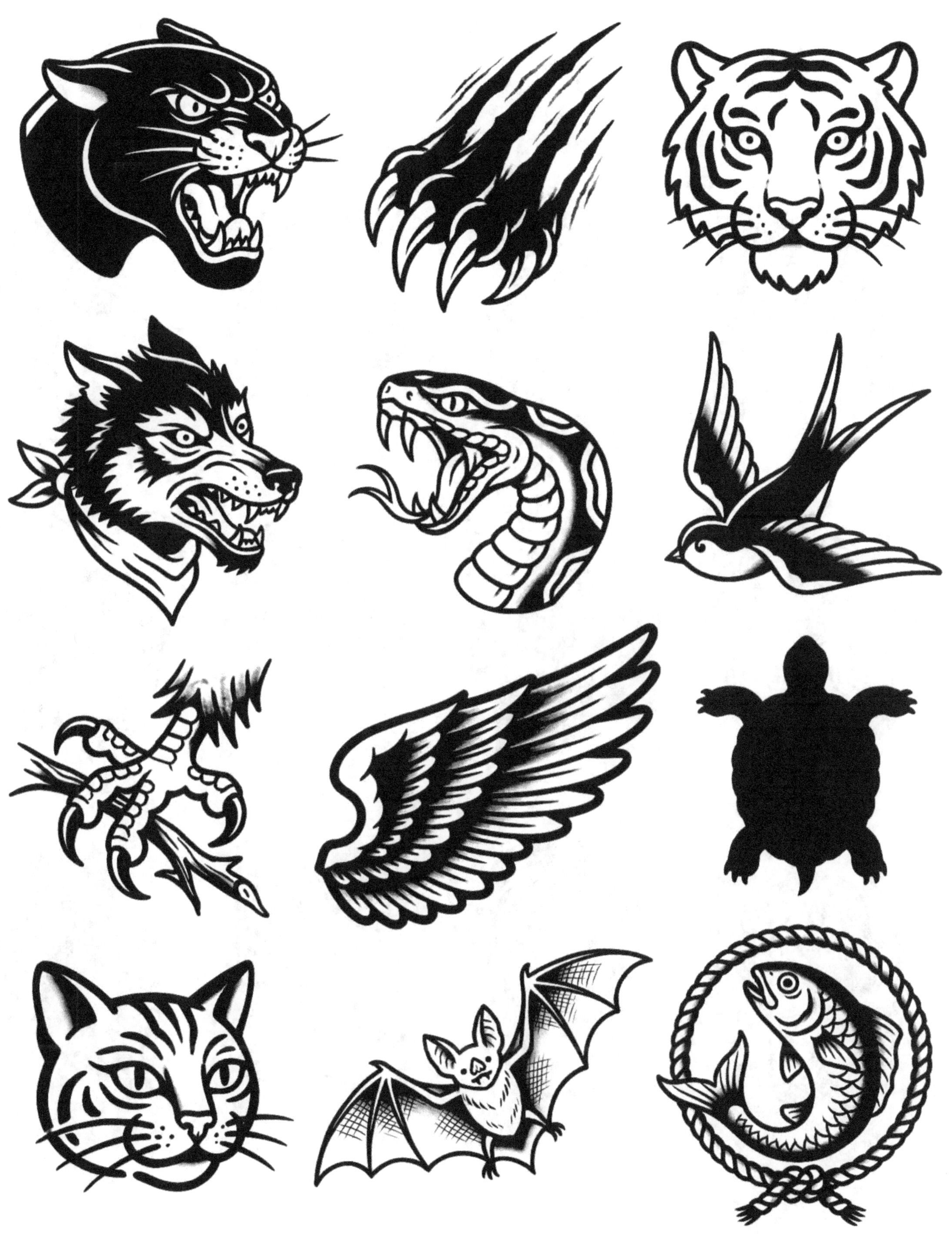

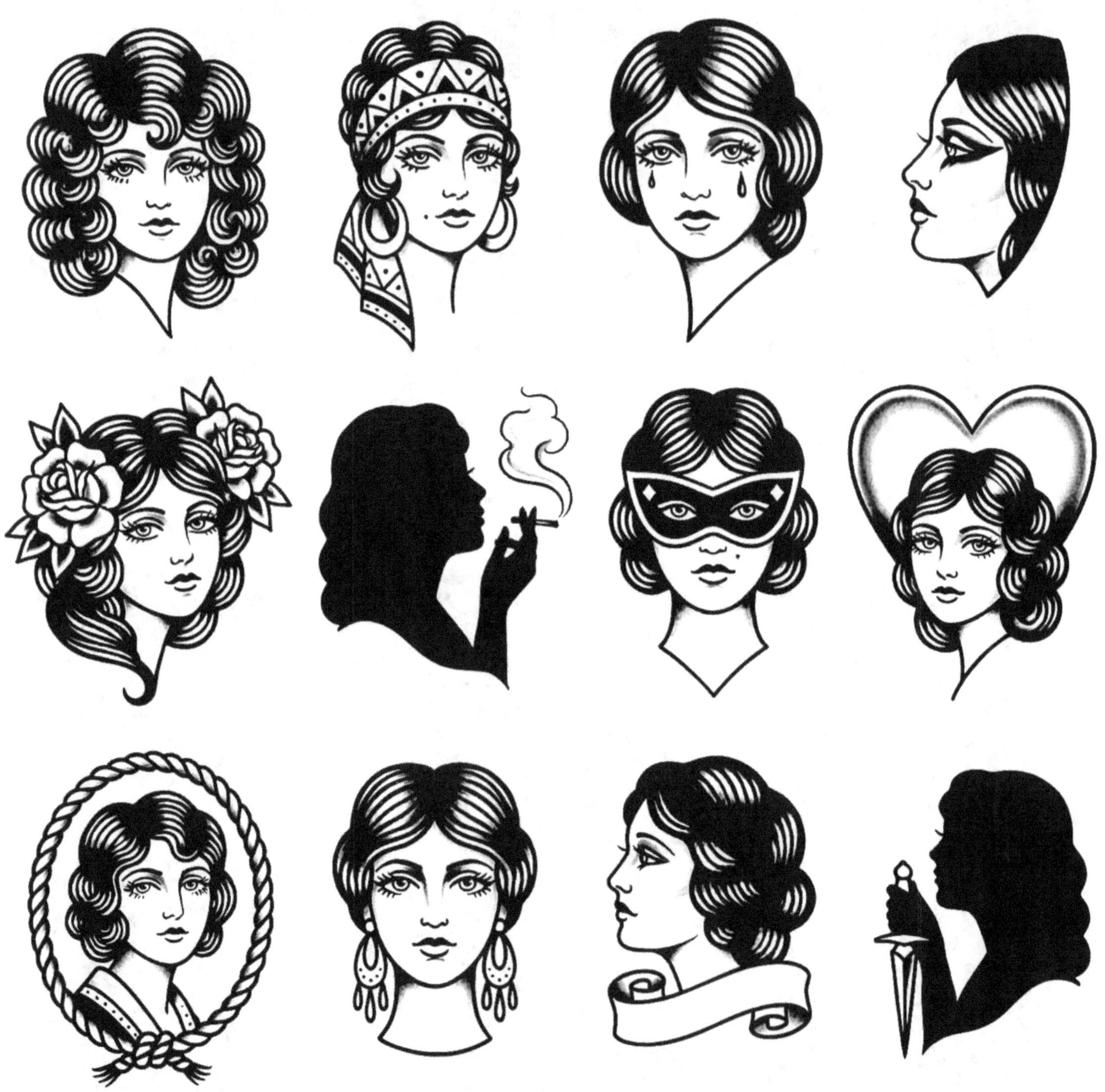

MOM
FOREVER

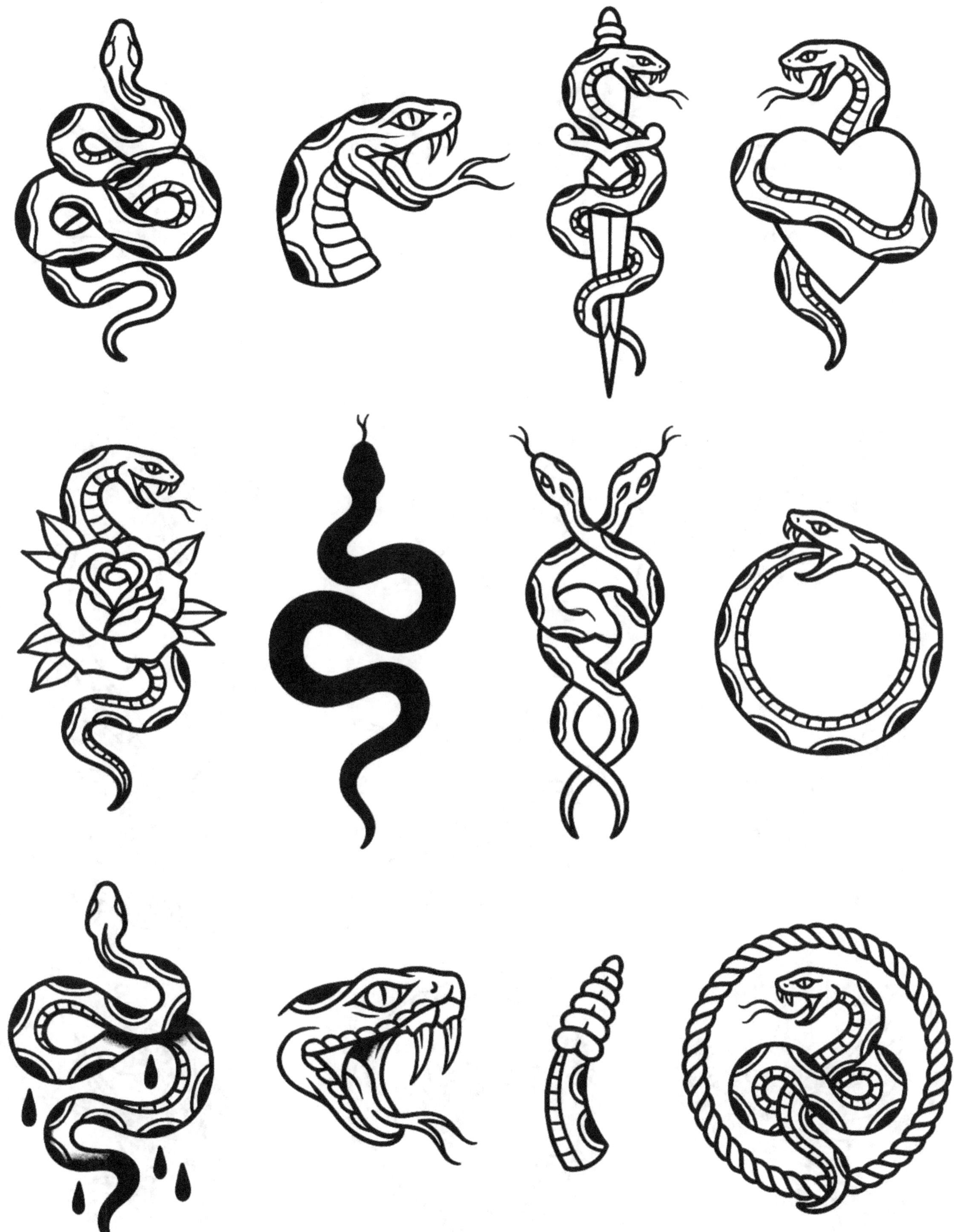

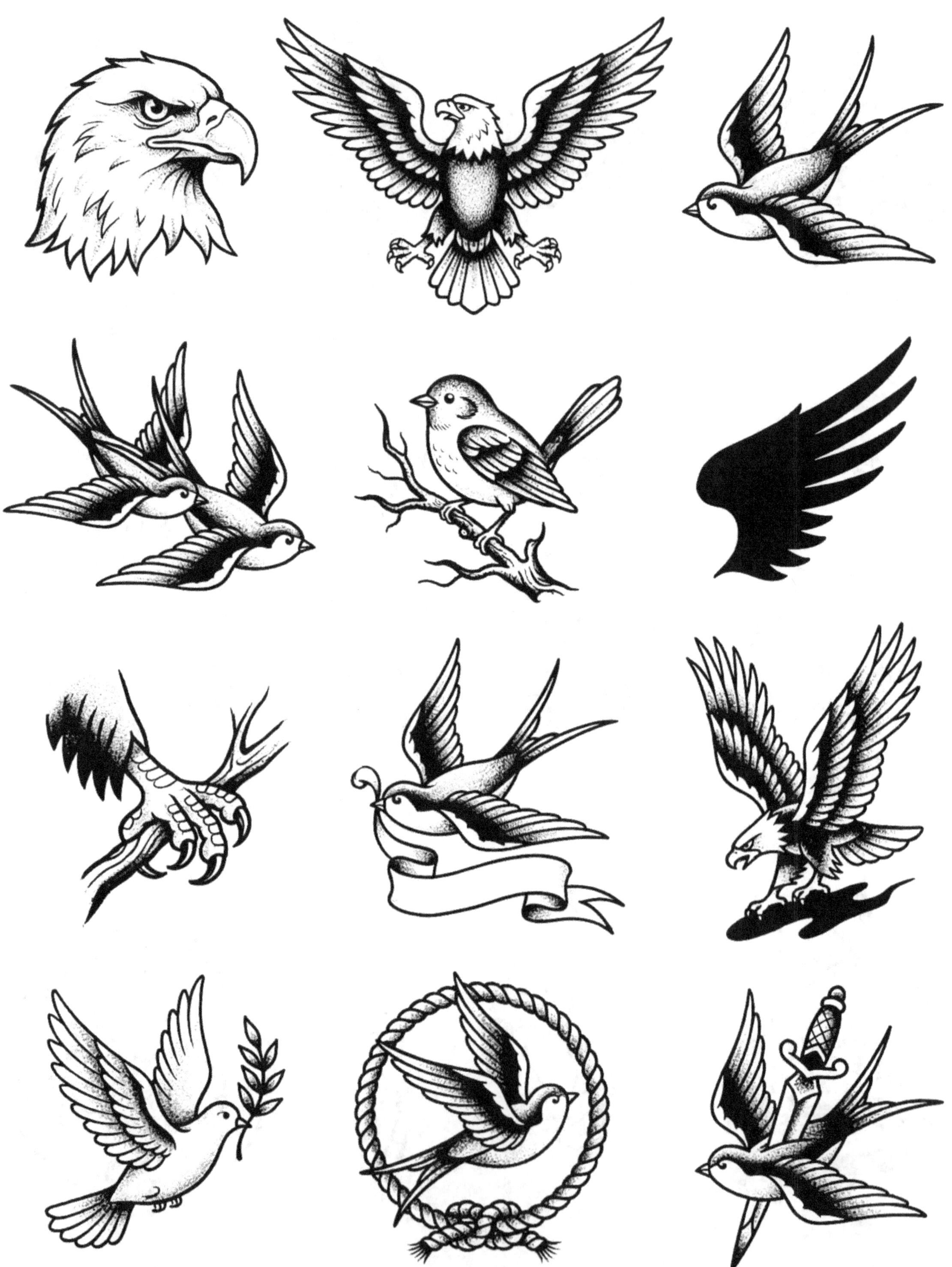

Tattoo art is a journey without a final destination. Styles evolve, techniques shift, tools change, and artists continually redefine what is possible with ink and skin. But one thing remains constant: the need for inspiration. The need to explore shapes, symbols, characters and stories that push your imagination forward. This book was created with that purpose in mind — as a companion to your creative process and a source of visual momentum whenever you need it.

As you move beyond these pages, remember that every design is only a starting point. What matters most is how you interpret, adapt and transform ideas into something uniquely yours. The strongest tattoos are those that carry the artist's voice — not just in the lines and shadows, but in the intention behind them. Let these designs spark new directions, challenge your habits and encourage you to explore themes you may not have considered before.

Take what resonates, reshape what calls to you, and leave space for your own style to grow. Tattooing thrives on experimentation and courage — the willingness to follow a concept even when it leads somewhere unfamiliar. Every sketch you make, every piece you refine, every client you collaborate with adds to your evolution as an artist.

Thank you for exploring these chapters and allowing this collection to be part of your creative world. May it serve you in your sessions, your studies, your sketchbook and your long-term artistic development. And may it remind you that inspiration is everywhere — in the shadows, in the symbols, in the architecture, in the creatures, in the stories and in the timeless traditions that shaped the craft.

This is not an ending, but another step forward.

The next design is waiting.

The next idea is already forming.

Keep creating — the world always needs more art.

Beneath the QR code you'll find a downloadable PDF containing a curated selection of the designs featured in this book — presented in full color, refined and ready to explore. These illustrations are provided as an additional source of inspiration, allowing you to study the details, lighting and color treatment of each piece. Simply scan the code to access the collection

Tattoo Design Book: A Guide to Getting Started

We appreciate the time and effort you've invested in exploring the "Tattoo Design Book." Your commitment to mastering the art of tattooing has been an inspiration to us all. As you continue on this artistic path, we're excited to see where your talents will take you.

Warm wishes,

The "Life Daily Style" Team